International Business and Society

International Business and Society

STEVEN L. WARTICK AND DONNA J. WOOD

Michael R. Czinkota, Consulting Editor,
North America Blackwell Series in Business

First published 1998

2 4 6 8 10 9 7 5 3 1

Blackwell Publishers Inc.
350 Main Street
Malden, Massachusetts 02148
USA

Blackwell Publishers Ltd
108 Cowley Road
Oxford OX4 1JF
UK

Library of Congress Cataloging-in-Publication Data

Wartick, Steven Leslie.
International business and society/Steven L. Wartick and Donna J. Wood.
    p.   cm.
    Includes bibliographical references and index.
    ISBN 1-55786-944-8 (pbk.:alk. paper) 0-631-20800-3 (hbk.)
  1. International business enterprises–Social aspects.
  2. Social responsibility of business. 3. Business ethics.
  4. Business and
politics. I. Wood, Donna J., 1949– . II. Title.
    HD2755.5.W376 1998
    658.4'08–dc21   97–11926
                                       CIP

British Library Cataloguing in Publication Data

A CIP catalogue record for this book is available from the British Library.

Typeset in 10 on 12 pt Meridien
by Graphicraft Typesetters Ltd, Hong Kong
Printed in Great Britain by MPG Books Ltd, Bodmin, Cornwall

This book is printed on acid-free paper

Contents

Figures

Exhibits

Tables

Preface

For a long time, international business meant little more than keeping up with currency exchange rates, banking procedures, and trade statistics, and making the necessary arrangements with border officials. Then, as transportation and communication technologies became faster and more sophisticated, international business itself began to change its character. Managers around the globe began to take seriously the idea that culture, language, and custom played important roles in international business. Ethnocentrism gave way to cross-cultural awareness.

Now, we have moved beyond cross-border issues toward a world economy, supranational legal agreements, multi-sourced manufactured goods that have no real country-home, and 24-hour stock markets around the globe. Managers must be as comfortable in Taipei, Sydney, Brussels, New York, Buenos Aires, London, Kyoto, Tel Aviv, San Salvador, Paris, Johannesburg, Riyadh, Atlanta, or Québec as they are in their own home cities. And the social, legal, political, ethical, and ecological issues facing business have never been more complex or more difficult to comprehend.

This book is designed to help managers navigate the modern rapids by making use of the analytical tools available for understanding these complex, socio-political environments of business. Some of the tools covered in the book are stakeholder mapping, ethical decision making, assessing corporate social performance, issues tracking and management, and managing government relations and regulatory compliance.

From the time we began writing this book until this time when you hold it in your hands, the particular issues facing business in international domains have changed several times over. Tools, fortunately, don't have to change as fast. With a single hammer, you can pound in almost any kind of nail. With a single management tool such as stakeholder mapping, you can configure almost any kind of stakeholder environment. So, our objective is to help you acquire a *toolkit*:

- that you can use to assess the nature of your company's socio-political environment, whatever it may be;
- that you can use to apply a broader vision and a more commonsense way of understanding how the socio-political environment affects your company and what you can do about it; and
- that will help you weather the changes and new issues that undoubtedly will arise.

The length of time it took to develop and put into words the ideas and frameworks presented in this book has been more than either of us expected. But along the way, the people and experiences encountered have been worth the effort. To our colleagues in IABS, the International Association for Business and Society, we express our thanks. This professional association, founded in 1989, has been a nexus of enormously valuable discussions, ideas, and critiques. We also thank Rolf Janke, our signing editor at Blackwell, who found us back at the beginning of this project and found us again near the end. His encouragement was most welcome at both places. Others along the way – Kathleen Tibbets, David Olson, Mark Cordano, Ray Jones – know what they have contributed to this work, and we thank them. The Blackwell production staff – Louise Spencely, Lisa Parker, Mary Beckwith, and Paula Jacobs – were most helpful and capable. Still, we want to give our greatest thanks to our families – Jake, Joey, Marty, Ryan, and Sam. Particularly when we sat face-to-face at a St Louis kitchen table for two weeks in the summer of 1993, our dueling laptop computers strained to the max, Joey and Sam off building rockets together at space camp, our families kept themselves going without us. For tolerating this and all the many other inconveniences associated with this work, we thank them all.

Steven L. Wartick
St Louis, Missouri

Donna J. Wood
Pittsburgh, Pennsylvania

Copyright Acknowledgements

The authors and publishers gratefully acknowledge the following for permission to reproduce copyright material:

Administrative Science Quarterly
Conference Board Incorporated
Fortune Magazine
Levi Strauss & Co
Management Reports Inc.
McGraw-Hill
Prentice-Hall Inc.
Reebok International Limited
The University of Western Ontario
The Wall Street Journal

The publishers apologize for any errors or omissions in the above list and would be grateful to be notified of any corrections that should be incorporated in the next edition or reprint of this book.

1

Business and Society: Global Issues and Global Environments

Before its 1996 merger with Sandoz, Ciba-Geigy Corporation was a Swiss-based producer of pharmaceuticals, specialty chemicals, and a great deal more. The US branch accounted for a third of the company's sales, but the company was a true global enterprise operating in 80 of the world's nations. In the 1990s, Ciba-Geigy adopted a new corporate vision statement, emphasizing a triad of objectives – economic, social, and environmental. In recent years, Ciba-Geigy has been involved in social and environmental issues such as local opposition to factory sitings, toxic waste clean-ups and regulatory fines, and developing environmentally sound packaging policies. The company's issues management team is busy trying to understand what, exactly, it means for a giant MNC to have "social" and "environmental" objectives as part of its corporate mission.

In 1910, world trade amounted to less than $40 billion; by 1990, the figure had reached almost $7 trillion, with most of the growth occurring since 1965. From 1980 to 1991, the market value of direct investments abroad by US companies had more than doubled, from $396 billion to $802 billion. During that same decade, direct investments by foreign companies in the United States grew from a little over $500 billion to almost $2.5 trillion (IMF, 1991: 2–3; US Department of Commerce, *Statistical Abstract*, 1993: 797). With growth has come increasing complexity in the business environment, more complicated management problems, and more serious consequences for more stakeholders if the problems are not addressed appropriately.

The nature of world business has also changed qualitatively, from international trade – identifiable two-party contractual exchanges of goods and money – to a global economy – an integrated, multi-party, cross-boundary flow of goods, services, capital, revenues, ideas, people, and technologies. *Fortune* magazine reported in 1988, for example, that the largest 200 multinational corporations in the world had affiliates in 20 or more countries (Alpert and Kirsch, 1988). More recently, researchers at the United Nations have identified at least 35,000 multinational enterprises and 170,000 foreign affiliates (Emmott, 1993). The new global stature of business has meant also the rise of multinational and global social and political problems for managers, requiring new ways of thinking about the business environment and new tools for managing within it.

Business and society is the study of relationships between business organizations and the social, political, technological, economic, and natural environments in which they operate. Over the past few decades, the field of business and society has emphasized the US business environment – the rise of social issues and demands affecting business, the increasing gap between business performance and social expectations, the role of public policy in implementing social objectives, and the ability of firms to meet social, ethical, and political challenges as well as economic and technological ones.

What is different about international business, the global marketplace? Nearly everyone acknowledges the reality of the global business environment. To understand the social and political consequences, however, we need to take a look at the differences between today's business environment and that of the past. As a benchmark for this comparison, let us consider the US-dominated world business environment of the 1950s.

THE BUSINESS ENVIRONMENT OF THE 1950s

In the early part of this decade, Europe and Japan were still recovering from World War II and had no significant economic hold on world markets. South Korea, also suffering war damage, was far from establishing its current economic prowess. Multicountry economic associations such as the European Economic Community (EEC, now known as the European Union, or EU) and the Organization of Petroleum Exporting Countries (OPEC) were not yet formed. The world monetary order was based on a gold standard largely tied to a fixed rate of exchange between gold and the US dollar. The US was dominant in oil, automobiles, steel, communications, weapons, and consumer goods. The US had already turned the corner toward becoming a service economy, but few had yet noticed this fact. Nor had most nonmanufacturing companies (for example, retail and service companies) begun thinking of national expansion, much less transnational strategies.

Technologically, we would barely recognize the business environment of the 1950s. Sputnik, the Soviet space satellite, was not launched until 1957; IBM had introduced its first computer – the room-sized 70 – four years earlier. In the US, gross revenue from radio-time sales still exceeded that from television-time sales; color TV had not yet hit the market, and many US families did not even own a television set. Many families, in fact, were making the transition from the icebox to the electric refrigerator, from the handfed clothes-wringer to the automatic washer; there were no microwave ovens or home freezers. To spur consumer spending, goods were designed with "planned obsolescence" in mind. Commercial jet travel was still in its infancy, as was the US interstate highway system. US production technology, the most advanced in the world, was built upon a "frontier mentality," that is, the assumption that when some resources were used up, there would always be more available beyond the frontier. Elsewhere in the world, technological development lagged behind. "Made in Japan" was synonymous with cheap, low-quality products. The simple and inexpensive Volkswagen Beetle was only beginning to appear on US highways. In the 1950s, the US had no rivals in technological development.

From a social perspective, the US of the early 1950s looked vastly different from today's global environment. The "baby boom" was in full swing; one out of every four people in the nation was under the age of fourteen. In this era of conformity to promote security, the suburbanization which followed urbanization led to a life style where only 29 percent of women worked outside the home. Employed women constituted only 34 percent of the labor force in the 1950s, and were concentrated in a few occupations, such as elementary teacher, secretary, nurse, librarian, sales clerk, and domestic service worker (US Bureau of Labor, 1989). The 1954 Supreme Court decision, *Brown v. Board of Education*, established the legal right of black children to equal education and paved the way for the next decade's civil rights movement. Environmentalism, consumerism, and feminism were still years from being major social and political issues.

Dinner (and often lunch) at home was the norm, and the words "fast" and "food" had not yet been coupled; McDonald's was just standardizing its hamburger at its first company store in Des Plaines, Illinois. (As we write this, almost a trillion McDonald's hamburgers have been sold worldwide, and the busiest stores are in Moscow and Budapest. Some readers may remember when McDonald's counted its hamburgers in the hundreds of thousands.) In the rest of the world, social problems related to rebuilding war-devastated societies, feeding and sheltering booming populations, and enhancing the quantity, rather than the quality, of life.

Global conditions and events did command attention in one environmental arena – the political one. The rebuilding of Europe, the Marshall Plan, and the United Nations occupied a great deal of political attention. Mao had begun his Cultural Revolution in a closed China. An even more potent political factor was the Cold War – a militaristic, menacing stand-off between the US and the Soviet Union – that focused US attention on the "red scare," communist expansion in the Third World, nuclear build-up and the implications of The Bomb. Schoolchildren learned to protect themselves against nuclear attack by hiding under their desks with their faces away from the classroom windows. For several years, the McCarthy hearings in the Congress focused on hunting down and getting rid of alleged communists in US society. Mikhail Gorbachev, then in his early twenties with no thought of the *perestroika* and *glasnost* that would eventually lead to the breakup of his country, watched new leadership take over in the Soviet Union after Stalin's death. Politics in the Middle East, South and Central America were dominated by American interests, and many African nations were still European colonies. Fidel Castro was a law student and promising baseball pitcher in Batista's Cuba until overthrowing him in 1959. The French, not the Americans, were fighting a war in Southeast Asia.

The business environment of the 1950s was anything but globalized. As Franklin Root (1973, p. 510) of the University of Pennsylvania's Wharton School has argued, globalization became significant only after the 1950s because: "Before that time the inadequacies of the global infrastructure of communications and transportation, as well as the pervasive influence of restrictive government policies, rendered global business strategies nothing more than utopian dreams in the minds of a few entrepreneurs." Economically, the world of the 1950s may have been ready to begin globalizing, but the entrepreneurs' dreams could not be fulfilled without technological, social, and political readiness.

TODAY'S GLOBAL BUSINESS ENVIRONMENT

Far removed from the US domination of the 1950s, today's business environment is marked by world markets, no single country dominance in a number of key industries, complexity, and rapid change. For multinational firms, the major issue today is competitiveness in the global environment. In 1988, of the world's 20 largest publicly-held companies (measured by market value), only three were US-based – IBM, Exxon, and General Electric. One, Royal Dutch Shell, was head-quartered in Europe, and the remaining 16 were Japanese. In 1990, the largest 100 multinationals accounted for $3.1 trillion of world-wide assets. Of this amount, $1.2 trillion was *not* in the MNEs' home countries, leading observers to estimate that these 100 companies control 40 to 50 percent of the world's cross-border assets (Emmott, 1993). By 1994, the Japanese stock market had experienced severe declines and only five of the world's largest firms were Japanese; eight were American, six were European, and one South Korean firm – the electronics giant, Samsung – had edged into the global elite.

Of the 20 largest multinational banks in the world in 1994, only four were American. The six largest banks were European, and only one was Japanese, down from 13 of the largest 20 banks in 1988 (Connor, 1994). In just a few years during the 1980s, the US changed from being the world's largest creditor nation to the world's largest debtor nation. Foreign investment in the US has now exceeded US investment abroad, though as recently as 1970, more than five invest-ment dollars flowed out of the US for every foreign dollar flowing in. In part because of the new system of free-floating exchange rates rather than a fixed gold standard, the value of US exports has not kept pace with the value of imports. South Korea, along with other newly developed nations, has emerged as an industrial power in such traditionally US-dominated industries as steel, automobiles, and elec-tronics. The European Union continues to progress toward complete economic integration, and the revolutions in Eastern Europe and the Soviet Union have opened undreamed-of opportunities and challenges. OPEC, although weaker now than in the 1970s and 1980s, has shown itself to be still a significant player in an oil-dependent world.

Technologically, today's managers no longer communicate; they telecommunicate. This has helped to make IBM one of the ten larg-est companies in the world. In fact, of 1993's 20 largest global firms, seven were primarily electronics companies (Farnham, 1994). Cable and satellite television, along with computer–telephone–fax–modem interconnections, bring world events in "real time" into offices and living rooms. In 1991's Persian Gulf war, national leaders (including Iraq's Saddam Hussein) as well as ordinary citizens around the world, got many of their reports about the war's progress from CNN – Cable Network News. The world's most modern factories produce via robot-ics and computer/machine tool technology, which encourages infinite product variety and diversity through small-batch processing. Produc-tion can be so well controlled that goods can be manufactured "just in time" for shipment, making the concept of "inventory" obsolete. "Outsourcing" has become commonplace, with a single product's components originating in many different countries and assembly taking place in one or two countries near large markets. Widespread recognition of the world's limited natural resource base has made energy and materials usage more strategically important than ever before. And "made in Japan," as well as "made in Europe," connotes quality, not inferiority.

In the social domain, the US's 1950s baby boomers became the dissidents and drop-outs of the 1960s, the "ME" generation of the 1970s, the Yuppies of the 1980s, and the national leaders of the 1990s. Now, only one in five US residents is under the age of fourteen, and well over half of American women are employed outside the home. The traditional US family of the 1950s – working dad, at-home mom, their children – has now almost vanished, constituting less than 8 percent of all family units. Throughout the world, the role of women has also changed substantially; career women are now commonplace in North America and Europe, and women have led Great Britain, Canada, France, Denmark, India, Pakistan, and the Philippines as prime ministers or presidents. Even Japan, one of the world's most tradition-bound societies, recently appointed a woman to a high-level government post. In several middle eastern countries, on the other hand, a decades-long trend toward modernizing women's roles has been cast back by leaders' return to religious fundamentalism.

Ecological and social issues such as destruction of the Amazon rainforests, global warming, acid rain, endangered species, and the protection of human rights have achieved worldwide prominence, emphasizing more than ever international interdependencies as well as intercultural differences. In the controversy over a worldwide ban on ozone-depleting CFCs, for example, the industrial world may readily give up its aerosol cans, but the developing world is desperate for refrigeration. In another example, a controversy over the possible pollution of central Europe's largest underground freshwater reservoir by a nearly-complete hydroelectric project is creating enormous tensions among Hungary, the Czech Republic, Slovakia, and Austria and has weighty implications for US, European Union, and former-East Bloc business interests (Wood, 1992).

Politically, civil and human rights, environmentalism, and consumerism are institutionalized as public policy activities throughout the industrialized world, not just in the US. The war between the world's two biggest ISMs – US/European capitalism and Soviet communism – has now become history, according to one popular author (Fukuyama, 1992), although as we write, the struggle of the ISMs continues in China, Korea, and southeast Asia, and the thriving capitalist center of Hong Kong was absorbed by mainland China in 1997. In the southern hemisphere, most developing countries continue their battle for independence, economic security, and world respect. However, issues of interest in the industrialized world – drug trafficking in Colombia, species extinction and soil erosion in many of the world's ecosystems – stand in the way of progress, as does the western world's economic power and ability to quickly move capital. The developing world's own inability to maintain intracountry political stability and to form intercountry coalitions also hold it back.

GLOBAL ISSUES AND BUSINESS INTERCONNECTEDNESS

The world is a far different place from the one that we knew only 40 or 50 years ago. On all dimensions, in all sectors, there is more complexity, greater turbulence (or change), more unpredictability, higher interdependence, greater awareness of the world's diversity, more threats and more opportunities for businesses and peoples. This makes it essential that every manager know something about the roles of business in social systems, to avoid the problems resulting from conventional thinking about markets, products, and corporate performance.

What does all this mean for the relationship between business and society or, more accurately, businesses and societies? Why does the globalization of economic activity affect the social and political environment of businesses, whether or not they are actually engaged in international trade? Here are some examples of current and recent social-political issues that would not exist outside a global economy:

- A political-religious leader in Iran condemns a book written in Britain, calls for his followers worldwide to kill the author and any users of the book, and thus forces US bookstores to remove the book from the shelves in fear of terrorist activity.
- Activists in Minnesota pressure their state government to divest stock of a Swiss-headquartered multinational company which is engaging in questionable marketing practices of infant formula in Jamaica.
- Saboteurs inject cyanide into a few Chilean grapes and disrupt the entire retail grocery business in North America for months.
- Involvement in a multinational corporation bribery scandal brings down an entire Japanese government and also threatens the next government.

• A massive leak of deadly chemical gas in a US-owned factory in Bhopal, India, results in the brief jailing of the company's American CEO, new safety regulations in Europe and in the US, the reviving of community evacuation procedures first established during the 1950s Cold War era, and lengthy international legal wrangles over corporate liability and fair compensation.

In the 1970s, the world experienced its rude awakening into the reality of global markets and global social issues. Throughout the world, sociopolitical changes triggered by the energy crisis, inflation and recession, Japan's increasing economic power, and the realignment of US-dominated industries such as steel and automobiles signaled a new business environment in which societal and intersocietal issues of culture, values, social structures, and politics were significant players. During the 1970s, for example, the Chilean government seized US-controlled copper mines along with the Chilean Telephone Company, 70 percent owned by ITT Corporation. In 1973–4, the Organization of Arab Petroleum Exporting Countries (OAPEC – a subset of OPEC, which also includes Venezuela and Nigeria) slapped an embargo on oil exports and virtually froze the world economy. Bauxite and coffee producers followed the Arab oil producers' lead in establishing worldwide cartel management of their commodities. In 1978, the Shah of Iran, a firm friend of the US and a modern though authoritarian ruler, was ousted by fundamentalist religious elements who nationalized foreign enterprises as Iran went once again "under the veil."

International quasi-governmental institutions, such as the EU and similar organizations in South America, the Caribbean, and Africa began to give a new dimension to business–government relations. Revelations of foreign payoffs and bribes in the Middle East, Japan, and Europe heightened awareness of internationally-oriented questions concerning ethics and business practices within diverse host country settings. In this decade, world attention began to focus on corporate social responsibility and responsiveness through such developing-country issues as the dumping of hazardous products and the inappropriate marketing of infant formula, pharmaceuticals, and pesticides.

Clearly it is not just the economy that is globalizing. Globalization of social and political issues is becoming the rule rather than the exception. The enduring impact of globalization on the business environment and thus on business and society relationships seems indisputable. Yet the effects of globalization are just beginning to be realized. In the 1990s, globalization and global thinking became imperative for business leaders:

> A few things seem certain, and one is that "globalization" will continue to be an inescapable buzzword. Businesses will operate in an even more interconnected world. With continuing advances in computers and communications . . . managers will have to shape organizations that can respond quickly to developments abroad. . . . With increasing globalization, companies will be unavoidably meshed with foreign customers, competitors, and suppliers (Kupfer, 1988).

These are challenging, interesting times for managers who work in multinational enterprises, in companies involved in international trade, in domestic companies dealing with foreign suppliers, or in companies that feel the impact of increasing foreign competition and ownership at home. For example, a South Dakota electric repair company owner says, "People keep buying more and more of these cheap, Red Chinese motors, so we have to learn how to repair them." *Fortune* comments, "Subtly or not, the world creeps in" (Farnham, 1994: 98).

To understand the global business environment, managers must be able to go beyond the traditional economic and technological factors in business management. To avoid unnecessary risks and to recognize opportunities, they must be able to appreciate the sources and impacts of changes along all dimensions of the business environment – social, economic, political, technological, ecological – in every country with which they are involved. To make timely decisions, they must be able to determine the interactive effects of environmental change in one country on events and conditions in other countries: "Complex global phenomena do not obey conventional logic or reasoning. They do not fall neatly into simple, mutually exclusive categories. Therefore they cannot be managed by conventional means" (Mitroff, 1987: 145). To avoid merely reacting to change, managers must be able to develop action plans that effectively incorporate sound knowledge of world cultures and events and the implications for the company.

WHAT IF . . . : THE NEED FOR NEW MANAGEMENT TOOLS

One way to explore the need for managers to use unconventional tools of analysis and understanding is to examine some "what if" questions, to generate some scenarios about possible world futures and their consequences for business. Consider, for example, the ideas in the inset box.

> - WHAT IF, in response to European integration, the United States and Pacific Rim countries form a common market?
> - WHAT IF Russia truly becomes a capitalist country? What if China does too?
> - WHAT IF human life expectancy moves to 100 years over the next two decades?
> - WHAT IF the US learns how to mine the mineral resources of other planets? What if the Japanese learn first?
> - WHAT IF global warming causes some countries (for example, the Netherlands) to disappear?
> - WHAT IF the United Nations is replaced in the next fifty years by a global conglomerate named "UN-r-Us"?

The implications of these scenarios for business could be enormous. How can they be recognized by using standard managerial tools of financial analysis, market analysis, corporate accounting and reporting, production and operations knowledge? Would these tools tell us anything useful about, say, the social, cultural, linguistic, and demographic changes that would be necessary for the US to form a common market with Pacific Rim countries? Would we be able to sort out the political as well as the economic consequences of one industrialized nation learning how to obtain valuable natural resources from space? What technological changes would follow the privatization of Russia and China, and how would that affect the world's balance of military and economic power? What new tools of production and distribution would be needed to feed, clothe, shelter, educate, and employ the world population that would result from a dramatic lifespan increase? Would overcrowded third-world nations band together, obtain nuclear capacity, and take over world political dominance?

None of these "what if" situations is far-fetched, any more so than some of the unexpected events we have witnessed in the past twenty years – for example, the political revolutions of Eastern Europe, the revival of religious fundamentalism in Iran and Algeria, the development of space shuttle technology, and the advances in worldwide human rights advocacy. What may be new, however, is the notion that these global events and trends affect the *business* environment and thus the ability of managers to perform their jobs and accomplish their objectives. This situation, more than anything, is what calls for nonconventional tools of understanding and managing global business environments. Some of these tools are developed and applied in this book, and the next section outlines them briefly.

GUIDING MODELS FOR BUSINESS AND SOCIETIES

To help readers begin to understand the international dimensions of business and society and the unconventional logic the subject requires, this section first defines some key terms, and then outlines a set of conceptual tools that have already proven useful in sorting out business–society interactions. These tools are the SEPTEmber model of the business environment and the institutional-ideological model built upon it, the stakeholder model of corporate environmental relationships, and the corporate social performance model. Later we will revisit these models, develop them further, and apply them to specific social and political features of the global business environment.

Terms such as international, multinational, global, home and host country, are now commonly used in business, but their meanings are not precise. We will use these terms as defined in the inset box.

Key Terms in International Business

Multinational. Vernon and Wells (1986) describe multinational enterprises as companies that are "made up of clusters of affiliated firms that, although in different countries, nevertheless share distinguishing characteristics as follows: 1. They are linked by ties of common ownership. 2. They draw on a common pool of resources, such as money and credit, information systems, trade names and patents. 3. They respond to some common strategy." Essentially, then, a multinational corporation is a single organization that accomplishes its objectives and has a physical presence in more than one country.

MNC or MNE. MNC stands for "multinational corporation." The term MNE – multinational enterprise – is sometimes used instead, to acknowledge that not all business enterprises are corporate.

International. This term is often used to refer to a firm's horizontal integration across national borders. That is, sourcing, selling, or other activities may expand across national boundaries although the firm or organization remains physically in only one location (Buckley and Casson, 1976).

Transnational. Traditionally, this term has been a synonym for "multinational," largely because the United Nations refers to MNCs as "transnational" rather than multinational corporations. Current usage, however, often equates "transnational" with "global" rather than with "multinational."

Global. There is also no widely accepted definition of this term, although it is much in vogue, along with the term "globalization" (see, for example, Rhinesmith, 1993). A global focus is one that targets a particular business activity or industry worldwide. It is a broader, more ambiguous term than the above three, and represents an integration of the concepts of international and multinational.

Home country. The home country is the nation in which a multinational enterprise originates and maintains its headquarters.

Host country. A host country is any nation, other than the home or headquarters country, in which a multinational enterprise conducts business.

THE "SEPTEMBER" ENVIRONMENT

As Figure 1.1 shows, we can view business as being embedded in an environment consisting of several different sectors. Actually, we have already been using the SEPTEmber model of the business environment (see Wilson, 1977, for the early development of the SEPT model; and Wood, 1994, for the extension to an SEPTE model) in our comparison of the social, economic, political, technological, and ecological conditions of the 1950s and 1990s. Wood (1994) explains that each sector is concerned with certain unique aspects of the environment:

- Social environment: culture, values, population, forms of social organization.
- Economic environment: conditions of production, distribution, and exchange.
- Political environment: influence, law, public policy, and governance.
- Technological environment: tools and methods of production, resource manipulation, communication, and knowledge production and use.
- Ecology or natural environment: natural resources, the emotional benefits of natural beauty or esthetics, and sustenance for life itself.

These components may be unique to each environmental sector, but events in one sector will have consequences for events and conditions in each of the other sectors – that is, the business environment is intricately interconnected. For example, the late 1980s and early 1990s saw dramatic political changes in Eastern Europe and the Soviet Union as one communist government after another toppled. For businesses and the *economic* environment in these countries, these *political* changes meant an end sooner or later to state-owned

Figure 1.1   The SEPTEmber model of the business environment

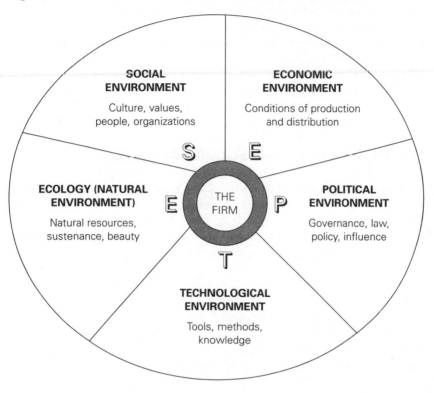

Source: Wood, 1994

enterprise and political decision making in economic organizations. Soft currencies hardened with resulting three-digit inflation; stock markets were established; the concept of private property gradually superseded the utopian idea of "ownership by all." In the *social* environment, values moved toward democracy and private enterprise, but societies also began to resurrect ethnic conflicts that had been underground for many years. As borders opened, labor and population migrations intensified. Though many people welcomed the changes as a joyful liberation, others were faced with the unwelcome task of redefining the past four decades, explaining and mythologizing their failed vision. Change appeared in the *technological* core, as western firms began technology transfers to support their new enterprises, and governments began to think about jumping to install the very latest cellular telephone systems. As the severe *ecological* damage done by communist production and governmental systems became visible,

questions of conservation and destruction of natural resources generated huge problems for managers in MNEs and governments.

This interconnection of global environmental sectors – one of the
central facts of today's world – requires nonconventional thinking
and new tools of analysis. The SEPTEmber model offers a first step
toward understanding the global business environment as a series of
interconnected human and material components, not merely as a
setting for the flow of money, goods, and technology.

THE INSTITUTIONAL–IDEOLOGICAL MODEL

From the SEPTEmber model, it is only a short step to the institutional–
ideological model (IIM), a way of thinking about how human activity
is organized, depicted in figure 1.2. This model places technology and
ecology at the core not because these two dimensions are the "most
important" environmental factors, but because technology and ecology
represent the foundations for what is possible, the set of opportunities
available to organizations and the people in them. The IIM then breaks
out the social, economic, and political sectors of the environment into
their ideological and institutional components. The ideological component consists of the ideas, values, and beliefs which underlie collective activity, and the institutional component represents the groups
and organizations that are the settings for that activity.

Figure 1.2   The institutional–ideological model (1)

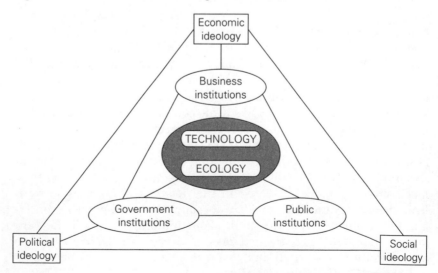

For example, talking about unemployment without identifying the specific economic ideology (for example, European-style capitalism) or the specific institution (such as, health care organizations) involved in the issue leaves too much room for misunderstanding of the problem. In some countries, there is no concept of unemployment, though some people may in fact be jobless, because the ideology makes it unthinkable that a nation would admit to being unable to provide all its people with employment.

The institutional–ideological model, then, is a refinement of the SEPTEmber model that distinguishes the ideological thought systems that drive human behavior from the institutional and organizational arrangements in which behavior is enacted. Chapter 2 expands on this model and provides several illustrations, and chapter 3 extends the discussion into the specific realm of business–government relations in the context of international business.

STAKEHOLDERS AND THE FIRM

The idea of a business stakeholder, a person or organization having a *stake* in a firm, extends the idea of *stock*holder, a person owning stock in a firm. Freeman (1984: 46) defines a stakeholder as "any group or organization that can affect or is affected by the achievement of the corporation's objectives." In figure 1.3, typical stakeholders of the firm are shown. These stakeholders are the various groups and organizations to which companies are related and with which they must interact.

Stakeholders' interests in corporate performance may be complementary or coexist peacefully, but often they are incongruent or even in dramatic conflict. Customers want high quality at low prices; owners

Figure 1.3   Some stakeholders of the firm

want to maximize their returns; employees want to maximize their compensation; financial analysts want the company to increase the value of its stock; the media want juicy stories; environmental activists want an end to pollution and may demand plant closings; communities may want jobs at any cost and corporate integration into community life; various governments want compliance with regulations, tax revenues, and good citizenship. These demands and expectations, it is easy to see, are not always compatible (although neither are they always in conflict), nor is it realistic that companies could meet *all* the demands placed upon them.

In a global marketplace, the stakeholders of business are dramatically expanded. For example, in *every* country with which a firm does business, a stakeholder map such as that shown in figure 1.3 will exist. Yet every country will have a *different* map, with different relations among the stakeholder groups, different expectations of business and its roles in the society, and different strategies and tactics available to influence corporate affairs. Also, international interconnectedness introduces new elements into corporate stakeholder maps, such as international economic and political associations, international terrorist and militarist groups, global copyright and trademark pirates, black market operators, governments-in-exile, revolutionary juntas, and world religious organizations, to name only a few. The effects of having global stakeholders are only dimly understood; for example, it is unclear what legal recourse companies have when faced with terrorism on the high seas or copyright piracy.

Stakeholders' expectations of corporations, and company impacts on stakeholders, make it essential for managers to be intensely aware of the processes and consequences of stakeholder relations. The corporate social performance model is helpful in this regard.

CORPORATE SOCIAL PERFORMANCE

Managerial beliefs and choices result in business behaviors that have consequences for stakeholders, the natural environment, and whole societies. The corporate social performance (CSP) model, shown in figure 1.4, shows linkages between the social responsibility principles that govern business–society relationships, the processes whereby companies attempt to put those principles into action, and the outcomes of corporate activity – intended and unintended, positive and negative, economic, social, political, and technological (Wartick & Cochran, 1985; Wood, 1991).

Figure 1.4   The corporate social performance model

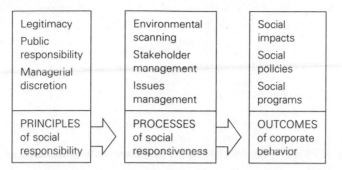

Legitimacy Public responsibility Managerial discretion	Environmental scanning Stakeholder management Issues management	Social impacts Social policies Social programs
PRINCIPLES of social responsibility	PROCESSES of social responsiveness	OUTCOMES of corporate behavior

Source: Wood, 1991

The CSP model is described and illustrated in chapter 4, and chapter 5 examines a number of specific issues involving corporate social performance and managing stakeholder relations. In addition, chapters 6 and 7 explore the ethical dimensions of international business, extending stakeholder and CSP analysis more deeply into issues of conflicting social values.

CONCLUSION

Managers who are trained only in traditional analytical methods involving economic and technological variables are going to be at a disadvantage in the global marketplace. Others, however, will have an advantage – those who also learn to analyze social structures, to map stakeholders and their interests, and to assess the social performance of their companies. The tools of social and political analysis outlined in this chapter and extended in future chapters can help managers grapple with the host of changes, challenges, threats, and opportunities in the global business environment.

REFERENCES

Alpert, Mark and Sandra Kirsch. 1988. "The Fortune 500." *Fortune* (April 25) D. 11–13.
Buckley, Peter, & Mark Casson. 1976. *The Future of Multinational Enterprise.* New York: Holmes & Meier.
Connor, David. 1994. "Top Twenty Take to Travel." *Banker* 144:816, pp. 49–52.

18   Business and Society

Emmott, Bill. 1993. "Multinationals." *Economist* 326:7804 (March 27): 555–8.

Farnham, Alan. 1994. "Global – or just globaloney?" *Fortune* (June 27, 1994): 97–9.

Farnham, Alan. 1994. "The Global 500." *Fortune* (July 25).

Freeman, R. Edward. 1984. *Strategic Management: A Stakeholder Approach.* New York: HarperCollins (formerly Pitman/Ballinger).

Fukuyama, Francis. 1992. *The End of History and the Last Man.* New York: Free Press.

International Monetary Fund. 1991. *Direction Trade Statistics Yearbook.* New York: IMF.

Kupfer, Andrew. 1988. "Managing Now for the 1990s." *Fortune,* (December 19) 133–40.

Mitroff, Ian I. 1987. *Business NOT As Usual: Rethinking Our Individual, Corporate, and Industrial Strategies for Global Competition.* San Francisco: Jossey-Bass Publishers.

Rhinesmith, Stephen H. 1993. *A Manager's Guide to Globalization: Six Keys to Success in a Changing World.* Alexandria, VA: American Society for Training and Development; Homewood, IL: Business One Irwin.

Root, Franklin R. 1973. *International Trade and Investment: Theory, Policy, Enterprise.* Cincinnati: South-Western Publishing Co.

US Bureau of Labor. 1989. *Handbook of Labor Statistics.* Washington, DC: US Government Printing Office.

US Department of Commerce. 1988. *Statistical Abstract of the United States.* Washington, DC: US Government Printing Office.

Vernon, Raymond, and Louis T. Wells, Jr. 1986. *Manager in the International Economy.* 5th ed. Englewood Cliffs, NJ: Prentice-Hall.

Wartick, Steven L., and Philip L. Cochran. 1985. "The evolution of the corporate social performance model." *Academy of Management Review* 10: 758–69.

Wilson, Ian H. 1977. "Socio-political forecasting: A new dimension to strategic planning." Pp. 159–69 in A. B. Carroll (ed.), *Managing Corporate Social Responsibility.* Boston: Little Brown.

Wood, Donna J. 1991. "Corporate social performance revisited." *Academy of Management Review* 16: 691–718.

Wood, Donna J. 1992. "'Dams or democracy?' Stakeholders and social issues in the Hungarian–Czechoslovakian hydroelectric controversy." *Proceedings of the International Association of Business and Society*, Leuven, Belgium, June.

Wood, Donna J. 1994. *Business and Society.* 2nd ed. New York: HarperCollins.

2

SEPTE and the Global ISMs

Business exists within societal contexts that involve customs and ethical rules, language and its influence on how things are perceived, law and public policy, governance processes, concepts of legitimacy, and much more. International business managers must be aware of these contexts and their effects on both organizational and individual performance.

Suppose, for example, that an American manager recently transferred to Brazil is assigned to set up a wholly owned subsidiary. It helps to know that interest rates in Brazil were around 700 percent in 1990, and that the Brazilian government had just emerged from a decade of military rule. In response, the central bank readjusted exchange rates, cut back foreign capital controls, and increased interest rates. One would want to be aware that Brazil's projected GDP growth rate for 1995 was 5 percent, the highest rate in several years (Ryser, 1995; "Finance," 1995). The manager would also want to know that Portuguese is Brazil's language and underlies the country's social traditions. Where the subsidiary is located will obviously be affected by existing transportation and labor force availability. The effects of technology and production practices on Brazilian rainforests and thus on the world's oxygen supply and ozone layer must also be considered.

How can a manager expect a firm to thrive abroad without a reasonable understanding of the social, economic, political, technological, and ecological dimensions of the host society? The prudent international manager must develop methods for gathering and interpreting information, and then developing meaningful, accurate understandings of societies' structures and functionings.

This chapter presents the institutional–ideological model (IIM), built upon the SEPTEmber model, and shows how it can be used to understand cross-cultural differences that relate to business and society issues. The chapter shows how societal-level definitions of institutional roles shape the possible actions of businesses. The world's major ISMs – for example, capitalism/socialism, pluralism/totalitarianism, individualism/collectivism – are used to provide the societal context, justification, and legitimization for institutional activity. The ISMs are compared to show their effects on business operations and global social issues.

WHITE-WATER CANOEING IN SEPTEMBER: THE EXCITING LIFE OF THE INTERNATIONAL MANAGER

Within the study of business and society, the SEPTEmber model is a common way to begin to sort out the dimensions of the business environment (Wilson, 1977; Wood, 1994). The SEPTEmber model is a planning tool that ensures that when a manager examines the macroenvironment of a business's operations, no major dimension is overlooked. *Social* dimensions (demographics, culture, values, power relationships), *political* dimensions (law, public policy processes, and the allocation of political power), and *ecological* dimensions (natural resources, beauty, sustenance of life) are accorded equal importance with the more commonly considered *economic* dimensions (GNP, market structures, conditions of competition) and *technological* dimensions (infrastructure development, tools and techniques, knowledge). Although the patterns of interaction may differ, all five dimensions of the SEPTEmber model are important factors in determining organizational and individual performance, and the conditions of each dimension have consequences for the other dimensions.

Ian Wilson, who originated the model while working as corporate planner at General Electric, liked to compare the macroenvironment of business with a river for white-water canoeists. At times the river is calm. Its banks are clearly defined, the currents are easy to read, major obstacles are readily visible, and even the least skilled of canoeists can navigate safely down the river. In such placid times the characteristics of the river are easy to observe and interpret. They present few problems and the canoeists' objectives are not threatened by the river itself. In fact, canoeists may take advantage of the opportunity to enjoy the scenery, have a cold drink, and relax as the world floats by.

Then, downstream, a faint roar begins to signal that rapids are upcoming. The rapids develop as the banks of the river bed change, causing the currents to become more turbulent and the obstacles more threatening. Once in the rapids, the banks of the river all but disappear, the currents come together with incredible force, and obstacles are invisible as they smash against the canoe. Only the skilled canoeist makes it through; the amateurs tip over, smash up, and go under. On the other side of the rapids, a new calm exists, a calm unlike any before it, a calm until the next rapids.

Like the white-water canoeist who only examines the banks, currents, and obstacles of the river during conveniently placid times, the international manager who only examines the macroenvironment during periods of calm will not be prepared for the rapids. Such a manager might even mistakenly assume that the roar of an approaching waterfall is nothing but more rapids. The changing riverbanks, currents, and obstacles cause turbulence for the canoeist; the SEPTEmber dimensions of a society's or a region's macroenvironment cause immeasurably more turbulence for the international manager.

Thus, knowing the gross domestic product (GDP) of a country or knowing that its political system rests with a military junta is certainly important, but understanding the junta's influence on economic development underlying GDP, or knowing that low levels of GDP prompted the coup which propelled the junta into power, leads to more meaningful understanding of societies. Knowing that technology is only effective when appropriately matched to skill levels of the labor force means that for each host culture, managers must know something about education, literacy, work values, and acquaintance with tools across social classes and regions. This knowledge, which will inform the MNC's technological decisions, may also tell the international manager something about political risk in these countries, or the likelihood of a rapid or steep change in GDP.

Linking the key dimensions of the SEPTEmber model, as in these examples, is what the institutional–ideological model (IIM) noted in chapter 1 is intended to do. The IIM can help international managers go beyond the simplicity of the SEPTEmber perspective and sort out the multitude of influences and interconnections which make up the macroenvironment of the societies in which they operate. This model, described in the following section, gives international managers a paddle they don't want to be up the creek without.

THE INSTITUTIONAL–IDEOLOGICAL MODEL

In the institutional–ideological model, shown in figure 2.1, institutional activity is the primary focus because, simply put, that's where the action is – where things happen in a society or among societies. In brief, the model suggests that technology defines a society's core

Figure 2.1   The institutional–ideological model (2)

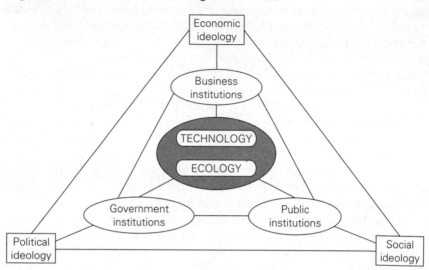

of possibilities, articulated through the institutional processes of business, government, and public activity, and shaped into specific forms and relationships by economic, political, and social ideology. The natural environment serves as the often-ignored but all-important physical setting for social systems, providing the resource core with which institutional activities become realized.

Business, government, and public institutions

An institution is an ongoing organized human activity that has some fundamental societal purpose. Societies can be viewed as having three types of institutional activity: business (economic), government (political), and public (social) activity. These institutions go beyond any single organization to reflect the basic processes necessary to make societies function. In fact, a single organization may represent two or even all three institutional processes, and any institution will be represented by many organizations (which can be mapped as an organization-set, similar to a stakeholder map as shown in chapter 1). Regardless of the particular forms, these institutions exist in all societies as the vehicles through which the problems and progress of society are realized.

The business institution is composed of those ongoing organized activities primarily intended to convert inputs (such as land, labor, natural resources, ideas, capital) into outputs (such as goods, services, employment, wealth, profit, income) which provide the society's material needs and wants. It is important to understand that when we use the term "business" in this institutional sense, we are not only talking about business firms, but about the material conversion process itself and any organizations that participate in this process. Privately owned capitalistic firms, of course, are part of the organization-set of the business institution. In addition, depending on the society's configuration of organizations and ideologies, organizations such as these may also be part of business:

- state-owned manufacturing enterprises that seek primarily to maximize employment or some other social or political goal,
- government-supported "incubators" that nourish small start-up ventures,
- not-for-profit hospitals and educational institutions,
- soup kitchens that convert leftovers and excess food products into meals for the hungry,
- municipal recycling programs that transform wastes into useable goods, and
- agricultural collectives that convert seed, soil, and labor into food for an entire community.

The government institution involves those ongoing organized activities primarily intended to structure society by defining and enforcing the "rules of the game" that apply to everyone, and legitimizing certain exceptions to those rules. Normally, the rules defined and enforced by the governmental institution will involve elements of social control as well as redistribution of the resources, benefits, and burdens of the society. Certainly, those organizations we usually think of as "government" belong in this category – leaders such as presidents or prime ministers; legislatures or parliaments; regulatory agencies, cabinets, bureaus, and ministries; courts – because their *primary* function is to define and enforce society's control and distribution rules. In addition, we can see industry associations performing the same functions for member companies, companies setting and enforcing rules for employees, and families doing the same for individual members, so that "government" as an institutional process goes far beyond the social structures and organizations that are typically given that name.

Public institutions such as family, education, religion, clubs, and voluntary associations reflect ongoing organized activities that primarily serve the interests of affiliation, socialization, and interpretation (or meaning). In any social system, people need to feel accepted as part of a group (affiliation); they need to learn acceptable behaviors and values appropriate to the society, as well as relevant knowledge and ways of learning (socialization); and they need to have the means for reaching some understanding of life's purpose and their own (interpretation).

With respect to US society, we normally think of families, friendship groups, clubs, professional associations, schools, religious organizations, and non-profit agencies of all types as "public" organizations in this sense of fulfilling affiliative, socialization, and interpretive functions. However, business firms and government organizations can also serve these same functions (though not as their primary purpose). Further interactions can be observed; for example:

- Most elementary and secondary schools in the United States are quasi-governmental organizations; in many other countries, schools through the university level are directly controlled by the government.
- Some nations have a state religion (for example Britain); some religious groups control a national government (for instance, Iran).
- Families in some countries can be more oriented toward economic or business functions (for example, in subsistence economies) than toward affiliation and meaning.

Institutional overlaps. It is common in US society to think of the social system being organized into business, government, and public institutions that are represented by organizations clearly distinct from one another in institutional purpose. Americans think in terms of corporations meeting business functions, regulatory agencies meeting governmental functions, and schools or churches meeting affiliative and interpretive functions. This strict segmentation of organizations by institutional function simply is not supported by the reality of organizations and what they do.

The institutional–ideological model represents a more interactive and realistic way of looking at social systems, institutions, and organizations. Practically every type of organization performs each of the three basic institutional functions, though in varying degrees. Using the IIM as a guide, we can readily trace the operations of these functions in our own organizations. We can see, for example, that a profit-oriented company may be organized primarily to meet the conversion function, but it will also be performing the functions of governance, affiliation, socialization, and interpretation.

An excellent example of this is the media in most developed countries. Is the media business, government, or public? The answer is "yes" – it performs all three institutional activities. In its business role, the media is converting inputs into outputs (primarily for profit in capitalist societies); in its public role, it is reporting and interpreting societal events; in its governmental role (for example, the "fourth estate" in the US) it takes on a control function, helping to spread ideas, values, and norms that become part of the culture.

Or, consider modern universities. They are engaging in business as they convert inputs such as knowledge, effort, and raw intelligence to outputs such as research, new ideas, and educated graduates. They serve a valuable public function of creating and disseminating knowledge through research, teaching, and consultation. Yet, universities may be criticized for being lax in performing governmental activities – especially control – for the daughters and sons under their custodianship.

Finally, consider any organization normally thought of as a "business." Its reason for being may be the conversion of inputs to outputs, but its governmental (that is, control and resource redistribution) and public (that is, affiliation, association, and interpretation) activities are also prominent.

ECONOMIC, POLITICAL, AND SOCIAL IDEOLOGIES

Among societies, business, government, and public institutional activities vary according to what and how inputs are converted into outputs, how the "rules of the game" are defined and enforced, and how the interests of affiliation, socialization, and interpretation are established and organized. This variability in institutional activity reflects two crucial underlying factors: the ideological foundations and the core technological and ecological capacity within a society. Here we consider the ideological bases for institutional forms; technology and ecology are considered in the following section.

Ideology is defined as the constellation of values that describe the ideas, or the blueprint, of the key dimensions of society (Cavanagh, 1990). In the institutional–ideological model, each societal institution – business, government, and public – is shaped by a corresponding economic, political, or social ideology. The types of ideology we will consider, and the range of activities they explain, are illustrated in figure 2.2.

Ideologies tend to be tied directly to particular areas of institutional activity. In fact, a "primacy of ideology" exists such that institutional activities are explained and justified on the basis of the fundamental underlying ideology attached to the institution. In addition, however, the ideologies attached to other societal institutions can also affect the shape and functioning of the focal institution. Thus, when business activity is explained, the explanation rests primarily with economic ideology and secondarily with political and social ideology. Similarly, government activity is explained primarily through political ideology, and public activity through social ideology, though each institutional activity is affected tangentially through the two indirectly related ideologies.

Figure 2.2   Ideological continua

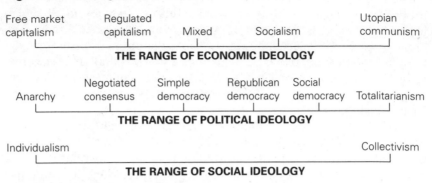

Free market capitalism — Regulated capitalism — Mixed — Socialism — Utopian communism

THE RANGE OF ECONOMIC IDEOLOGY

Anarchy — Negotiated consensus — Simple democracy — Republican democracy — Social democracy — Totalitarianism

THE RANGE OF POLITICAL IDEOLOGY

Individualism — Collectivism

THE RANGE OF SOCIAL IDEOLOGY

Economic ideology

Economic ideology is intended first and foremost to explain the *ideals* of business activity – how people think business should be organized. Interestingly, these ideas about business activity have relatively little to do with concepts that managers normally associate with business – for example, productivity, employment, profit, or distribution of goods and services. Instead, economic ideologies are collections of values (an idea examined more fully in chapter 7) oriented toward structuring economic activity so that society itself can fulfill certain goals or desired states of being.

Economic ideologies fall along a continuum describing the degree of collective (or government) control over property use and market functions, from pure capitalism with no community or government control over property use and market functions, to utopian communism, with total community (or government) control over property use and market functions. These end-points are "ideals" in the sense that neither can actually happen in a society because of the complexity and turbulence of large social systems. In between, however, are several types of economic ideology that do exist and that have different institutional and organizational consequences. We will briefly consider the entire range, because the "ideal" end-points represent dramatic contrasts that are reflected in the more realistic intermediate points.

Pure capitalism is the idea that society's material wants and needs should be satisfied by privately-owned producers and vendors (entrepreneurs) operating in a free market of exchange, constrained only by the supply and demand of desired goods or services and the consequent price signals of the market. Producers and vendors try to attract investors to lend them capital, in exchange for a hoped-for return on their investment. Capital is invested in growth ventures, and the profit that results from successful operations is the reward for both the investor (for risking capital) and the entrepreneur (for efforts and ideas). According to pure capitalism's defenders, the abstract, impersonal workings of the marketplace are the best way to ensure that the utilitarian philosophical goal of "the greatest good for the greatest number" is met in the society. Nobel-prize-winning economist Milton Friedman (1962) holds this view, and believes also that capitalism is the best path to securing human liberty, not only because each investor and entrepreneur is free to risk capital and efforts and to profit or lose, but also because the impersonal forces of the marketplace do not operate according to any political or social ideology, and therefore do not constrain the free expression of ideas or the individual's search for success.

Utopian communism, in contrast, holds the idea that society's material resources should be produced according to people's abilities and distributed according to their needs. A utopian society would have no poor members and no rich ones, even though the society as a whole may be rich or poor in comparison to other societies. No one would suffer unfair burdens, and each member would contribute to the collective good. Small communistic communities may operate as consensus-based collectives; larger ones impose a more complex governance structure that officially merges the economic function of converting inputs to outputs, with the governmental function of defining and enforcing social control and distribution rules. Pure communism is dominated by the philosophical goal of justice – achieving a fair distribution of society's benefits and burdens.

In between these two end-points are many varieties of business ideology that combine the characteristics of capitalism and communism, and the related goals of liberty and justice. *Regulated capitalism* favors the capitalistic ideal, but recognizes a need for government to intervene in establishing rules (a) that make capitalism possible, as in antitrust and deceptive practices regulation; and (b) that implement society's noneconomic objectives such as equal opportunity and environmental protection. *Socialism* favors the communistic ideal and is likely to be characterized by a centrally planned economy (that is, government control of major portions of production and distribution). But a socialistic ideology also recognizes the need for small private entrepreneurial ventures to "fill in the cracks" of a large economic system. In between regulated capitalism and socialism are various forms of *mixed* economic ideologies, attempting various blends of the personal liberty focus of capitalism with the collective-good and justice orientation of communism or socialism.

One primary difference between the end-points of economic ideology is the degree to which the institutions of business and government are distinct from each other, as in pure capitalism, or are merged, as in communism. In between, various degrees of distinction and overlap exist between business and government. These economic ideologies, in turn, have to do with how societies believe they can best achieve their desired mix of individual liberty and collective justice, which represents the other primary difference between the end-points.

Political ideology

Political ideology is the prevailing force behind the institution of government – how a society defines and enforces social control and distribution rules. Political ideology explains the ideals of government activity as they fall along a continuum from anarchy, or total personal freedom, to totalitarianism, or total state control of individual behavior. The key question, one relating to the degree of individual participation in government, is this: Who shall govern, and how much? As with economic ideology, we will examine briefly the ideal-type end-points as well as the intermediate ideologies that better reflect political reality.

Anarchy answers the prime question of "who governs" by saying, "No one, none of the time, no way." The true anarchist is opposed to *any* formally constituted government, believing that all governments are oppressive and corrupt and that free decision-making is the individual's fundamental human right. The institutional functions of government – defining and enforcing rules of social control and distribution – would be fulfilled in free exchanges and bargaining among individuals. Anarchists believe that no person has any right to exert power over another person; consequently, no organization or institution has the right to intervene in an individual's free decision-making. (As we write this chapter, the people of Rwanda are being destroyed by a disastrous anarchy – not ideologically driven, but resulting from a complete collapse of government authority.)

Totalitarianism, in contrast, is an ideology whereby individual freedom is completely suppressed in favor of some definition of collective well-being. A government operating according to totalitarian ideology has a leader or small coalition with absolute power over members of society. The leader's power may derive from religious, monarchical, traditional, or military authority, and is normally backed up by societal members' belief that the leader can and will use force. Social control and distribution policies of a totalitarian government may or may not be stable, and may or may not be oriented toward justice. Because the leader has absolute power, the rules can change on a whim. Science fiction often depicts totalitarian societies, and many people think of the former communist countries as totalitarian.

In between the two extremes of anarchy and totalitarianism are numerous forms of governance ideologies that have different configurations of individual versus collective power over social control and distribution rules. A *negotiated consensus* ideology embraces the anarchist's emphasis on bargaining and adds a collective decision making element; that is, every person can attempt through argument and bargaining to influence others, but once the group reaches a decision, that becomes the rule by which all must abide. This type of government is most likely to be found in extremely small and isolated societies that emphasize egalitarianism. Some residential religious communities, for example, might display this type of governance.

In a *simple democracy*, each citizen can vote on all governmental issues. The majority rules, although safeguards may be established to protect rights of minorities. This form of governance is time-consuming and cumbersome, and cannot be executed in large, modern societies. A *republican (or pluralistic) democracy* is characteristic of nations like the United States, in which governmental representatives are elected by citizens to make decisions on their behalf. The prevailing belief is that complex societies cannot operate on the basis of simple democracy, but that each citizen can exercise political choice through chosen representatives. A *social democracy*, characteristic of many European nations, balances the law-making power of elected representatives with the rule-making and enforcement powers of a large, permanent civil service bureaucracy, charged with overseeing many aspects of the public interest. A *bureaucratic* ideology, which might characterize Japan, would emphasize the continuity and stability of a permanent bureaucratic government regardless of the fate of leader-politicians, and with little input from individual citizens.

Social ideology

Public institutions – those designed to meet people's needs for affiliation, socialization, and interpretation – are governed by social ideology. Social ideology is intended to explain the ideals of public institutional activity as they fall along a continuum from individualism to collectivism.

· *Individualism.* Cavanagh (1990: 41) defines individualism as "a view that all values, rights, and duties originate in the individual and that the community or social whole has no value or ethical significance not derived from the individual constitutents." This social ideology puts individual rights above anything else, and does not acknowledge any superior right of the community.

Collectivism. At the opposite end of the social ideology continuum is the idea that the social whole, the collectivity, is everything, and that no individual has any value or meaning apart from the larger community. Perhaps an ant colony is the best example of pure collectivism – it seems unlikely that any free human society could be purely oriented toward the community.

All human societies are built upon both individual and collective values in varying mixes. The United States holds individualism as a core social value, although many of its institutional and organizational forms and processes serve collective interests in addition to, or rather than, individual ones. Japanese culture has a stronger emphasis on collective values, with individual rights, duties, and actions being less important. Some US forces for change have been oriented toward collectivism – moves toward enhancing social welfare, achieving just distribution of society's benefits and burdens, and protecting the natural environment are examples. On the other hand, forces for change in Japan have an individualistic tone, as workers begin to rebel at the high economic and emotional cost of living in a collective-oriented society.

Interactions of ideologies and institutions

Ideally, institutions and ideologies are mutually supportive. Ideologies define what ought to be, and institutions attempt to carry out the objectives and desired end-states expressed in the ideologies. Ideologies are sets of ideas; institutions are the processes and structures that attempt to make the ideas concrete. Ideologies define what can be imagined; institutions describe what is possible. For example, a society with a socialistic economic ideology would engage in central planning of business activity, and a society with a simple-democracy political ideology would have a governmental institution that facilitated citizen decision making.

Realistically, however, institutions and ideologies are not entirely consistent and may even be in conflict at times. For example, in the United States, a free-market-capitalism ideology prevails in the economic domain, but business actually operates in a regulated, or even a mixed, economy. Similarly, US citizens think of their political ideology as simple-democratic, but in fact the US government is a combination of republican democracy (with its representative legislature) and social democracy (with its big, stable bureaucratic agencies). Figure 2.3 illustrates the main and secondary interactions among

Figure 2.3 Institutions and ideologies

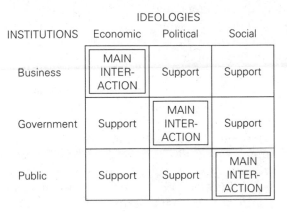

the institutions of business, government, and the public, and the corresponding economic, political, and social ideologies.

THE TECHNOLOGICAL AND ECOLOGICAL CORE

At the core of any social system is the natural environment and the available technology. Both define the possibilities for human action in the society – the natural environment through its resources and constraints, technology through the tools and processes available for human use. To some extent the ecology and technology are interdependent; technology is always built upon what is physically possible in the natural environment, and the natural environment can be degraded or enhanced, made more productive for human uses or depleted for any use, by the application of technology. In this section we will focus first on the natural environment, and then on the technological core of societies.

The natural environment ultimately is the source and support of everything used by businesses (and almost any other human activity) – every raw material, every energy source, every life-sustaining factor, even every waste disposal site.

The natural environment determines what can get done in a society and how institutions can function. Resource availability is the fundamental factor in the development of business in societies. Some world regions are rich in natural resources; some have only a few; and some are virtually barren of resources. Several areas rich in natural resources, such as Western Europe, Russia, and North America, have experienced vast economic growth fueled first by mercantilist trade and industrial production. Other areas whose natural resource base is less extensive, or less amenable to industrial use, or less accessible, have not experienced the same degree of economic growth.

The natural environment is a commons, and therefore is not entirely subject to the same laws and processes of self-interested actors that govern economic markets, even though some nations are attempting to apply market forces to control pollution emissions or environmental hazards such as oil spills. Political processes, balancing and compromising among the wishes and interests of a variety of stakeholders, are therefore highly salient to natural environment issues.

Technology includes the tools – both machines (hard technology) and ways of thinking (soft technology) – available to solve problems and promote progress between, among, and within societies. Technology determines what can get done in a society. SubSaharan countries, for example, might hold to a socialist ideology emphasizing just distribution, and might want to have an economy and government that could feed all their citizens and generate excess agricultural products for export. However, if the people do not have the knowledge to increase agricultural productivity, or if they have the knowledge but do not have the tools, they will not be able to accomplish their goals because the natural environment is harsh from the perspective of supporting human life. As another example, many people would agree that computers represent a technological advance that is liberating and increases productivity. However, there are people in modern societies who should be able to use computers but refuse to do so, because they don't have the soft technology (the knowledge) or the will to make use of these tools.

Technology defines how institutions can function. In the 1992 US presidential election, for example, independent candidate Ross Perot suggested that public policy issues be resolved through computerized "town hall meetings," where issues would be posed and citizens would register opinions via touchtone telephone, interactive cable TV, and computer networks. This suggestion, if offered in the 1972 presidential election, would have met with a giant, collective "Huh?" However, the technology to implement Perot's suggestion is readily available, and makes it theoretically possible for the US government to adopt a simple, rather than a representative, democracy. By 1993, the Clinton administration had established an e-mail address so that the millions of Internet users and commercial on-line services could have direct access to the White House and its decision makers.

Technology can be a progressive influence on institutional activity because it is available for anyone to use. Theoretically, technology is equally available to all institutions within a society, and the extent to which a technology is actually used by an institution depends on choices made by those acting for that institution. For example, differences in the degree of computer usage among business, government, educational, and family institutions in a society are normally matters of resource allocation and choice, and not a matter of the physical availability of computers. As another example, the technology for high-speed magnetic levitation trains is readily available, and has been implemented for a number of years in France, where social and political ideologies support collective efforts and large government technology programs. In the US, however, where social and political ideologies lean toward individualism (and private automobiles), maglev trains have not caught on.

The major differences in the ways that ideology and technology influence the accomplishment of a society's institutional activity relate to the breadth of influence of each. In some societal contexts, ideology is likely to be a stronger, deeper influence than technology. For example, in a highly ritualistic, ceremonial society, technological development may be suppressed or hindered because the society's ideology constrains the flow of new ideas and their pragmatic implementation. Or in a society based on religious principles emphasizing spiritual growth, technology may be almost irrelevant, and therefore receive no attention or investment. In contrast, in a society with an ideology that is based on growth, progress, and knowledge, technology may proceed far ahead of people's ability to accept it, as has been true of computer technology, medical procedures, and bioengineering.

In other societal contexts, technology may dominate ideology or force it to change. For example, technologically less-advanced societies have been acquiring modern industrial and telecommunications technology over the past few decades, and such technology transfer changes the possibilities for individual and social life in a way that forces concurrent change in ideas (ideology) about what constitutes a proper life. As another example, some people believe that the technological inability to block incoming telecommunications – television, telephone, e-mail, fax – was ultimately responsible for the late 1980s break-up of the Soviet bloc. No amount of ritualism or totalitarian rule could prevent telecommunications technology from reaching people and giving them new ideas.

INTERACTIONS OF IDEOLOGIES, INSTITUTIONS, AND THE CORE

To further illustrate the interplay of ideology and technology, consider that ideological influences can limit the theoretically universal availability of technology in a society. For example, because the government is based upon a conservative religious ideology, Saudi Arabian women are not permitted to drive cars. This limits their mobility and personal freedom and ties them to the local neighborhood, public transportation, or a male driver. This is not simply a matter of resource allocation, but instead is one of ideologically-based prohibition against some of society's members having access to a readily available technology. As another example, several predominantly Catholic countries of Europe and South America prohibit access to birth control technology. Again, resource availability is not the issue, but rather control over the values and behavior of society's members. On the other hand, the US's ideology of separation of church and state, personal freedom, and price-based markets means that all citizens can buy wide-screen color TVs, VCRs, car phones, fax machines, or personal computers, whether or not they need them, whether or not they can afford them, and regardless of who or what they are in the social system.

Summary. Business always involves converting inputs into outputs which are intended to satisfy society's material wants and needs, but how this conversion process is accomplished is a function of ideology and technology, within an ecological context. For example, China's Marxist ideology and relatively unsophisticated technology mean that business is conducted via state-owned and managed enterprises driven by national employment and production goals (not by profit or wealth maximization goals), and via tiny entrepreneurial enterprises serving local needs. In the US, by contrast, a pluralist, democratic, free-market ideology encourages a wide variety of business organization types and discourages nationalized businesses.

Government always involves defining and enforcing the overall "rules of the game," but how this activity is accomplished is a function of ideological and technological influences. For example, in late 1991, the government-owned airline of Saudi Arabia required its female flight attendants to wear veils and long skirts, bowing to the conservative religious majority seeking a return to traditional Islamic rules. In this case, ideological concerns outweighed the technological need for airline attendants to be able to move rapidly, as the government bowed to the demands of conservative religious leaders seeking a nationwide return to traditional Islamic rules. To compare, Max Weber's classic study, *The Protestant Ethic and the Spirit of Capitalism*, showed how religious-based political ideology and the development of industrial technology operated in tandem to create and sustain the economic form of capitalism in Europe and America in the late 1800s.

Finally, *public* institutions normally involve fulfilling the affiliative, socialization, and interpretive needs of a society's people, but how these institutions are created, organized, and maintained is a function of ideology and technology. For example, in the US, union dues can be deducted from employee paychecks (sometimes against the employee's wishes), but church contributions cannot. In Germany, which does not have such a strong ideological bias for separation of religious activity from other institutional activities, charitable contributions can be deducted from paychecks, and payroll contributions to either the Lutheran or the Roman Catholic church are mandatory unless the employee specifically designates "none." As another example, families in the US are constituted strictly on the basis of the participating adults' choice, but in India, marriages are arranged by the parents of the individuals. Finally, education in most countries is considered of interest to the government, but ideological differences drive the degree to which government controls the educational institution, and technology influences educational organization, content, and teaching methods. Countries without a reliable supply of electricity will not use videos, computers, overhead projectors, and so on in their educational organizations.

Institutions, ideologies, and social issues

The link of the institutional–ideological model to social issues is a crucial one for international managers. It helps us to understand how social issues "flow" through a social system, through institutions and organizations, with various meanings and consequences. For example, consider the problem of pollution. The basic technological problem is that we produce wastes that we can't dispose of – "byproducts looking for a use." If technology could prevent pollution, or dispose of wastes in an acceptable manner, there would be no pollution problem. The issue of pollution is manifested in business activity because the byproducts arise through converting inputs into outputs. At some point, pollution is raised as a problem by voluntary or public activities. After pollution is recognized as a social problem, government activities attempt to control the problem and to redistribute resources according to a new assessment of societal values with respect to the issue. For example, tax revenues may be redirected from social welfare programs to environmental clean-up efforts, from aerospace research to research on environmentally-friendly production processes.

When the issue enters a public forum for debate, every institution is represented by its primary ideological base; that is, people who speak from a certain institutional perspective will speak with the ideology that underlies that institution. In western capitalist societies, the discussion would go something like this:

- Business: "We can't do anything about pollution; it's too expensive not to pollute and we wouldn't be competitive in the global marketplace. We wouldn't make a profit."
- Public groups: "Clean up what you mess up. We don't care what it costs you."
- Government: "Let's look for a compromise. Either that, or we'll figure out the rules and make sure that all of you obey them."

These positions, and the action gridlock they may produce, reflect the business ideology of free enterprise, the government ideology of pluralistic or representative democracy, and the social ideology of individualism and personal responsibility.

In contrast, an authoritarian government would theoretically have the power to either stop the problem of pollution at its source, or to ignore or suppress public opinion against it. A non-capitalist business institution could simply absorb the cost of pollution control as part of its operating costs. Public institutions that derive from a fatalistic worldview would merely shrug and say, "So be it," ignoring pollution until the earth was destroyed. In the United States, these latter alternatives do not exist, or are difficult to implement, because of the overall influence of ideology on institutions. Elsewhere in the world, they do exist and are implemented, for the same reason.

THE IIM AND INTERNATIONAL MANAGEMENT

The institutional–ideological model uses the SEPTEmber model as a starting point, then extends the social, economic, and political dimensions of that model by examining the interplay of ideological and technological influences on institutional activity. This is a more realistic way of looking at social organization. It reflects how social institutions really function – across organizational boundaries, in conjunction with people's beliefs and ideas, and dependent upon available technology and resources. Furthermore, the IIM helps us to see that each institutional function is influenced primarily by its directly related ideology, but is also indirectly influenced by each of the other ideologies. Finally, placing technology and ecology at the core of the model indicates that the tools available to a society set the limits on how the society can accomplish its necessary functions. In addition, the state of technology and the ecological foundations of a society tell us what will and will not be a social issue, and what possibilities exist for understanding and managing social issues and problems.

In exhibit 2.1 is a checklist based on the IIM model for international managers considering expanding their business into a new country. The checklist is built around the structures, functions, and fit of the technological, ideological, and institutional dimensions of the country being considered, and the fit of these dimensions with the manager's business. Of course, the checklist will not provide a device for quick-and-dirty decision making. But, if the objective is to make a meaningful fit between the company and the country, and to minimize social, political, and ecological problems as well as economic and technological ones, the IIM checklist will help.

Exhibit 2.1   IIM checklist

(1) Technological dimensions

What is the soft-technology core?
What are the country's education/literacy levels, its technical know-how?
How do people learn – through science, magic, religion, formal education, elder teaching, peer socialization, consensus decision making, violence?
What do people think can be learned?
What are the country's sources of new understandings and new knowledge? How and where is research supported?

What is the hard-technology core?
What is the level of technological development in terms of machinery, equipment, production capacity?
Are there internal suppliers for needed hard-technology, or not?
What are the country's primary energy sources?
Can the infrastructure support the technology we need?

Investment
What investment is necessary to get the soft-technology or hard-technology to the level you want it?
What do we have to do to match existing soft and hard technology with our company's technological needs?
What is needed, and what is our role?

(2) Ecological dimensions
What is the natural resource base?
What ecosystems are represented? What's the position of endangered species?

What is the state of health of ecosystems? How does this affect human health, animal life, and plant life?
What is the current state of environmental pollution?
What are the ecological dimensions of transportation, communications, population siting, and waste disposal?

(3)   Ideological dimensions

Economic ideology
What are the prevalent beliefs about the business's role and status in society?
What are the expectations placed on business?
How is private property viewed?
What's the apparent mix of free enterprise and socialistic ideas?
Is monopoly accepted? Are competitive markets favored over monopolies or vice versa?
What are the assumed rights of owners, employees, managers, customers, communities?
Is the country's economic ideology consistent with this firm's culture?

Political ideology
What are the prevalent beliefs about government's role and status in society?
What are the expectations placed on government?
To what extent is political will to be exercised through government?
Do people believe in or accept bureaucratic or democratic or totalitarian government forms?
Is the country's political ideology consistent with this firm's culture?

Social ideology
What are the prevalent beliefs about the role and status of public institutions in the society?
What are the expectations placed on public institutions?
To what extent is membership in public institutions believed to be voluntary?
Is the country's social ideology consistent with this firm's culture?

Interactions
What is the relationship among the economic, political, and social ideologies of the country?
Are there inconsistencies or conflicts that would cause trouble for the company?

(4)   Institutional dimensions

Business institutions
What is the structure of business in this country?
Are business organizations large or small?
What is the ownership structure – corporate, proprietor, state, cooperative?
Is decision making centralized or decentralized?
What is the mix of business functions (a) externally – manufacturing versus service, and (b) internally – production, marketing, finance, accounting, personnel, external relations?
What are the competitive conditions in the country – monopolistic, oligopolistic, partially competitive, completely competitive?
Is the country accustomed to international or global business, or is the scope of business more local or regional?
What limits are placed on business decision making, and by whom?
Does the company have structures, processes, and people appropriate for interacting with the country's business institutions?
To what extent are business organizations expected to perform government and public activities?

Government institutions
Are government organizations large or small?
Do they exist at different levels (local, regional, state, national)?
What is the governmental power base – military, electorate, tribal, monarchy, consensus?
How does government exercise its function of social control?
How are rules established, enforced, and changed?
How does executive, legislative, and judicial decision making occur?
What is the government's role in redistributing the society's resources?
What legal protections for private property exist?
Does the company have structures, processes, and people appropriate for interacting with the country's government institutions?
To what extent are government organizations expected to perform business and public activities?

Public institutions
What is the mix among types of public institutions – family, education, religion, press, voluntary associations?
What are the roles of women and men, ethnic or racial minorities and majorities, in public institutions?

Do public institutions tend to be large or small?
How is their expected role in the society accomplished?
What legal or other protections exist for public institutions?
To what extent is membership in public institutions actually voluntary?
Does the company have structures, processes, and people appropriate for interacting with the country's public institutions?
To what extent are public organizations expected to perform government and business activities?

Interactions
What is the relationship among the business, government, and public institutions of the country?
Are there inconsistencies or conflicts that would cause trouble for the company?

FINALLY: Is the company prepared to do business in this country, given its mix of technology, ecology, ideology, and institutional arrangements?

CONCLUSION

Students of business and society and managers of MNEs must approach the international arena with their eyes wide open. Those who ignore any major dimension of the international business environment or who focus too narrowly on just one specific aspect will be vulnerable to the sheer complexity they face.

Managers need to carefully examine each aspect of a society and its interactions with other societal aspects. The institutional–ideological model is one device for sorting and making sense of international complexities. Ideologies, institutions, technologies, and ecosystems determine both the structures and processes of modern societies.

REFERENCES

Cavanagh, Gerald F. 1990. *American Business Values*. 3rd edition. Englewood Cliffs, NJ: Prentice-Hall.
"Finance Watch." 1995. *Business Latin America* 30:11 (March 20): 7.
Friedman, Milton. 1962. *Capitalism and Freedom*. Chicago: University of Chicago Press.

Ryser, Jeffrey. 1995. "Brazil, si! Mexico, no!" *Global Finance* 9:2, pp. 42–7.

Weber, Max. 1958. *The Protestant Ethic and the Spirit of Capitalism*. Translated by Talcott Parsons. New York: Charles Scribner's Sons.

Wilson, Ian H. 1977. "Socio-political forecasting: A new dimension to strategic planning." Pp. 159–69 in Archie B. Carroll (ed.), *Managing Corporate Social Responsibility*. Boston: Little, Brown.

Wood, Donna J. 1994. *Business and Society*, 2nd edition. New York: Harper Collins.

3

Managing International
Business–Government Relations

Just before leaving office in 1992, President George Bush, along with the leaders of other UN member nations, committed troops to a United Nations relief effort intended to provide food to starving Somalians. The government of Somalia had broken down and the country was being "governed" by warring armies of thugs. Food intended to relieve mass starvation was being comandeered for the gangs, resulting in continued starvation and social chaos. The UN troops entered Somalia to combat the gangs and to guarantee orderly food distribution to those who desparately needed the relief effort.

The UN involvement in Somalia gets us thinking as much about the future of business–government relations as about the present and past of this important aspect of international business and society interactions. If some supranational government such as the UN becomes accepted as the authority for resolving within-country conflicts, if the world accepts a UN role that draws military might from the world's industrialized nations, if the UN becomes a multinational government, then what are the implications for MNEs and international business–government relations? In this chapter we outline some of the many roles of business–government relations in the context of global business.

THE IMPORTANCE OF NATION-STATES

How do we define the three elements in the phrase "business–government relations"? Consider this:

The study of business–government relations is predicated on the way each of these three elements is conceptualized. Forms of business which are marginal in the United States may occupy center stage in other cultures. For example, to what extent is it possible to consider as equivalent research units a large private bank in the United States, and an equally large, democratically-run credit union in Quebec, each filling the same economic purposes? Defining the concept of government is another source of concern. For example, to what extent should European neocorporatist structures, which are run by private parties (mostly unions and employer associations) be considered as part of government? To what extent should the personalized states of Africa or Italy (Balducci, 1987) be considered the conceptual equivalents of the classic impersonal bureaucratic states of western tradition? As for the problems of business–government relations, thorny questions of equivalence arise with cultures in which the limits between state and private ownership, and especially the limits between state and private control, are uncertain. What is government, what is business, and what is the relationship between the two in economic organizations of which both are owners and managers, and in which both are parties to internal exchanges of resources? (Pasquero and Wood, 1992.)

In chapter 2, government was defined as "those ongoing organized activities primarily intended to structure society by defining and enforcing 'the rules of the game' that apply to everyone, and legitimizing certain exceptions to those rules," and business was defined as "those ongoing activities primarily intended to convert inputs . . . into outputs . . . which provide the society's material needs and wants." Business as an activity appears to be relatively constant over time, but since the 1500s, multiple forms of government organizations (for example, monarchy, democracy, parliamentary, military, totalitarian), exercised through nation-states, have been the norm in European, North American, and Asian societies. In fact, many people equate the term "society" with the nation-state.

Although US business rhetoric often seems to dismiss governmental activities as being of little value or even destructive, government in nation-states serves a number of irreplaceable functions for business, and the role of government is well-accepted in most nation-states. Even free-market capitalism's strongest defenders acknowledge the importance of government to business. Milton Friedman (1962), for example, notes four necessary functions that government performs for business:

(1) to serve as rule maker and rule enforcer;
(2) to provide a common monetary authority;
(3) to control the negative consequences of monopoly power; and
(4) to take care of those who cannot legitimately participate in the system (for example, "madmen" and children).

In most nations, these vital roles of government in relation to business are readily accepted. In Japan, for example, one key task of government is to coordinate the intra- and international operations of important industries and to support Japanese MNEs for the benefit of the domestic economy. In many European countries, the government is expected to provide for social welfare and to conduct its international affairs for the benefit of domestic MNEs. The United States stands virtually alone among the world's nations in its ideological hostility to government taking an active role in business.

From the point of view of business, government provides the needed context within which business organizations can operate. The substance of governmental involvement in business activities has been and will continue to be a source of debate, but the legitimacy of these involvements is generally acknowledged and accepted. In fact, when governments crumble (as in the Somalian case, or in South Africa or the former Yugoslavia), business as much as any other societal component seeks out a new authority which can provide the context and clarity of a societal framework.

In addition, government is a *customer* of business (contracts, supplies), a *financier* of business (subsidies, joint research), a *promoter* of business (trade policy), and a *protector* of business (tariffs, quotas, regulations). Furthermore, even in countries as free-market-oriented as the United States, we find government as *owner* of business-like operations (for example, the Tennessee Valley Authority, a giant water management and power generating organization, or NASA, the National Aeronautics and Space Administration). In many countries, government owns essential service industries such as utilities, telecommunications, and even mining and some heavy industry (see McCraw, 1984).

Government activities through the nation-state are far too important to business to be ignored or cavalierly dismissed. Business organizations convert inputs to outputs to satisfy society's material needs and wants *within a context created by government activities*. Business–government relations, then, are a central focus of business and society analysis, whether in a single nation or internationally.

KEY ASPECTS OF BUSINESS–GOVERNMENT RELATIONS

As we saw in chapter 2, underlying any business–government relationship are the fundamental societally accepted economic and political ideologies of business and government, respectively. Where on the continuum of capitalism to utopian communism does a society's economic ideology fall? Where on the continuum of anarchy to totalitarianism does the political ideology fall? Answers to these questions tell us a lot about a society's business–government relations because answers must take into consideration different combinations of business–government relations variables.

For example, business–government relationships will also be strongly influenced by the technological and ecological cores of societies. Countries with limited technological development or sparse natural resources must trade and attract investment in order to have growing economies. Policies and multinational agreements directed at trade and investment are established or negotiated by government activities. In addition, business–government relations involve implementation factors that bring managers' attention down from the broad matters of ideology, technology and ecology to the more specific concerns of public policy scope and focus.

As well, regardless of ideology, business–government relations both within and across societies will be partially determined by the degree of cooperation between the two institutions and by the degree of self-interest that motivates private and public decision makers. Figure 3.1 illustrates combinations of a society's business–government relations tendencies in terms of cooperation (a collective motivation) and self-interest (an individualistic motivation). The top part of figure 3.1 illustrates how these two variables interact to determine the scope of regulatory activities within one society. The bottom part illustrates influences of the coupled variables across societies. Any of these

Figure 3.1   Business–government relations: motivations and interactions

WITHIN SOCIETIES

Decision maker interaction:	Decision maker motivation:	
	Self-interest	Other interest
Cooperative	Industry regulation	Infrastructure regulation
Adversarial	Economic regulation	Social regulation

ACROSS SOCIETIES

Decision maker interaction:	Decision maker motivation:	
	Self-interest	Other interest
Cooperative	Trade and integration compromise	Economic assistance
Adversarial	Limits and restrictions on trade	Extraterritorial regulation

combinations may exist within a particular ideological domain such as pure capitalism combined with simple democracy, or negotiated consensus coupled with utopian communism; they are not ideologically bound. The typology is intended to describe, not predict, the general tendencies within the public policy scopes and focuses of business–government relationships.

An interesting point illustrated in figure 3.1 relates to the extreme adversarial nature of US business–government relations in comparison to other societies in the world. Business historian Thomas McCraw (1984) has argued that US business–government relations are more adversarial than in other societies because in America, big business evolved *before* big government. However, the evolution of these institutions occurred in reverse in most other modern societies. Thus, in the US, much government policy has been more of a reaction to business practices, a countervailing power, rather than a partnership interaction with business.

Another coupling of variables which helps clarify the specifics of business–government interactions relates to the degree of pluralism (access by many political players) within a public policy development process and the type of public policy process (for example, one-step-at-a-time incrementalist versus rational planning) which prevails. The result of the combinations of these two variables relates mostly to the general public's perceptions of the results of the public policy process, and helps explain why, for example, Japan or Sweden often appear to have a much more orderly public policy process than the US or Britain (see figure 3.2).

An interesting extension relating to this coupling of the degree of pluralism and the type of public policy process concerns the acceptance of industrial policy. Again, the United States seems to be at an extreme in terms of their acceptance of the need for industrial policy since other countries of the world more readily accept the idea that government has an appropriate and important role in providing incentives and inducements to promote business activity in designated

Figure 3.2   Business–government relations: pluralism and types of public policy

TYPE OF PUBLIC POLICY DEVELOPMENT	DEGREE OF PLURALISM	
	Homogeneous	Pluralistic
Incrementalist	Logical, orderly, evolutionary	Piecemeal, chaotic, ambiguous
Rational planning	Focused, consistent, future-driven	Controversial, idealistic, "coercive"

sectors. David Vogel (1987) has argued that American rejection of industrial policy is more rhetorical than real since for decades we have had agriculture, housing, and aerospace industrial policies. Nevertheless, the US has consistently rejected overarching industrial policy, even though some experiments in this direction were made during the Great Depression of the 1930s and during World War II in the next decade. This is likely to be the result of the incrementalist/pluralistic character of US public policy.

A final combination of variables which helps to differentiate the specifics of business–government interactions relates to definitions of "the public interest" and predominance of different lobbying techniques. Is the concept of "the public interest" focused more on minimizing interest group dissent (maximizing the mix of self-interests), or does it rest more with a collective view of societal good? Does lobbying focus more on information to help decision makers reach rational conclusions, or on financial/political favors to buy, or facilitate, a wanted decision? Answers to these questions help us understand what seems to get accomplished through the public policy process.

Underlying the logic of coupling the concept of "the public interest" and the influence of lobbying techniques is the important role which the media plays in reporting and interpreting public policy (see figure 3.3). As the media has globalized through advances in telecommunications (for example, CNN International) and as the "media-selected" events of the world become the cornerstones of individuals' knowledge and understanding, the influence of international media operations becomes an important issue for all businesses to consider. For example, consider the 1993 statements of the Japanese Minister which were reported in the US press as condemning American workers for being lazy. Actually, the comment was a criticism of increasing laziness of Japanese (not American) workers, and the criticism was merely being placed in the context of a worldwide phenomenon affecting European, Canadian, American and Japanese workers. Business managers must become more concerned and sophisticated

Figure 3.3 Business–government relations: lobbying and "The Public Interest"

CONCEPT OF "THE PUBLIC INTEREST"	LOBBYING FOCUS	
	Informational	Financial
Interest group satisfaction	Localistic results	Pecuniary results
Broader societal interest	Multinational results	Elitism results

about media influences in selecting and interpreting world events if they are to understand what appear to be the results of international business–government relations.

There are a multitude of other variables which could be introduced to help explain the specifics of public policy and international business–government relations, but the six factors noted above (degree of cooperation, degree of decision makers' self-interest, degree of pluralism, type of public policy development process, definition of "the public interest," and the influence of lobbying techniques) provide sufficient background and framing in order to understand public policy and business–government relations both within a single society and across societies. Attention can then be turned to the realities of alternative business–government relations at the multinational level of analysis.

ALTERNATIVE INTERNATIONAL BUSINESS–GOVERNMENT RELATIONSHIPS

Most multinational corporations are relatively skilled at business–government relations. The field of "political risk assessment" focuses on determining and comparing the political stability within and among particular societies, assessing the likelihood of change in public policy, and analyzing the impacts of government actions on investment climates. Many techniques have been developed to fulfill these tasks, including case studies, scenario building, cross-impact analyses, Delphi techniques, Bayesian forecasting, events studies, simulations, and content analysis (see Rogers, 1983).

Events of the last several years have also meant that those interested in business and society interactions must become more concerned about intersocietal business–government interactions. The integration of the European Union, the creation of the North American Free Trade Agreement (NAFTA), the splintering of Eastern bloc countries, the merging of the Germanies, and the changing emphases within existing institutions such as the General Agreement on Tariffs and Trade (GATT) and UN agencies such as the World Health Organization (WHO), have brought to the fore the importance of intersocietal business–government relations.

Economic integration

In absolutely free markets there are no restrictions placed on the movement of products (that is, goods and services) or on the transfer of resources and factors of production (that is, labor, capital, natural resources, and information). Restrictions on either products or factors of production are government creations intended to somehow protect domestic input or output markets. Conversely, various forms of economic integration between countries are intended to minimize if not eliminate the restrictions on the movement of products and factors of production. These forms of integration (from most restrictive to least restrictive) are free trade areas, customs unions, common markets and economic unions (see table 3.1).

Free trade areas permit the free flow of products across borders of those countries who are a party in the free trade agreement, but they allow member countries to maintain their own external tariffs. So, the NAFTA means that products from Mexico may enter the United States or Canada without being subject to Canadian or American tariffs. Similarly, American goods can go tariff-free to Canada and Mexico, and Canadian goods can go tariff-free to the United States and Mexico.

Customs unions permit the free flow of products among member countries and establish common external tariffs. Thus, if the United States and Mexico created a customs union, products could move across borders with no restrictions but there would be a common external tariff for all goods imported into the customs union regardless of the member country which imports the goods.

Table 3.1 Types of economic integration

	Free trade area	Customs union	Common market	Economic union
Tariffs on goods are abolished for trade among member countries	Yes	Yes	Yes	Yes
Common external tariffs on goods imported into member countries are created	No	Yes	Yes	Yes
Restrictions on the movement of factors of production are abolished	No	No	Yes	Yes
Member country economic policies are "harmonized"	No	No	No	Yes

Source: adapted from Daniels and Radebaugh, 1989

A common market allows for not just the free flow of products, but also for the unrestricted flow of factors of production. So, if the United States, Canada and Mexico set up a North American Common Market, then labor, capital and information as well as products could flow unhindered across the borders of the three countries in order to take advantage of whatever benefits might exist. Some NAFTA analysts believe that a common market-like situation is an inevitable result of the new ability of US, Canadian, and Mexican firms to shift production, goods, and jobs among the three countries.

Economic union – the process which Europe is going through right now – seeks to go beyond a common market and to "harmonize" economic factors such as government regulation, currency and the monetary system, property rights, inflation and growth rates, and unemployment rates as well as a few other governmental activities such as social programs and military organizations.

These are theoretical categories of economic integration. The reality of integration is likely to be less tidy. Europe, for example, has had more trouble moving toward a common currency and monetary system than even the gloomiest analysts had predicted. The pound, deutschmark, franc, and other national currencies of the European Union are deeply embedded in the culture and values of their countries, and the ecu – European Currency Unit – simply does not have the same clout or acceptance.

It takes little imagination to appreciate the troubles which these various forms of economic integration can create in a world so dominated by nation-state mentalities. It is also easy to understand how difficult it is to achieve each of the various types of integration. Exhibit 3.1 reviews the post-World War II experience of Europe in moving from a continent at war to a "Europe without frontiers."

The motivation for creating any form of economic integration must be extremely strong. Given, for example, the historic and deep-seated animosities among the nations of Europe, it is remarkable that total integration of the European Union is even a thought. Yet, these countries are making progress toward total integration and when complete, they will end up with the largest consumer market in the world. Under integration, the "domestic" market of a German producer in 1989, for example, increases from a gross domestic product, at current German exchange rates, of DM1.5 trillion to more than DM7.4 trillion (from US$929 billion to US$4.5 trillion). The current drive toward reduction of economic transaction costs should not be understated and, in the face of an increasingly independent global business system, seems likely to win out ultimately over even the deepest of historic social and political differences.

Exhibit 3.1   The evolution of the European Union

1944   Holland, Belgium and Luxembourg create the Benelux customs union.

1952   Benelux countries join with Italy, France and West Germany to form the European Coal and Steel Community (ECSC), a free trade agreement only for coal and steel.

1957   ECSC countries sign the Treaty of Rome creating the European Economic Community (the EEC, a common market) and the European Atomic Energy Community (Euratom).

1959   UK along with Denmark, Norway, Sweden, Portugal, Austria, and Switzerland create the European Free Trade Association (EFTA).

1961   Finland joins the EFTA.

UK seeks entry into the EEC, but (in 1963) France vetoes the UK entry. French concern is with agricultural policy.

1962   EEC adopts a "Common Agricultural Policy."

1967   The Brussels Treaty (of 1965) merges the EEC, the ECSC and Euratom into the Commission of European Communities (the EC). The EC consists of four parts: a commission, a council, a parliament and a court system.

The UK again applies for membership in the EC, but again the move is vetoed by France.

1970   Iceland joins the EFTA.

1973   Denmark and the UK withdraw from EFTA and join (with Ireland) the EC.
Norway is admitted to the EC, but Norwegians reject the treaty.

1979   The European Monetary System (EMS) is created to reduce the restrictions on capital movement. The EMS consists of a European Currency Unit (ECU), credit facilities, transfer arrangements and exchange-rate stabilization programs.

The UK refuses to participate in the EMS.

1981   Greece joins the EC, but declines to participate in the EMS.

1986   Portugal and Spain join the EC.

The EC passes the Single European Act which sets 1992 as the date for fully implementing the conditions set out in the 1957 Treaty of Rome.

1992   The EC continues to work toward total integration, but in June, citizens of Denmark reject the Maastricht Agreement on monetary union, slowing progress toward a unified currency.

1993   Negotiations begin to enlarge the EC by adding Austria, Sweden, Finland, and Norway. EC leaders establish strict criteria for the possible admission of Poland, Hungary, the Czech Republic, Slovakia, Romania, and Bulgaria.

In May, citizens of Denmark approve the Maastricht Treaty in a second vote. German federal courts confirm the compatibility of Maastricht with the German constitution, ending delays to monetary union begun with Denmark's earlier rejection of the treaty.

The Uruguay Round of the GATT (General Agreement on Tariffs and Trade) is signed, to be implemented by July 1995.

1994   The EC becomes the EU, or European Union. Plans for the single market are nearly complete, although some key directives are still undecided by the Council of Ministers. EU finance directors order the directors of national mints to discuss the coinage problem. Paper currency can be produced for all member nations within a year, but coins may take 5–7 years, making the paper useless until change can be made with coins.

Source: Adapted from chronology offered in Wright 1992; updated with *Business Europe*, various issues, 1993–4

To illustrate the difficulty which the EU currently faces as it works toward integration, consider so-called "harmonization" of factors such as unemployment rates, inflation rates, and tax policy. All member nations of the EU have, for example, a "value added tax" (VAT) which provides substantial revenues. Without harmonization, companies in low-VAT countries have a distinct advantage over those in higher-VAT countries. The question becomes one of creating a system of an appropriate range of VATs which minimize advantages from one country to the next.

As another example, consider the recent negotiations among EU countries which focused on the community's competitiveness and the structure of their social safety net programs. The following passage captures the conflict and controversy:

Britain used the debate for a frontal attack on the "folly" of stringent EC labor rules, while Denmark rejected any emulation of a "US model" as an invitation to "societal problems, crime and hopelessness." While Germany's Chancellor, Helmut Kohl, advocated open markets and longer working hours, French President François Mitterand raged at what he called "unfair competition" from low-cost producers, especially in Asia, and stressed the need for a united EC front against the US in world trade talks. (*Wall Street Journal*, 6.22.93: A12.)

Not only are the leaders of each member country identifying different issues for the competitiveness agenda, they are suggesting different solutions. It seems safe to predict that until there is a "meeting of the minds" on relevant issues *and* viable solutions, policy resolutions for the issue of EU competitiveness and the levels of social safety nets will not occur.

Several other policy matters relating to different integrative forms could be raised, but the point remains – integration among countries creates change in the contexts and frameworks of international business–government interactions. Shortly, we will take a closer look at managerial options for dealing with the change occurring because of integration, but first, other types of intersocietal business–government relations need to be considered.

INTERNATIONAL BUSINESS–GOVERNMENT INSTITUTIONS

While Western European countries are pulling together through economic integration, Eastern European countries are splintering through political disintegration. The collapse of the Soviet Union and the elimination of attendant structures such as COMECON (the eastern bloc common market) have led many businesses to see new opportunities as the Eastern European countries restructure their governments to be more supportive of and complementary to market-based economies. New political economies which could possibly emerge will be discussed in chapter 10, but the obvious point is that business–government contexts are changing. How the newly emerging business–government relations of Eastern Europe will ultimately play out through treaties, internal reform, and even new economic integrations poses considerable uncertainty for managers.

One factor which is likely to play an important role in the developing business–government relations of Eastern European countries (as well as other countries undergoing change in business–government relations) is the actions of existing institutions such as GATT and WHO.

Both organizations were created in the 1940s as specialized agencies of the United Nations. GATT focuses on trying to reduce tariffs and other trade barriers; WHO focuses on global health issues.

To illustrate how these organizations might play a particularly important role in the future of international business–government relations, recall that one of the major issues discussed in the recent Uruguay Round of GATT talks was the issue of using environmental regulation as a trade restriction. Environmental regulation is very uneven across countries. The United States, for example, has stringent environmental laws relating to automobile emissions. The extent to which these restrictions limit auto imports into the United States is a continuing GATT concern. Variability in environmental regulations also underlies the enormous controversy over exporting and importing hazardous waste and products, and minimizing cross-country influences of environmental damage and accidents.

In 1984, a panel of MNE leaders and international environmental experts released recommendations for dealing with global environmental problems. Among their recommendations for developing countries were:

- Make environmental regulations explicit and predictable.
- Rely on performance criteria for attaining environmental objectives, rather than mandate procedures or technology.
- Strengthen the position of . . . environmental protection agencies in their dealings with planning, finance, and development ministries.
- Improve enforcement of environmental regulations, but in doing so treat multinational companies the same as domestic enterprises in order to prevent abuse by local firms.
- Remove trade barriers and domestic economic policies that impede environmental protection, such as underpricing energy and water or restricting imports of pollution-control equipment. ("Multinationals," 1984: 25)

The obvious principle underlying this "wish list" is standardization with the environmental stringency of Western societies. But standardization may mean the loss of some competitive advantage in the production opportunities of developing countries, or it may be interpreted as a loss of "self determinism." So, even voluntary collaborations of non-governmental groups are likely to go nowhere without the "force" of government. Kalmbach (1987: 835–6), discussing various attempts by international bodies to regulate the export of hazardous chemicals banned in home countries, points out that all such regulatory efforts fall short for lack of enforcement: "The essence of a meaningful regime is its ability to coerce, through international and domestic legal mechanisms, compliance with provisions. Without such coercive means, plans and regimes remain impotent, and developing nations, viewing such grand schemes, think 'Yes . . . isn't it pretty to think so?'" Simply, environmental policy in any other context than international business–government relations makes little sense.

The potential importance of WHO can be illustrated in the role this organization eventually played in the widely discussed and analyzed infant formula controversy of the 1970s and 1980s. The marketing of infant formula in developing countries by such large MNEs as Nestlé and Abbott Labs was fraught with ethical issues relating to health, sanitation, literacy, and distribution. Several countries attempted to deal with the issue through their own public policy initiatives, but it wasn't until the WHO was brought in as somewhat of a supranational authority that anything other than piecemeal actions resulted. Through the WHO, a worldwide code of conduct for the marketing of infant formula was finally developed. The issues in this area are generally the same as those outlined above for pollution. To the extent that this specialized agency of the United Nations takes on a role of multinational "government" for health issues, the issues finally get resolved. Given that in 1977 WHO set "Health for All by the Year 2000" as its overriding priority, we can add yet another important institutional dimension to international business–government relations.

MANAGING WITHIN CHANGING INTERNATIONAL BUSINESS–GOVERNMENT RELATIONSHIPS

Because both the process and structure of international business–government relations are continually evolving, business managers must learn to cope with future uncertainty as their reality. Managers who believe that the business–government interactions of today will be those of tomorrow will be caught off guard and are likely to become the victims of change. How can international managers deal with the uncertainties of changing business–government relations?

Reaction, proaction and interaction

As a beginning point, we can use James E. Post's (1976) concept of reactive, proactive, and interactive response choices. One approach to responding to changing business–government relations is to be *reactive* – wait until a change occurs or is mandated, and then adapt to it. Organizational performance and policies remain the same until it is clear that they must be changed to meet a new condition. Being reactive minimizes unnecessary costs that can arise from incorrectly anticipating change, but it is a passive choice and makes the organization subject to the dictates of others.

Conversely, the *proactive* response attempts to alter the impending change in business–government relations so that organizational performance and policies will not be affected. This use of proaction is somewhat different than use of the term in other areas of study (for example, strategic management uses proaction to mean anticipation only), but Post's point is that proaction is the exact opposite of reaction. Proactive response choices promote more involvement and activism on the part of the business organization in terms of changing business–government relations, but it also can be more costly unless the organization effectively influences the change, and can be anti-change in nature.

Between reaction and proaction is the *interactive* response choice. An interactive approach starts with diagnosing the underlying problem that is prompting the change in business–government relations, and then seeks a positive-sum solution to address the underlying problem. This alternative also involves organizational activism, but the potential costs of changing organizational performance or policies are likely to be offset through gains in more effective business–government relations.

To illustrate the use of the reaction, proaction, and interaction response choices as they might be applied in the international arena by a decision maker in an MNE, consider the following situation.

Terrorist attacks in London have historically been covered by private insurance, but in 1992, insurers dropped all coverage for commercial and property damage caused by terrorists. The British government stepped in to establish an insurance pool (Pool Re) consisting of voluntary corporate premiums plus a government guarantee. A major bombing attack in the City of London, however, depleted the entire pool, causing the government to require a 300 percent increase in premiums. Companies reacted angrily, and the *Economist* observed that the government might as well abandon the insurance pool, since its high premiums would mean few companies would be covered, and the government would end up paying for damage anyway. (*Economist*, June 12, 1993, p. 91.)

Now, what are the implications of various response choices in a situation like this? Decision makers with substantial operations in London may take a reactive approach and do nothing until government dictates policy. If premiums go up 300 percent and London remains the best location for their business operations then so be it – the insurance component of the costs of doing business merely goes up

300 percent. Some reactive managers might choose to move out of London as a result of the premium increases, but again, the costs would be absorbed or passed along to some constituent or constituents. In either case, the reactive approach is still the same; let government decide on a course of action and then adjust company performance and policy to meet the change.

Given the problems with the Pool Re fund, the proactive manager would take action to maintain the existing cost structure for insurance but change the definition of the issue. The end of the illustration above suggests one way that this might take place: by articulating the issue as both a government problem and a government responsibility, the proactive manager attempts to shift the financial consequences to another party. If this approach is successful, nothing changes for the business, since the issue has been redefined to eliminate or reduce the business's costs and responsibilities.

Finally, turning attention to the interactive manager, the chief problem may be defined as trying to eliminate the terrorist bombings in London as well as elsewhere in Britain. Is there anything more that businesses might do (especially in conjunction with government) in terms of increasing security or decreasing the exposure to bombings? Barring a positive response to this question, is there any alternative measure within the insurance system which would allow for spreading the risk among several societal constituencies? If no mechanism exists, then are there alternative after-the-fact methods for compensating businesses which have been bombed; are there alternatives which will keep the companies in business? The interactive manager recognizes that change must occur to reduce or eliminate the underlying problem through interactively developed solutions.

As another example of possible responses to changing business–government relations, consider American business response to the Foreign Corrupt Practices Act (FCPA) of 1977. The FCPA has been controversial since its passage. Companies are required to keep detailed records of all foreign payments to officials, but the guidelines for determining what is and is not acceptable are still not clear. Facilitating payments to officials, for example, are permitted under the law, but no dollar value is specified for the cut-off between an illegal bribe and legal "grease."

But, problems with the applicability of the FCPA go well beyond the definition of "grease." Language problems and cultural differences make the area of bribery an extremely confusing one for international managers. Fadiman (1986: 122–3) recounts an example from his own experience in Africa, when he walked away from a business deal, greatly offended, because at the conclusion of negotiations, he was asked to provide money and a radio to the negotiator. What he failed to understand was that the request had been made in the context of his superior wealth and social status; the money would be used to throw a party in his honor and for his benefit; the radio would set the proper mood at the party. He concludes: "What may initially appear as begging, bribery, or blackmail may be revealed as local tradition, cross-cultural courtesy, or attempts to make friends" (Fadiman, 1986: 123).

Further, Fadiman (1986) points out that payments in many Asian, African, or South American countries may serve a much broader purpose than merely bribery or extortion within a single economic transaction. He argues that gift giving and favor exchanges are intended to build trust and obligation (where contract law may not be the norm); "Western interests lie in doing business, non-Western in forming bonds so that business can begin" (p. 128). So, under the FCPA, what is an MNE which wants to do business in these non-Western cultures supposed to do?

A *reactive* response to the FCPA might suggest: don't make payments unless it is absolutely clear that they are legal. This may cost the company business, but so be it. The FCPA may provide a convenient excuse for refusing to pay a bribe, but it might also prompt managers to find other ways of establishing business relationships.

A *proactive* response is to go after the law or try to change home country public perceptions about foreign payments. Going after the law may mean working through government to get parallel laws passed in other countries (for example Germany or Japan) where foreign payments are not questioned. It may mean working through a supranational government to "level the playing field." Regardless, changing the context of foreign payments becomes the goal.

Finally, an *interactive* response suggests that solicitations and payments, when deemed culturally appropriate, may be handled publicly, avoiding the fact or appearance of bribery and still establishing the desired long-term relationship (Fadiman, 1986: 126). For example, if a developing country minister requests a large cash payment "for a hospital," the solicited firm could actually build a hospital instead. A request for "wildlife management" funds could be met by the importation of equipment needed by wildlife managers (as one British company did in Tanzania). According to Fadiman, such approaches "further social progress while offering local status instead of US funds" (p. 136).

Some scholars who study business and society relationships like to argue that the interactive approach to dealing with change in business–

government relations is always the best approach. Especially in terms of the international environment, this assertion is a stretch. Reaction or proaction may be best in some circumstances. Overall, however, the interactive approach is probably the most effective at solving long-term problems and developing productive business–government relations.

Focusing on outcomes

Another factor to be considered is the question of goals for the manager as well as for the organization. What is to be accomplished as a result of the business–government relationship? What are the organization and its managers willing to accept; against what do they want to fight?

Earlier in this chapter, several roles of government vis-à-vis business were noted. The type of interaction with government – government as customer, financier, promoter, and protector – will certainly be a determinant of desirable outcomes of a business–government relationship. When government is a customer of goods or services and when government is a supplier of capital, promotion and protection, mutually beneficial transactions between business and government will be the goal. The mutual benefit will often be described as going beyond the organizational interests of a business or a government and will be couched in terms of societal gain.

For example, justifications for setting up trade barriers or for strict enforcement of international competition laws (for example, anti-dumping laws) are not usually defended by public or private decision makers as intended to improve the profitability of a specific business or the popularity of a specific government decision maker, even though these are in fact outcomes. More often, the action is justified as enhancing some societal good – maintaining jobs, solidifying a key industry, or supporting a basic ideology (for example, free enterprise competition). Cynics will argue that the "real" motivation is always to support the societally powerful, but the fact is that when government is a customer or supplier, the business–government interaction seems to rest with some identifiable mutual benefit.

What about when the business–government interaction is based on conflict or competition? When government competes with business through state-owned enterprises or when government regulates business to force business to do something it would not do on its own, then both the justifications and the statements of ideal outcomes change. Under competition and conflict, both business and government place more emphasis on being the agent for some other group. Business managers like to appeal to the notion that they are just a vehicle representing the interests of owners; government representatives like to appeal to the notion that they are just the vehicle representing the multiple interests of the citizenry.

To bring these ideas back to the question of managing international business–government relations, figure 3.4 suggests that managers of MNEs can see their companies as operating in a complex of multiple governmental influences, interactions and contexts. (Actually, the situation illustrated in figure 3.4 is rather simple since the MNE is operating in only four countries, but the basic issues are still apparent.)

Figure 3.4　Operations of a hypothetical multinational enterprise

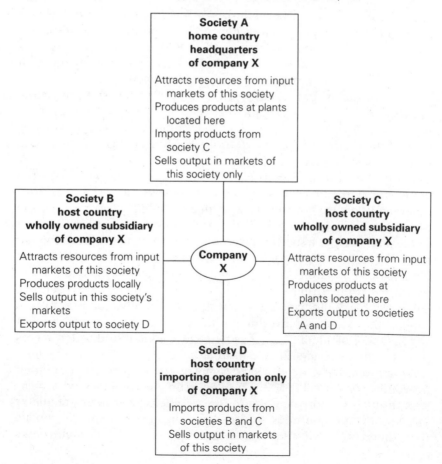

Given this complexity, MNE managers must focus on outcomes and their consequences and implications across societies as well as within societies. For example:

- Government policies of Societies A, B and C are all likely to be focused on the important societal issue of maintaining and increasing employment in Company X. But, what are the alternatives to Company X if Society B passes a plant closing law? What happens if Society D tries to guard employment by limiting or severely taxing imports from those companies which do not have production operations in Society D?
- Governments of all four societies are interested in maintaining capital for reinvestment and economic growth within the borders of their own societies. What happens when Society C places a limit on the amount of profit which can be repatriated back to the home country?
- Suppose that the goods and services which Company X produces have "high-tech" military significance and the home country (Society A) places limits or restrictions on the technology transfer out of Society A. What does the restriction imply for the production and exporting of the facilities in Societies B and C, and how will their governments respond?
- What might happen in business–government interactions if, because of international competition, Company X begins to lose market share in the home markets of Society A? Where will the government of Society A focus its policies, and how will the governments of Societies B, C and D respond?

Although certainly not exhaustive of all possible concerns in managing business–government relations, these questions illustrate the complexity that business managers face when their companies operate within the international arena.

As discussed in chapter 2, effectively addressing the complexity of managing international business–government relations will involve the full understanding of technology and ecology; of social, political and economic ideologies; and of business, government, and public institutional operations. For example, smart MNE managers understand that legal issues in the international arena sometimes arrest technological development. For example, Highbarger (1988: 47) points out that global information systems may suffer because of import restrictions on computer technologies, country differences in telephone encoding systems, and restriction of transborder data flows.

In the US, businesses can freely communicate information electronically both in and out of the country and import technology hardware
and software as desired. Outside of the US, this is not always the case.
Many countries restrict the use of electronically encoded data, particularly when it relates to the transport of data beyond borders.

In a few countries, such as Indonesia, transborder telecommunica-
tion of data is prohibited. In other instances, information communicated in and out of the country may be subject to review. The typical
American MIS executive has not encountered these concepts in the
past . . . [T]hese restrictions may seem like silly bureaucracy, but many
countries are extremely serious about these laws; companies and persons found in violation of the laws are subject to substantial sanctions
and criminal penalties. (Highbarger, 1988; 47.)

MNE managers must also recognize that the increased complexity
of international operations means that new allies for resolving conflict may be available. For example, when the US government placed
sanctions on Dresser Industries because Dresser's French subsidiary
sold pumps to the Soviet Union for the Soviets' pipeline, the sanctions were not lifted because of negotiations between Dresser and the
US government; they were lifted because of negotiations between the
US government and the French government.

The final point to be raised is the question of how the manager's
organizational interests can be factored into this societal equation,
and how, more specifically, business–government interactions can
support and enhance rather than constrain and restrict organizational
performance. MNEs have proven themselves inventive at achieving
their goals despite government intervention. Aggarwal (1989) points
out, for example, that the ancient practices of bartering and countertrade, accounting for 20–40 percent of world trade by some estimates,
are increasingly popular ways of avoiding regulatory trade barriers.
Yet, such inventiveness is generally short-lived as governments eventually discover and eliminate such inventiveness. So the question again
is how to achieve business objectives *within* business–government
relations, not in spite of them.

One way of understanding how individual business organizations
are factored into the equation of international business–government
relations is to examine the *strategic uses of public policy* (Mitnick, 1981;
Wood, 1985, 1986; Marcus et al., 1987). Business organizations can
and do gain competitive advantages from public policy initiatives.
Within a society, such factors as patents, copyrights, trademark protections, and government regulation of monopoly can actually eliminate all potential competition and serve the strategic interests of the
monopolist by protecting the market. Within industries, one firm can

gain a competitive advantage by promoting regulation of product safety, employment, or any other issue which that one firm has resolved but the competitors have not resolved (for example, Du Pont began to strongly support limits on CFCs once they could envision a substitute technology). In the US, antitrust law has served in many instances as an effective tool for restraining the market development of large firms in order to give competitive advantages to smaller firms. Giant competitors may attempt to use antitrust law to prevent each other from getting bigger. We miss the point if we always view public policy as a constraining force for individual businesses.

Considering strategic uses of public policy at the international level reveals some interesting axioms for MNE managers. For example, *regulation can push new technology*. In Europe, "green regulations have often helped speed up research into advanced processes and led to early competitive successes. In the race to develop ceramic engine technology, which will make cars both cleaner and more fuel-efficient, British Petroleum's . . . Carborundum Co. recently made a major breakthrough when it developed the first ceramic engine part – a seal ring – for mass production" (Bruce, 1989: 25).

In addition, *an environment of multiple governments allows for multiple opportunities*. For example, the EU strictly regulates pollution emissions, creating costs but also opportunities for businesses operating in EU nations. At the end of 1988, 9,000 companies in Europe existed to deal with pollution, and about two million workers owed their jobs directly or indirectly to environmental regulation (Bruce, 1989: 25). In July of 1993, the EU adopted its Environmental Management and Audit Scheme (EMAS), which mandates a wide range of compulsory eco-audits at various industrial sites, creating yet more business opportunities in pollution control and regulatory compliance. In the international area, working through governments therefore becomes as important as working with governments.

MNE managers must also recognize the enormous number of opportunities available through business–government relations in a world characterized by economic integration (for example the EU as discussed above) and political splintering (such as Eastern Europe). Those MNEs which established a sufficient presence in EU countries once integration had been announced but before 1992 were taking advantage of the strategic uses of public policy. Those companies which are lobbying the EU decision makers in order to get their products or technologies supported by the "new" social, economic and regulatory policies currently being constructed, or by the quality and environmental standards of ISO 9000 and 14000, are participating in the process of strategic uses of public policy. Those second and third level bureaucrats in the formerly communist governments of Eastern Europe who have seized the business opportunities presented to them through access and information of their earlier positions understand strategic uses of public policy.

Simply put, managing business–government relations in the international arena of today demands that MNE managers throw off any remaining baggage of adversarial relations with government and adopt the perspective of a search for opportunities.

We are only just beginning to comprehend the need for managers and scholars alike to seriously examine business–government relations in the international domain. Some of the ideas for doing this, and some of the payoffs, are described as follows by Pasquero and Wood (1992):

> Raising the question of the equivalence of our concepts, research units, and theoretical partitioning of the reality in foreign settings opens the door to a critical look at their true significance, not only as universal concepts, but also as valid American concepts to explain American reality. Myths may then be revealed about the way American scholars conceptualize their country's economic environment. One potential myth is that of the so-called adversarial relationship between business and government in the United States, which might well appear as an epiphenomenon masking an otherwise well-entrenched structure of government support to business. (Pasquero and Wood, 1992.)

CONCLUSION

Let us return to where we began – with a comment about US military involvement in Somalia. This chapter has focused on the enormity of the changes taking place in international business–government relations. The importance of nation-states, key aspects of business-government relations, alternative business–government interactions, and managing both the process and outcomes of international business–government interactions help us to understand what exists. The Somalian situation forces us to consider the future.

As we write, UN presence exists in Bosnia and Rwanda, and other peacekeeping and humanitarian missions are under consideration. Does the US involvement in Somalia as an agent of the United Nations suggest movements beyond social, political and economic integration such as the EU or NAFTA and on to more supraregional integration? Does an increasingly activist UN on matters such as world health and the environment imply a future development of an accepted global authority? What would business–government relations in the international arena look like if the UN or some other body gained real authority to regulate MNEs and to resolve legal conflicts among nation-states? And, given the US terrorist bombing of the federal building in Oklahoma City as a "protest" against both domestic government and the concept of supranational government, will businesses have even more to fear in the future? Questions such as these could well define the business–government interests of the MNE manager of the twenty-first century.

REFERENCES

Aggarwal, Raj. 1989. "International business through barter and countertrade." *Long Range Planning* 22:3 (June), 75–81.

Balducci, Massimo. 1987. *Etat Fonctionnel et Décentralisation: Leçons a Tirer de l'Expérience Italienne.* Bruxelles: Editions Story-Scientia.

Barnes, Pamela. 1994. "A new approach to protecting the environment." *Environmental Management & Health* 5:3, pp. 8–12.

Bruce, Leigh. 1989. "How green is your company?" *International Management* (Jan.): 24–7.

Business Europe. 1993–4. Various Issues. 1993 issues: Feb. 8–14, Mar. 8–14, May 10–16, May 24–30, July 5–11, July 26–Aug. 1, Oct. 18–24, Dec. 13–19, Dec. 27, 1993–Jan. 2, 1994. 1994 issues: Jan. 10–16, Jan. 17–23, Mar. 21–27, May 30–June 5.

Daniels, John and Lee Radebaugh. 1989. *International Business: Environments and Operations.* 5th ed. Reading, MA: Addison Wesley.

Fadiman, Jeffrey A. 1986. "A traveler's guide to gifts and bribes." *Harvard Business Review* 64:4 (July–August). 122–36.

Friedman, Milton. 1962. *Capitalism and Freedom.* Chicago: Free Press.

Highbarger, John. 1988. "Diplomatic ties: Managing a global network." *Computer World* 22:18 (May 4): 46–8.

Kalmbach, William C. III. 1987. "International labeling requirements for the export of hazardous chemicals: A developing nation's perspective." *Law and Policy in International Business* 19:4: 811–49.

Marcus, Alfred A., Allen M. Kaufman and David R. Beam. 1987. *Business Strategy and Public Policy.* New York: Quorum Books.

McCraw, Thomas K. 1984. "Business & government: The origins of the adversary relationship." *California Management Review* 26:2 (Winter): 33–52.

Mitnick, Barry. 1981. "The strategic uses of regulation – and deregulation." *Business Horizons,* 71–83.

"Multinationals in the third world: Environmental role is studied." *Chemical Marketing Reporter* (July 30, 1984): 4, 25.

Ohmae, Kenichi. 1989. "Managing in a borderless world." *Harvard Business Review* 67:3 (May–June), 152–61.

Pasquero, Jean, and Donna J. Wood, 1992. "International business and society: A research agenda for social issues in management." Conference paper,

"Perspectives on international business: theory, research, and institutional arrangements," University of South Carolina, May.

Post, James E. 1978. *Corporate Behavior and Social Change.* Reston, VA: Reston Publishing Co.

Rogers, Jerry. 1983. *Global Risk Assessments: Issues, Concepts and Applications*, Riverside CA: Global Risk Assessments Inc.

Vogel, David. 1987. "Government–industry relations in the United States: An overview," in *Comparative Government–Industry Relations: Western Europe, United States, and Japan*, Stephen Wilks and Maurice Wright (eds.). New York: Oxford University Press, 91–116.

Wall Street Journal. 1993. 22 June: A 12.

Wood, Donna J. 1985. "The strategic use of policy: Business support for the 1906 Food and Drug Act." *Business History Review*, 59, 403–32.

Wood, Donna J. 1986. *Strategic Uses of Public Policy: Business and Government in the Progressive Era.* Marshfield, MA: Pitman Publishing.

Wright, John W. (general editor). 1992. The Universal Almanac. Harrisonburg, VA: The Banta Company.

4

Corporate Social Responsibility and Responsiveness

- What are the social responsibilities of a company headquartered in Germany, obtaining natural resources from South America and the Soviet Union, manufacturing components throughout the Pacific Rim, and selling its goods in North American and European markets?
- How can a Japanese parent firm understand the practice of social responsibility as its US subsidiary must understand and deal with it?
- In a world where companies are driven to a large extent by economic imperatives, but people and nations are driven by all sorts of other goals, how can issues such as companies' need for cheap labor and natural resources and countries' need to be free from exploitation be reconciled?
- To whom, exactly, is the multinational enterprise responsible?

Questions such as these plague international managers and scholars alike. There are no easy answers. And yet, questions of social responsibility and responsiveness are central to any thorough understanding of the roles of economic organizations in the modern world, their relationships with societies and peoples, and how those roles and relationships may change over time.

This chapter examines the concepts of corporate social responsibility and corporate social responsiveness in the international arena. We take primarily an organization-level perspective on the relationships between responsibility and responsiveness within and between cultures, showing some of the problems and opportunities managers experience in determining their organizations' social responsibilities in various cultures, and how to think about operationalizing responsive processes to meet those responsibilities. After presenting the concepts of responsibility and responsiveness and how they apply to managerial behavior, we illustrate their international relevance through a global social issue affecting and affected by business – environmental pollution.

CORPORATE SOCIAL RESPONSIBILITY AND RESPONSIVENESS: DEFINING THE CONCEPTS

Corporate social responsibility and responsiveness, as we saw in chapter 1, form the first two units of the three-part corporate social performance (CSP) model (Wood, 1991a), with outcomes being the third unit. Responsibility, responsiveness, and outcomes are so conceptually linked that we cannot completely isolate them even for purposes of analysis and application. In this chapter, however, we will focus primarily on social responsibility and responsiveness; subsequent chapters examine outcomes more closely.

Defining corporate social responsibility

Corporate social responsibility is a term that has been applied to US companies for several decades. Originally the idea was that businesses were not isolated organizations working to meet a single societal function (that of economic production and distribution), but were integrated with the whole of society and had dramatic effects on that society's problems, structure, and future. However, the idea of business's isolation and independence had taken hold of the US's economic ideology in the 20th century, which meant that business's impacts on social and political conditions were consistently overlooked both in academic theory and in managerial decision making. Since the 1970s, the concept of social responsibility has taken stronger root and is now more readily accepted as a fact of US business life. This history does not necessarily apply elsewhere in the world, for a variety of reasons.

In comparison, German executives have a difficult time relating to the idea of corporate social responsibility. This is not because German companies are more irresponsible than US ones, but because German culture has its own rather definite, historically rooted ideas about business–society relationships, and has institutionalized these ideas in its business organizations and legal institutions. For example, when Chrysler was forced by federal bail-out provisions to put the United Auto Workers president on its board of directors, US business executives were scandalized at this interference of government into corporate private affairs. But the idea of labor-management codetermination, and its expression in functioning labor councils and labor membership on boards, is a well-established feature of German business. Additionally, while US companies consider themselves in a free-market situation with respect to labor, German companies expect to serve as partners with the government and the schools to train young workers and find them jobs. Finally, the idea that businesses exist to maximize stockholder wealth, prevalent among US firms, is considered a curiosity by German executives, who prefer and are expected to manage for the long-term well-being of the company and the society. However, in Germany, support for social services and the arts is provided by the government, not by charitable contributions, so the American attention to corporate philanthropy seems strange and inappropriate to German executives.

As another example, recall from chapter 2 that until very recently, the idea of corporate social responsibility (CSR) would have been seen as completely alien in the (former) Soviet Union. In the first place, with no privately-owned corporations and no free-market ideology, there was no institutional location for the idea or the practice of CSR. That is, there literally could not be any "corporate social responsibility" because there were no corporations distinct from the government. Additionally, the philosophy behind state ownership of economic enterprise is that the *sole* duty of companies is to be socially responsible, to serve society's interests and enhance its well-being through jobs and production. Thus, theoretically, the question of whether or not economic organizations were acting in the society's interest or were meeting social expectations would never arise.

As a final example, there are many developing countries in the world where "corporate social responsibility" exists only to the extent that foreign companies are willing to engage in it. In the Mexican *maquiladora* assembly factories, workers may earn higher-than-normal wages but they have long hours, no benefits, and no job security (Russell, 1984), and their purchasing power remains at subsistence level (Van Buren, 1995). The impact of Union Carbide's Bhopal disaster was only worsened by the company's initial offer to compensate victims at the rate of $100 per death and $5 per injury, an apparently reasonable rate for the local culture, but an outrageously low rate in the light of world public opinion. And a US oriental rug importer boasted to one of the authors, "Those women in Pakistan work 15 hours a day, six days a week, to handweave these beauties for you."

On the other hand, MNC activities in developing countries bring vital capital, technology, know-how, and social projects into those countries, raising the quality of life and contributing to economic and social development. One writer argues that "well-intentioned terms such as 'corporate responsibility' and 'social involvement' only isolate the notion of 'good behavior' or 'altruism' as a marginal activity. And using those terms paves the way for detractors of MNCs to claim 'tokenism,' 'window dressing,' 'cosmetics,' 'do-gooding,' or 'conscience money'" (Micou, 1985: 10). Unfortunately, this argument has some truth to it. However, our view of corporate social responsibility in this book is not the "do-gooding" version to which so many business voices object; it is a broad, integrated, strategic view of business's vital roles and responsibilities in every society and in the global environment.

Taking the concept of corporate social responsibility global has immense consequences, only some of which we can observe in these comparative examples. Some consequences, such as those implicit in the opening of this chapter, are still ambiguous and troubling. It is easy to defend the idea that businesses should be responsive to the expectations of their societies. After all, businesses are organizations existing within a society. They draw their human and material resources from that society, produce goods and services for use by society's members, emit wastes into the society's natural environment, and so on. But it is truly not always clear to whom, to which societies, the multinational enterprise should be responsible, or what the MNE should do about conflicting expectations among its various host countries. The social responsibilities of firms engaged in international trade or foreign operations are not self-evident.

Nor is it obvious that multinational enterprises *should* always follow the dictates of the societies in which they operate:

> if we really mean to say that companies are obligated to abide by societal values, we must be prepared to go all the way, grounding corporate social responsibility completely in societal values. If we really don't mean it, then we need to decide which of our own values we are prepared to defend as universal and abide by in our worldwide transactions, whatever the result. In the first case, we must be able to say that companies in communist states are obligated to provide all personnel information to the government; companies in the Middle East are obligated not to hire women; companies in South Africa [were] obligated to enslave black workers; companies operating in Nazi Germany were obligated to produce poison for the gas chambers; companies operating in Libya (replace with any other relevant nation) are obligated to help the government acquire nuclear weapons. In the second case, we must examine these distasteful possibilities to surface those values we are willing to uphold. (Wood, 1991b: 69.)

The corporate social performance (CSP) model, briefly described in chapter 1, can be helpful in sorting through what social responsibility means at the global level. Building on the earlier work of Frederick (1978), Carroll (1979) and Wartick and Cochran (1985), corporate social performance is defined as "the exercise of the principles of social responsibility, the processes of social responsiveness, and the social impacts of business activity" (Wood, 1991a). The CSP model begins with three structural principles of corporate social responsibility. These principles express institution-level, organization-level, and individual-level statements of what business's social responsibility means. (A structural principle expresses a sociological relationship, unlike a normative principle, which would specify what *should* happen under specified circumstances.) In the following sections, we examine these structural principles in greater depth and try to discover what happens to them when they are applied in an international business context.

The principle of legitimacy

Society grants legitimacy and power to business. In the long run, those who do not use power in a manner which society considers responsible will tend to lose it.

This institution-level principle, derived from the work of Keith Davis (1973) and Davis and Blomstrom (1975), defines the *institutional* relationship between business and society and specifies what is expected of *any* business simply because it is a member of the business institution (Wood, 1991a: 696). The principle of legitimacy expresses two ideas: (1) that business is society's economic institution, serving society's functional need for production and distribution of goods and services; and (2) that business firms are organizations by which society's economic institution accomplishes its work. Society grants legitimacy to business; that is, the economic institution of business is given certain rights to exercise power. In exchange for these rights, business therefore has a responsibility to society to perform the functions allocated to it for society's benefit, and to avoid using its power in inappropriate ways. Every business organization, then, because it is part of society's economic institution, has a responsibility to perform its functions and avoid abusing its power simply *because* it is a member of that economic institution.

As we saw in chapter 2, the organizational and ideological components of business institutions can look quite different from one society to the next. In Western Europe and North America, capitalist business enterprises accomplish the bulk of economic activity. In Eastern Europe and the former Soviet Union, state-owned enterprises were the rule throughout much of the 20th century, and in

China and parts of South America, state-owned enterprises are still the predominant form of economic organization. In some tribal societies, there are no business organizations as we think of them, but instead there are complex networks of individuals and kinship groups engaged in barter and trade. In whatever form, all societies make arrangements for economic activities to be performed.

Economic activity, however it is organized, requires some exercise of power over materials, natural resources, and people. It is this power that is at issue in questions of legitimacy. Do businesses have a right to exercise power over those resources they require? If so, they have social legitimacy. But the right to exercise power is matched by a reciprocal responsibility to use the power in appropriate, socially sanctioned ways and *not* to use it in unapproved ways. According to the principle of legitimacy, for example, an auto manufacturer headquartered and operating in the United States might have the right to buy the materials it needs at whatever price it could negotiate, but not a right to force suppliers to lower their prices at gunpoint. It might have the right to manage workers to accomplish organizational tasks, but not a right to require them to act in a way that would injure them or make them ill. And the company might have the right to sell its products to those who want to buy them, but not a right to use misleading or deceptive advertising. These prohibited behaviors would be considered abuses of business power, and a business that continually engaged in them would lose its legitimacy because it was not acting as US society expects every business to act. Furthermore, if people came to believe that these prohibited behaviors truly characterized business activity, then the overall legitimacy of business as an institution would be threatened, and moves might be made to replace capitalistic business with some other form of business enterprise.

In international business, does the principle of legitimacy hold true? To the extent that business activities are governed by the nations in which they operate, we can answer "yes," because the legitimacy of the business institution and its organizations is a matter of public policy. It is easy to see the principle of legitimacy in operation when a government undergoes radical transformation and nationalizes foreign firms operating within its borders. One can see nationalization as a raw power grab by a government, an illegal seizure of wealth and assets. But nationalization can also be a sign that the seized company has lost its legitimacy in the society and no longer has a right to autonomously exercise power. The same phenomenon is at work, with opposite effects, in the privatization of state-owned enterprises in Eastern Europe and the former Soviet Union. As these societies change from socialist to capitalist ideology, state ownership of economic organizations comes to be seen as an illegitimate form of economic power, and thus state-owned enterprises lose their right to exist.

The principle of public responsibility

Businesses are responsible for outcomes related to their primary and secondary areas of involvement with society.

This organization-level principle (Preston and Post, 1975), speaks not to the responsibilities of business as a social institution, or of a business firm as a member of that institution, but to the responsibilities of a *particular* organization because of what it, specifically, does. Simply put, this principle tells every business to "clean up what you mess up, fix what's in your backyard." While the principle of legitimacy captures the idea that *all* businesses have some responsibilities in common, the principle of public responsibility expresses the idea that *each* business also has its own unique set of responsibilities because of the type of business it is and how it conducts itself.

In developing the idea of public responsibility, Preston and Post (1975: 11) were trying to bring the concept of corporate social responsibility out of the clouds to make it real and meaningful to managers. They maintained that managers have public, or external, responsibilities defined by public policy, just as they have internal planning, budgeting, supervisory, reporting, and other responsibilities defined by the firm's economic function. These external responsibilities were to be found in the areas of the firm's primary and secondary involvements with society.

The area of primary involvement includes behaviors and transactions "that arise directly from [the firm's] specialized functional role . . . . Without them, the organization cannot be what it is" (Preston and Post, 1975: 10). An automobile manufacturer would necessarily be concerned with public policy issues such as technical standards for auto safety, energy conservation policy, driver education programs, and public funding for road maintenance, because these issues are directly related to the company's particular economic role of producing cars. A bank would necessarily be concerned with issues such as neighborhood viability, economic development, and discriminatory lending practices. A chemical distributor would necessarily be concerned with issues such as environmental pollution, product safety, and product labeling.

The area of secondary involvement includes "impacts and effects not intrinsic to the character of the organization but generated by its primary involvement activities" (Preston and Post, 1975: 10). The automobile manufacturer would reasonably also be concerned with issues such as public transportation and trade restrictions on oil and steel, because these issues, though not directly related to the firm's primary economic function, are either (a) concerned with outcomes of the company's activities, or (b) related to the company's ability to fulfill its objectives. On this dimension, even social issues that seem fairly far afield from auto-making could fall within the firm's public responsibility: the firm might need literate workers, for example, and thus participate in adult literacy programs; or it might sponsor high school drug and alcohol education seminars, hoping to contribute eventually to drug-free (safer, more reliable) workplaces.

What happens to the principle of public responsibility when we take it into the global marketplace? Simply put, nothing changes. The principle that a company is responsible for the outcomes and impacts of its behavior is applicable to any company, operating anywhere in the world, in any number of countries, with any number of product or service lines, using any type of technology. In less academic language, the rule is easy to understand: "If you broke it, fix it," or, "If you don't want it done to you, don't do it to others." Likewise, the idea that a company can take responsibility for trying to solve social problems that affect it is also easily transferrable: "If it can break you, try to fix it," or, "if it can mess you up, clean it up."

The principle of managerial discretion

Managers are moral actors. Within every domain of corporate social responsibility, they are obliged to exercise such discretion as is available to them, toward socially responsible outcomes.

Corporate social responsibility has been viewed as "the management of discretion" (Ackerman, 1975: 32–3). This individual-level principle of managerial discretion captures the idea that people in organizations are not robots, unquestioningly following orders that cover every detail of their working lives. People at work face choices every day, in a wide variety of situations. This principle suggests that they have a responsibility to make responsible choices rather than irresponsible ones, and they need to add moral reflection (Epstein, 1987) to their managerial toolkits. They need to be able to reflect upon their responsibilities in various domains of corporate and human activity, and to apply a process of moral reasoning in reaching decisions (Velasquez, 1992).

Managerial discretion is one of the important domains of corporate social responsibility (Carroll, 1979; Wood, 1990, 1991a). These domains are:

- *Economic responsibilities* – the firm's duty to make a profit and generate wealth, to produce and distribute goods and services, and to provide employment and income for workers.
- *Legal responsibilities* – the firm's duty to obey the law.
- *Ethical responsibilities* – the firm's duty to abide by the society's core ethical values concerning right and wrong behavior.
- *Discretionary responsibilities* – the firm's duty to use its resources for social betterment in ways of its own choosing.

Discretionary responsibility is too often defined as charitable giving and very little else. Wood (1991a) insists, however, that "managerial discretion – the ability to make choices – applies to *each* domain, and one can find socially responsible actions and outcomes in each." Economic responsibilities, for example, involve choices about products, services, markets, production technologies, and advertising. Legal responsibilities involve choices not only about obeying or disobeying, but also about *how* laws shall be met. Ethical responsibilities involve choices about how people are to be treated. And discretionary responsibilities, if they center on philanthropy, involve choices about how slack resources are to be allocated among charitable or social service organizations. As Dickie and Rouner (1986: 13) note: "Ultimately the ethical questions are intensely personal. How responsibly a corporation acts (or, more accurately, to whom a corporation acts responsibly), is a function of the values, thoughtfulness, and wisdom of the individuals within the corporation to whom power is entrusted." That is, a company's social responsibility ultimately depends on how people within the company use their discretion.

Does the principle of managerial discretion apply in international business? Of course; as long as organizational members are free from coercion and have sufficient information, managerial discretion exists in virtually any business activity anywhere. These conditions of non-coercion and access to information, however, may vary across cultures.

Britain, for example, has an Official Secrets Act that permits a vast amount of corporate and industry information to be classified as confidential. In the US, under the Freedom of Information Act, this same information would be accessible to the public. This situation can both enhance and limit the discretion of British managers. They may be freer from stakeholder interference if stakeholders do not know "secret" information, and they have some confidence that their own confidential data, used as evidence in lawsuits, will not be released to the public. But they themselves will likewise not have access to the "secrets" of competitors and cannot readily gain competitive information by suing, as US companies can.

As another example, in the former communist nation of the German Democratic Republic (East Germany), managerial discretion was limited by the coercive powers of the government's secret police. Decisions and actions that did not appear to be "politically correct" could subject the decision maker to loss of promotion opportunities or even the job itself, and also could affect the entire family's life circumstances (for example, housing, foreign travel, and educational opportunities for children). It was never clear exactly who, or how many, were secret police agents, and this constant threat of coercion was a definite limit on individual decision making and discretion.

In sum, the structural principles of corporate social responsibility do not appear to be particularly culture-bound. These principles can be restated as follows. First, society is the source of legitimacy for forms of economic activity (for example, privately-owned business firms or state-owned enterprises), and society can choose to withhold or withdraw legitimacy from certain forms. Second, business organizations are not responsible for solving all the world's problems, but they are responsible for solving the problems they have caused and for helping to solve the problems that affect them or are indirectly connected to their core functions. Third, business managers have personal responsibility for their own acts, for the systems and procedures and products they design and sell, and for the people they manage. In each domain of corporate social responsibility – economic, legal, ethical, and discretionary – managers normally have choices about how to fulfill their many obligations.

Processes of corporate social responsiveness

Processes of corporate social responsiveness, the second leg of the corporate social performance model, are tools that allow managers and companies to put the principles of corporate social responsibility into action. Ackerman (1975: 65) proposed that companies go through three phases in responding to a social issue:

- *Phase I, Policy* – the chief executive becomes aware of the issue, decides that it is of significance to the company, and gives it personal attention. Policy is formulated, at first on the basis of sketchy analysis and evidence, and later evolving as the company gains experience with the issue.

- *Phase II, Learning* – the issue is defined as a technical one, and a specialist is appointed to act as a change agent, to develop and coordinate the organization's response to the issue. Learning is accomplished both as the specialist increases his/her skills and learns to overcome barriers to change, and as other organizational members become more aware of the issue and the company's attempted responses.
- *Phase III, Commitment* – the issue is no longer seen as in the exclusive domain of the specialist, but as something that must be owned and implemented by middle management and integrated into daily business operations.

Ackerman also proposed that responsive firms share three characteristics: they monitor the environment, respond to stakeholder expectations, and manage responses to social issues and trends. These characteristics correspond to the fundamental processes of corporate social responsiveness:

- *Environmental scanning* allows firms to monitor and assess environmental trends, events, and conditions.
- *Stakeholder management* allows the firm to pay attention and respond appropriately to the many stakeholder demands placed upon it.
- *Issues management* allows the firm to design and implement plans and policies to respond to emerging trends and changing conditions.

In brief, responsive processes have to do with gathering and evaluating *information*, managing relations with *people* and other organizations, and dealing with *issues*, events, and trends in the larger environment.

Each of these responsive processes is explored in more depth elsewhere in the book. Here, we want to quickly assess whether these seem to be appropriate and workable processes in a global marketplace. Two aspects of this assessment must be distinguished: (1) intracultural and comparative crosscultural similarities and differences in the conditions under which responsive processes are applied, and (2) transcultural, multinational, or global problems, relationships, and opportunities to which those processes are applied.

Intracultural and cross-cultural aspects. Across cultures, different things need to be scanned. Firms operating in the US, for instance, have relatively little need to conduct political risk assessment or to guard their assets from seizure by the government, as they would do in many other parts of the world. Furthermore, the available environmental scanning tools may be somewhat different across cultures. For example, managers from industrialized nations who are used to getting their news from television and print media may be in for a rude shock when trying to scan issues and events in developing nations that still depend on radio and word-of-mouth for news transmission.

Similarly, a company's stakeholder groups may change from one nation to the next. In the US managers are now accustomed to thinking of stakeholders as stockholders, employees, government, customers, suppliers, environmental activists, and so on. Companies doing business in certain parts of Central America, Africa, the Middle East, or Southeast Asia, however, might list a different set of stakeholders, including leftist guerillas, rightist guerillas, terrorists, a variety of religious activists, missionary organizations, nomadic healthcare workers traveling in vans, customs officials, ethnic and linguistic political parties, tribal or extended family leaders, revolutionary governments, criminal organizations, governments-in-exile, military factions, gunrunners, diplomats, spies, counterspies, and politically powerful drugdealers, to name just a few possibilities.

Finally, different issues will arise in different cultures. Familiar US issues involving the separation of church and state would be considered impossible, even unethical, in countries governed by religious leaders, who would see it as their duty to enforce religious precepts using state powers. In such countries, likewise, social and political issues will exist with which US managers have no experience, such as government policy requiring women to be veiled in public. As another example, companies operating in Western Europe do not have to guard their employees against outbreaks of malaria, nor would they be necessarily interested in supporting medical research to prevent or cure the disease (unless they are pharmaceutical firms). But companies operating in parts of Africa and Central America do have to be concerned about malaria, and might indeed participate in preventive research.

Transcultural, multinational, and global aspects. In addition to the intracultural and comparative aspects of applying processes of corporate social responsiveness to international business, it is clear that the global business environment is more than a collection of national environments; it is itself a whole system and a force in business. Environmental scanning, then, has to take into account political, technological, economic, social, and ecological conditions and changes that *cross* national borders and affect conditions *among* nations. In the Cold War era of the 1950s and 1960s, for example, communism was not confined to the Soviet Union, but extended through China, Cuba, parts of Europe and Southeast Asia, Africa, and elsewhere. It was a multinational phenomenon with global implications and consequences. Similarly, cross-national dependencies created by trade patterns, currency exchanges, or labor mobility make the international economic environment something that does not necessarily respect national borders.

Stakeholder management has transnational and multinational aspects as well, particularly in these days of rapid communications and relatively easy travel. Some activist stakeholder groups are themselves multinational. For instance, in the late 1980s, state-owned companies engaged in building a huge hydroelectric project along the Danube River between Hungary and Czechoslovakia found themselves opposed by domestic environmentalists who were supported physically and financially by groups from other nations (the Austrian and West German Greens) and by international groups such as the World Wildlife Fund. The emergence of these stakeholders was a surprise to company managers, in part because they were not local groups (Wood, 1992). As other examples of multinational stakeholders, consider the activist Catholic groups who organized the infant formula boycott against Nestlé, the Islamic Jihad which has conducted a variety of terrorist activities against businesspeople, Greenpeace which disrupts whaling and fishing operations around the world, and the United Nations which serves as a forum for international political positioning and a barometer of political risk.

Finally, issues management has clear transnational aspects because issues themselves are not always contained within political borders. In particular, a transnational firm needs a transnational issues management function to track the development of social and political issues worldwide, to assess their impact on the firm, and to devise responsive strategies where needed or desirable. The issue of environmental pollution, which we outline in the next section of this chapter, exemplifies the need for companies to be alert to the global business implications of social issues and problems.

In sum, what we find is that the responsive processes of environmental scanning, stakeholder management, and issues management are not only "workable" in international business settings, they are absolutely essential. The world is too small and too closely linked these days for business managers to ignore what is happening beyond their own small corners. Awareness and responsiveness are necessities, not luxuries.

Putting the principles and processes to work

In the remainder of this chapter we will explore the global dimensions of corporate social responsibility and responsiveness by outlining some of the sociopolitical issues related to environmental pollution. These issues have true international scope, impact, and visibility; and their relationship to business activity worldwide cannot be questioned. Through these issues we should glimpse both the complexity and difficulty of enacting principles of social responsibility and processes of social responsiveness in a global setting, as well as the possibilities that exist for businesses to help solve or to exacerbate serious social problems worldwide.

GLOBAL SOCIAL RESPONSIBILITY AND ENVIRONMENTAL POLLUTION

In 1974, Toni Yogurts of Switzerland responded to rising ecological awareness by initiating a project to market its yogurts in recyclable glass containers. Over the next decade, Toni had to solve technological problems with their bottle sealants, distributor problems in handling returned glasses, customer problems with motivation to recycle, and economic problems resulting from poor brand acceptance. However, their solutions were so successful that their competitors were forced into "an ecological head-on race," resulting overall in substantial energy and natural resource savings from a variety of ecologically-conscious packaging innovations in the industry (Dyllick, 1989; quote on p. 661).

Pollution is a global problem, not respecting national boundaries but threatening the future of every people. Wasteful production and consumption practices deplete natural resources and consume irreplaceable energy; the wastes of both the industrialized and developing nations poison the water, dirty the air, destroy the soil. As we see in exhibit 4.1, pollution is a problem in which business has a significant stake, and not just because business is the primary source of pollution.

Exhibit 4.1   Business stakes in global pollution

Resource effects
Pollution destroys natural resources that business must use for production and operations.

Regulatory effects
Pollution eventually generates tighter government control of business activities within countries.

Trade policy effects
Global pollution problems push international treaties and create international law.

Inefficiency effects
Pollution means waste; waste costs money; wasteful spending negatively affects corporate profits.

Stakeholder effects
Pollution generates activist stakeholders who can dramatically affect a company's operations.

James Gustave Speth (1987: 21), president of the World Resources Institute, observes that pollution in the developing world is a tremendous challenge to western business:

> The way the developing world meets the challenges of managing resources, generating energy for economic growth, and providing food for its expanding population can affect American business's access to both materials and markets. Failure to meet these challenges may lead to economic restrictions, social turmoil, and even political upheaval. Sustainable economic development, political stability, careful resource management, and appropriate international accords are all preconditions to continuing this access on an affordable, long-term basis.

With so much at stake, and with such serious effects on world populations, global pollution would seem to be an ideal locus for corporate social responsibility.

The first step in examining global pollution from a CSR perspective is to apply the principles of corporate social responsibility and see if there are any obvious flaws. The question is this: what are multinational corporations obliged to do about pollution, wastes, and environmental safety and health?

Applying the principles

(1) The principle of legitimacy demands that corporations, at a minimum, must abide by the environmental standards of their host-country governments. At the rock-bottom level, this may be merely a matter of obeying host-country law. This obligation may not contribute very much to the clean-up of the natural environment, for many developing nations do not have any environmental protection laws or compliance mechanisms.

At a more sophisticated level, the principle of legitimacy means fulfilling the requirements of legitimacy in the home country. Most MNEs are headquartered in developed countries with relatively strong pollution control laws. So, MNE legitimacy at home can be a driving force for exceeding legal environmental standards in host countries and for being "ahead of the game" when international pollution control regulations begin to be accepted via United Nations activity.

(2) The principle of public responsibility goes further to suggest that corporations should not only clean up their own messes, but should also help to clean up the messes that will negatively affect their operations. This is a powerful principle, giving companies a mandate both to internalize all the external costs of production and to take a broad, long-term view of their own positions and responsibilities within larger societal and international contexts. Under this principle, MNCs would be obliged, for example, to think through the entire lifespan of a product – design, manufacturing, distribution, use, and disposal – to try to reduce the product's negative environmental impacts, whatever they might be (as is now being required in Germany, by the way). Furthermore, some of those negative impacts might be related to characteristics of transporters, sellers, buyers, and users, so that a company would need to think through and handle its environmental responsibilities and possible actions on all these fronts.

(3) The principle of managerial discretion suggests that within every domain of their responsibilities, managers can try to make environmentally sound choices. This may mean spending extra effort to identify what those choices might be. It may mean bringing new factors into the decision making process. It will undoubtedly mean that previously unconsidered problems and opportunities will now be on the table. It can even mean applying a higher standard than is required by any government, justifying this path as a good business decision and sound business ethics. Because this principle emphasizes the ability of individuals to change organizational behaviors, it is perhaps the most powerful of all the CSR principles.

It is not yet clear whether operating according to principles of social responsibility will put a company at a competitive advantage or disadvantage, and there is evidence for both results, depending on the company, the industry, and the problem being addressed. It is known, for example, that industry self-regulation (which can be a form of CSR) can take the place of costly and cumbersome government regulation to the advantage of all firms in an industry. Self-regulation can also turn CSR operations into a competitive advantage for members of the industry by leveling the playing field and requiring socially responsible operations as a condition of industry participation. This approach is seen in the US chemical industry's Responsible Care program, borrowed from the Canadian chemical industry in 1988 and now a condition for membership in the industry's most powerful trade associations ("Responsible distibution," 1993; Shon, 1993; Reisch, 1994).

The Responsible Care program, promoted by the Chemical Manufacturers Association (CMA), requires chemical manufacturers to increase communication with the public and to meet industry standards for health, safety, and environmental protection. As of 1992, adherence to Responsible Care standards became also a condition of membership in the National Association of Chemical Distributors (NACD), and CMA members were required to use distributors that agreed to comply with Responsible Care standards. Responsible Care standards cover the following areas:

- community concerns and emergency reponse,
- distribution,
- pollution prevention,
- process safety,
- employee health and safety, and
- product stewardship.

Understanding the problems

Exhibit 4.2 shows a few of the many issues involving environmental pollution, along with underlying problems, consequences, perpetrators, and possible solutions. What does this example tell us about global corporate social responsibility and responsiveness?

(1) Social issues are symbolic as well as substantive. A single issue such as "environmental pollution" only serves as an initial point of analysis; it is actually an incredible tangle of related, subsidiary, and spin-off issues. This means that no solution can be found to "environmental pollution" – that term is a *symbol*, a powerful shorthand way

Exhibit 4.2   Environmental pollution – the global issues

Ecological problems
Ozone layer destruction; destruction of oxygen-producing rain forests; global warming (the greenhouse effect); acid rain; radioactive and toxic waste disposal; solid waste disposal; air, water, and ground contamination; soil erosion; contamination and dissipation of drinking water; ecoterrorism; plant and animal species extinction; destruction of commercial species habitats (e.g., seafood); proliferation of chemical compounds with unknown environmental effects.

Underlying problems
Poverty, overpopulation and underproduction of food, illiteracy and lack of education, developed-world arrogance, irresponsible production and consumption patterns, nationalism, war, inability to govern commons areas.

Consequences
Destruction of ecosystems; increasing rates of cancer, asthma, and other environmentally-linked diseases; long-term degradation of and irreversible harms to the natural resource base, especially water and soil; changes in weather and temperature patterns with possible geopolitical consequences;

Perpetrators
Nations, governments, cities, businesses, other organizations, farms, families, individuals.

Solutions
International regulation; international collaborative agreements such as multilateral treaties; intranational government policies; corporate and organizational social responsibility; changes in consumer/user behavior.

---

of referring to an entire package of problems. Each problem must be dealt with individually as a technically distinct issue, but all problems must also be dealt with as interrelated and interdependent.

The symbols attached to social issues engender strong emotions – notice, for example, how people will respond to words like "Love Canal" or "Bhopal" or "Chernobyl." This means that technological solutions alone will not suffice; people must be reassured, confident that the experts can be trusted and that the problems are indeed solved. Such reassurance is as much a function of politics and public relations as it is of scientific expertise, knowledge, and organizational and governmental financial commitment to solutions. Technological solutions to institutional problems must be consistent with the dominant ideology, or public unease and conflicts are likely to result.

(2) Issues of interest to corporations derive from larger underlying social issues. Observe, for example, that the problem of global export and import of toxic wastes is related to macrosocial issues such as racism; third-world poverty and lack of education; a lack of international regulatory structures; and the failure of developed-nation producers, consumers, and governments to take responsibility for their own wastes.

Even among developed countries, environmental issues are entangled in a welter of social, political, technological, and economic factors. The European Union, for example, in moving toward a unified internal market, has permitted some internal trade barriers to stand on the grounds that member countries having higher environmental standards than the EU overall should be able to enforce those standards. Thus, Denmark requires returnable bottles for beer and soft drinks, Germany requires deposits on plastic bottles, and Italy places limits on all plastic packaging ("The freedom," 1989: 22). Underlying issues in reaching common EU environmental standards include country differences in industrial and political structure, demographic differences and trends, and international and intercultural tensions that are rooted in many hundreds of years of European history. Observers believe that the recent addition of Austria, Finland, and Sweden to EU membership will mean even more stringent environmental protection pressures on all EU companies and a "growing prospect of prison sentences, costly court cases, and crippling fines" in response to environmental liability judgments ("Green or bust," 1995).

(3) Consequences of environmental pollution reflect the complex interweaving between human populations, other living species, and the natural environment. Ecology has been a branch of biological science for decades, but the message of ecological interconnectedness is only recently getting through to large numbers of people. For example, rainforest destruction in the Amazon is driven in part by developed-nations' demand for exotic lumber and for beef, and in part by developing nations' desire to "catch up" with the industrial world in wealth and quality of life. The forests, however, not only generate a sizeable portion of the globe's oxygen, but they also absorb substantial amounts of carbon dioxide and other airborne wastes, and they are the sole source of numerous pharmaceutical and chemical raw materials. Eventually, rainforest destruction reduces the entire

world's ability to breathe. As another example, pollution of under-ground aquifers by the run-off of agricultural chemicals is spurred by farmers' need for cash crops, but it has negative consequences on all who draw their water from those underground sources. As a final example, Kalmbach (1987: 828–9) observes that exported carcino-gens banned at home can nevertheless appear unexpectedly in home markets: "the pesticides aldrin and dieldrin are produced in the United States only for export but return in Ecuadorian cacao, Costa Rican coffee, and Indian sugar and tea."

(4) The perpetrators of global issues affecting business include practically everybody. Corporations are by no means blameless in con-tributing to global environmental problems. But they are joined by consumers who demand throw-away goods and who fail to demand environmentally sound products and reductions in packaging; gov-ernments that themselves generate enormous quantities of waste and that do not use their regulatory powers wisely to control environ-mental problems; farmers who use deadly pesticides and herbicides to increase their yields; schools that use disposable plates and cups every lunch period.

"Not-in-my-backyard" (NIMBY) issues have surfaced recently to exacerbate the problem of who is responsible for generating and for cleaning up wastes and pollution. These issues express people's deep concern with environmental health and safety hazards, but they can be serious impediments to solving environmental problems because they represent the failure of all parties to take responsibility for their own contributions to the problems. For example, developed-country residents do not want power lines crossing their property, dumps or toxic disposal units in their neighborhoods, or belching smokestacks nearby. Nevertheless, they continue to increase their demands for electricity, for wastefully-packaged products, and for the jobs and economic benefits of manufacturing facilities. So, in whose backyard should the power lines, smokestacks, and disposal sites be? The temp-tation is to export the problems, but this tactic, of course, rebounds, as is easily seen in the current controversy over the exporting of toxic waste to developing countries. It is still cheaper for many companies to use a waste broker to export their toxic byproducts for disposal than it is to abide by in-country environmental protection regula-tions. However, legislation in environmentally-aware countries, as well as new awareness of environmental dangers in toxic-importing countries, will likely erase this economic advantage in the near future (Chester, 1993).

Backyard concerns can become the spark for more concerted ac-tion to solve a problem. In 1986, for instance, when the European

Community began wrestling with regulations to reduce global warming, interest in the issue was pushed by the Dutch, out of concern for their below-sea-level nation and the drastic consequences of polar icecap melting ("Controlling carbon dioxide," 1986: 57). The backyard of the Netherlands is the Atlantic Ocean; understandably, the Dutch are very interested in not having a rise in oceanic water levels. Not being able to solve the problem alone, however, they were forced to take the issue up in a larger, collective setting.

(5) *Solving these problems will require multi-level, multi-party approaches.* Unilateral actions by some nations, some peoples, can certainly help delay the onset of negative consequences, but they do not solve the "prisoner's dilemma," one of the central problems of collective action (Olson, 1971): why should one act in the collective interest when others are acting in self-interest? Scott Barrett of the London Business School observes that "every country has some incentive to protect the global environment. The crux of the problem is that this incentive is often small" (Barrett, 1990: 48).

Similarly, *The Economist* (1989: 13) editorializes that countries will not be willing to unilaterally impose pollution-control costs on their own businesses unless other countries do the same ("The First Green Summit", 1989). In addition, solving global environmental problems will require sensitivity to global divisions of rich–poor, North–South, white–nonwhite, and so on. *The Economist* editorial comments that third-world countries do not like to be lectured about global pollution problems by countries that have created most of those problems in the first place. And, finally, the editorial continues, developing countries cannot escape their own responsibilities, or the fact that their failure to do so hurts them and their developing-country colleagues ("The First Green Summit," 1989: 13).

Accepting the opportunities

Concern for the environment is often given a great deal of attention in international business, both pro and con. Arguments continue about whether it is economically viable and morally justifiable to transfer pollution problems to less developed parts of the globe, or whether pollution is just one of the unfortunate but unavoidable side effects of industrialization and the improved standards of living that accompany it. Despite continuing controversy, global pollution is becoming more subject to multinational as well as national regulation. The new European Union pollution guidelines, ISO 14000, provide an example.

ISO 14000 is designed to make concern for the environment a mandatory part of the global business environment. Two key components of ISO 14000 – the standards of environmental management systems and environmental auditing – were to be implemented in 1996. By the time ISO 14000 is fully implemented, four additional areas will be addressed: performance evaluation, environmental labeling, life cycle assessment, and environmental assessments of product standards. This standardization of environmental protection in the EU is expected eventually to make certification of ISO 14000 compliance a requirement for virtually all multinational enterprises ("ISO," 1995; Harris, 1994).

The emergence of important regional environmental protection standards means that multinational businesses will need to develop strategies to incorporate concern for the environment into their everyday operations. Here are some examples of what will be required in a business environment governed by ISO 14000 (Ottman, 1995; Powers, 1995):

- Adopt management strategies that will enable firms to obtain ISO 14000 certification in their industry.
- Reduce pollution and conserve resources as a means of meeting stringent environmental regulations.
- Shift from product changes to behavioral and manufacturing process changes, so as to manufacture products in a more environmentally sound manner.
- Reduce solid waste by incorporating recycling into the manufacturing process.

Similarly, recommendations of a panel of multinational corporation leaders and international environmental experts concerned with global environmental problems included the following:

- Comply fully with all host-government environmental and health laws and regulations, and establish workplace health and safety standards that may go well beyond local regulations.
- Make certain that a corporate environmental policy is firmly supported by top executives, widely circulated in the company, and publicized in the host country.
- Carry out – and make public – environmental impact assessments for all major investments, including analysis of on-site and off-site environmental effects, technologies for moderating adverse affects, social impacts such as the displacement of local residents and the influx of workers, and ways to manage emergency pollution hazards.

- Take responsibility for the environmental behavior of joint venture partners and sub-contractors, and [do] not sub-contract hazardous operations to avoid direct responsibility for worker protection.
- Regulate . . . hazardous exports, individually and through trade associations. ("Multinationals," 1984: 25.)

Accepting that complex global environmental problems have no simple cure can mean new opportunities for technological developments, sales, and markets. If MNEs spend all their energies complaining about environmental regulations, differing standards, increasing costs, and so on, or shifting their capital around the globe in search of yet another pristine unregulated environment, they will miss opportunities to obtain competitive advantage, to build stable relationships in host nations, and to enhance the global quality of life through their own actions. They will also eventually run out of pristine environments to which to move, and will have to face a much worse problem than exists now. There is "considerable evidence that MNCs pollute less than indigenous companies. In fact, they often provide the main channel for transfer of pollution-control technology" (Micou, 1985: 13).

CONCLUSION

In this chapter we have examined the first portion of the corporate social performance (CSP) model – principles of social responsibility – to see how well they can be applied by international companies. We also explored briefly the international fit of the CSP model's second portion – corporate social responsiveness. Finally, we used the global issue of environmental pollution to try to understand the complex interactions among cultures, values, peoples, and organizations when companies try to implement principles of social responsibility globally.

Recently, Joel Makower (1994: 21), in his study of socially responsible businesses, emphasized that "one of the most socially responsible things most companies can do is to be profitable: providing sustainable jobs at fair wages for their employees, solid returns for their owners and investors, and prosperity and sustainability for the communities in which they operate." Max B. E. Clarkson (1988: 263), reporting on an intensive study of the social and economic performance of 17 large Canadian corporations, offers some evidence for this perspective. He concluded that

> average or above-average economic performance, in an industry group over several years, is related to the integration of social, ethical, and

discretionary responsibilities and goals within the strategic planning of the company, which is, in turn, linked with management performance and decision-making at the operating level. To be socially responsible is to be ethically responsible and profitable. (Clarkson, 1988.)

Facing the challenges of global economy requires facing also the problems and opportunities of global social and political issues. The multinational corporation is going to be held accountable in many different venues, by an enormous host of stakeholders (see Thompson, Wartick and Smith, 1991). Abiding by the principles of corporate social responsibility will be a major step towards profits and effective world citizenship for MNCs.

REFERENCES

Ackerman, Robert W. 1975. *The Social Challenge to Business.* Cambridge, MA: Harvard University Press.

Barrett, Scott. 1990. "After you." *Report on Business Magazine* 6:7: 48.

Carroll, Archie B. 1979. "A three-dimensional conceptual model of corporate social performance." *Academy of Management Review* 4: 497–505.

Chester, Elaine. 1993. "Toxic exports." *Environment Risk* (July/Aug.): 19–21.

Clarkson, Max B. E. 1988. "Corporate social performance in Canada, 1976–86." Pp. 241–65 in Lee E. Preston (ed.), *Research in Corporate Social Performance and Policy.* Greenwich, CT: JAI Press.

"Controlling carbon dioxide: The view from Europe." *Chemical and Engineering News* 64 (Nov. 24, 1986): 57.

Davis, Keith. 1973. "The case for and against business assumption of social responsibilities." *Academy of Management Journal* 16: 312–22.

Davis, Keith, and Robert L. Blomstrom. 1975. *Business and Society: Environment and Responsibility.* New York: McGraw-Hill.

Dickie, Robert B., and Leroy S. Rouner. 1986. "Introduction." Pp. 1–16 in *Corporations and the Common Good.* Notre Dame, IN: University of Notre Dame Press.

Dyllick, Thomas. 1989. "Ecological marketing strategy for Toni Yogurts in Switzerland." *Journal of Business Ethics* 8: 657–62.

Epstein, Edwin M. 1987. "The corporate social policy process: Beyond business ethics, corporate social responsibility, and corporate social responsiveness." *California Management Review* 29:3 (Spring): 99–114.

"The first green summit." 1989. *The Economist* 312 (July 15): 13–14.

Frederick, William C. 1978. "From CSR1 to CSR2: The maturing of business and society thought." University of Pittsburgh working paper; published as a Classic Paper in *Business & Society* 33:2 (July, 1994).

"The freedom to be cleaner than the rest." 1989. *The Economist* (Oct. 14): 21–2, 24.

"Green or bust?" 1995. *Business Europe* 35:9 (March 6): 1–3.

Harris, Paul. 1994. "Companies should prepare for global E-management standards." *Environment Today* 5:12 (Dec.): 7.

"ISO 14000 standards update" 1995. *Environmental Manager* 6:10 (May): 3–5.

Kalmbach, William C., III. 1987. "International labeling requirements for the export of hazardous chemicals: A developing nation's perspective." *Law and Policy in International Business* 19:4: 811–49.

Makower, Joel. 1994. *Beyond the Bottom Line: Putting Social Responsibility to Work for Your Business and the World.* New York: Simon & Schuster.

Micou, Ann McKinstry. 1985. "The invisible hand at work in developing countries." *Across the Board* 22:3 (March): 8–15.

"Multinationals in third world: Environmental role is studied." *Chemical Marketing Reporter* (July 30, 1984): 4, 25.

Olson, Mancur. 1971. *The Logic of Collective Action: Public Goods and the Theory of Groups.* Cambridge, MA: Harvard University Press.

Ottman, Jacquelyn. 1995. "New and improved won't do." *Marketing News* 29:3 (Jan. 30): 9.

Powers, Mary Buckner. 1995. "Focus on environment." *ENR* 234:21 (May 29): 30–2.

Preston, Lee E., and James E. Post. 1975. *Private Management and Public Policy: The Principle of Public Responsibility.* Englewood Cliffs, NJ: Prentice-Hall.

Reisch, Marc S. 1994. "Chemical industry tries to improve its community relations." *Chemical & Engineering News* 72:2 (Feb. 28): 8–21.

"Responsible distribution: A code for chemical distributors by chemical distributors." *Chemical & Engineering News* 71:10 (March 8): 20–1.

Russell, James W. 1984. "US sweatshops across the Rio Grande." *Business and Society Review* 50 (Summer): 17–20.

Shon, Melissa. 1993. "Chemicals '93." *Chemical Marketing Reporter* 242:1 (Jan. 4): SR23–4.

Speth, James Gustave. 1987. "An environmental agenda for world business." *Across the Board* 24 (March): 21–6.

Thompson, Judith K., Wartick, Steven L. and Smith, Howard L. 1991. Integrating corporate social performance and stakeholder management: Implications for a research agenda in small business. In James E. Post (ed.), *Research in Corporate Social Performance and Policy.* Greenwich, CN: JAI Press, Volume 12, 207–30.

Van Buren, Harry J. III. 1995. "The exploitation of Mexican workers." *Business & Society Review* 92 (Winter): 29–33.

Velasquez, Manuel G. 1992. *Business Ethics: Concepts and Cases.* 3rd edition. Englewood Cliffs, NJ: Prentice-Hall.

Wartick, Steven L., and Philip L. Cochran. 1985. "The evolution of the corporate social performance model." *Academy of Management Review* 10: 758–69.

Wood, Donna J. 1990. *Business and Society.* Glenview, IL: Scott, Foresman/Little, Brown.

Wood, Donna J. 1991a. "Corporate social performance revisited." *Academy of Management Review* 16: 691–718.

Wood, Donna J. 1991b. "Toward improving corporate social performance." *Business Horizons* 34:4 (July–August): 66–73.

Wood, Donna J. 1992. "'Dams or democracy?' Stakeholders and social issues in the Hungarian–Czechoslovakian hydroelectric controversy." *Proceedings of the International Association of Business and Society*, Leuven, Belgium, June 1992.

5

Managing International Stakeholder Relations

Do your company's managers know to handle customers, suppliers, stockholders, government agencies, environmental protection advocates, and competitors, not to mention kidnappers, extortionists, corrupt customs officials, and so on? Do you know how your company's stakeholders differ from country to country? Does your company have strategies and procedures for managing stakeholder relationships of various types?

Too many companies still do not have explicit strategies and procedures for managing stakeholder relationships. This is easy to understand; corporate–stakeholder relations at home (in whatever nation) are usually complex and difficult to handle. For international companies in global markets, the problems of identifying, tracking, and managing stakeholder relations worldwide are simply immense. Nevertheless, stakeholders have so much real and potential influence on business decision making that no manager, no business organization, can afford to overlook them.

This chapter presents the stakeholder model of the firm, showing how it builds upon older neoclassical and behavioral theories. The chapter examines specific business–stakeholder relationships, showing how stakeholder relations are more complex and difficult, but also richer and potentially more rewarding, in international contexts. The process of identifying and mapping stakeholder relationships is examined, as are the processes of international stakeholder management. The chapter provides examples of how a company's key stakeholders may differ considerably across cultures, how a single worldwide stakeholder may have different interests and power relations in different parts of the world, and how stakeholder relations may shift over time. Finally, we examine a dynamic model of stakeholder characteristics that allows us to predict when and how stakeholders will be actively seeking to meet their interests.

THE STAKEHOLDER THEORY OF THE FIRM

The stakeholder theory of the firm is an image of business organizations existing and operating in a network of relationships with other social groups and organizations. Before outlining this theory, we first explain the theoretical context in which it became necessary. In the twentieth century, though numerous theories have been proposed, two theories of the firm have predominated management thinking – the neoclassical economic theory and the behavioral theory. Each of these theories has serious deficiencies that have made it necessary to frame a more comprehensive theory of the firm.

Neoclassical economic theory of the firm

Economists such as Milton Friedman (1962) posit a theory of the firm based upon rational, self-interested behavior of managers acting in the firm's interests. The interests of the firm are held to be identical with the interests of the firm's owners, or stockholders, and are assumed to be purely economic. That is, owners are interested in financial gain – dividends, stock appreciation – and managers are obliged to act in that interest. Accordingly, managers are said to make decisions that maximize long-term shareholder wealth.

Currently, the neoclassical theory undergirds the field of finance and influences most other areas of management thought and practice as well as corporate law. Subsequent theoretical developments in economics, including public choice theory, transaction costs economics, and agency theory, are variations on the theme of rational self-interest and maximization of economic value. The shortcomings of neoclassical theory have been widely discussed (see, for example, Galbraith, 1975; Thurow; 1983). In brief, they include (1) a failure to account for externalities – the costs of doing business not borne by those who purchase products or services, (2) an inability to accommodate individual or organizational values or choices that are neither economic nor narrowly self-interested (for example, spiritual values or altruistic choices), and (3) oversimplicity in dealing with human and organizational relationships in the business environment.

In addition, the neoclassical approach permits and even promotes a very short-term perspective on maximizing shareholder wealth. Managers are encouraged to ignore the long-term consequences of current business behavior with a simple rationale: if people are worried enough about those consequences, they will pay more to prevent them, and then market forces will have automatically adjusted price and demand. For example, if the market truly wants to reduce environmental pollution, then it (that is, millions of individual customers) will be willing to pay a higher price for goods and services in order to pay for less-polluting technology and packaging. However, this model does not acknowledge that people do not have very good information about the environmental effects of the products they buy. As well, the model fails to consider the short run costs attendant to long run market adjustment. More seriously, it does not allow for the definite possibility that by the time people realize the destruction they are causing and are willing to pay to clean it up, it may be too late for the ecosystem to regenerate. The commons cannot be protected under a completely free market system.

Market-based theories of firm behavior depend upon adequate, accurate information. When such information is not available, market mechanisms will not work to achieve social goals. These theories also depend on assumptions that human motivation and behavior is rational, self-interested, and individualistic. When these assumptions are not met (as when behavior is spiritually or emotionally driven, other-interested, or collaborative), market theories cannot explain human or company actions.

Behavioral theory of the firm

In contrast to the neoclassicists, Cyert and March (1963) proposed a behavioral theory of the firm, based upon the idea that managers, as human beings, (1) are unable to behave completely rationally, and (2) have all sorts of interests and motives aside from their formal organizational ones and their narrow self-interest. Thus managers can only incompletely achieve the best interests of stockholders. The behavioralists point out also that *maximizing* shareholder wealth is an impossible task; managers cannot know all information relevant to complex decisions, nor can they adequately sort and synthesize the information they do have available – they operate from a position of "bounded rationality" rather than complete rationality. Nor, when it comes down to it, are they likely to behave only in owners' best interests, because they have too many interests of their own to be met. Instead of maximizing, then, managers "satisfice," reaching merely for an acceptable and defensible outcome.

The behavioral theory of the firm is, more than anything else, a theory of interpersonal politics, perceptual limits, and noneconomic influences on human and organizational behavior. It has the advantage over neoclassical theory of examining these vaguely defined but real factors explicitly, rather than assuming them away or considering them irrelevant to managerial decision making. But like neoclassical theory, behavioral theory narrowly focuses on just the firm and cannot accommodate the interorganizational and societal networks within which firms are enmeshed.

Stakeholder theory of the firm

In recent years, business and society scholars have been moving away from traditional neoclassical and behavioral theories, toward a stakeholder theory of the firm. The intent of such a theory is to express more accurately what happens in the real world, and to provide a sound theoretical understanding of the complex interweaving of business organizations with other societal institutions and with the sociopolitical environment:

> By focusing the understanding of business on the traditional relationships between customers, employees, suppliers, owners, and domestic competitors, managers are constantly surprised by governments, consumer advocates, environmentalists, terrorists, media, local communities, foreign competitors, and other groups who perceive that they have a stake in a business. There is a constant source of tension between business strategy, traditionally conceived as the appropriate means to an end of profitability, and the demands of society and ethics as seen through the eyes of other stakeholders in a business. (Freeman and Gilbert, 1987: 397.)

Though some scholars used the concept of stakeholder earlier (Ackoff, 1970), R. Edward Freeman (1984) was the first to systematically outline a way of thinking about stakeholders that could lead eventually to a stakeholder theory of the firm. A stakeholder is defined by Freeman (1984: 24) as "any group or individual who can affect or is affected by the achievement of the firm's objectives." This definition is broad enough to include practically any type of group, and is not narrowly focused on a particular type of stakeholder – for example, owners – whose interests are held to be prime. Achieving and sustaining a workable balance among competing interests, rather than "maximizing" the interests of a single stakeholder, is the core concept of stakeholder theory for managers.

The idea of stakeholder relationships now rings true with managers, and these relationships imply a number of things: varying interests, give and take, potential for conflict, reciprocal or boomerang effects of an organization's actions, and relationships among stakeholders themselves as well as between stakeholders and the focal organization. Yet theory in this area has proceeded very slowly, probably because it is a truly complex subject and because most empirical research has focused on quantitative measures of firm performance or aspects of managerial decision making, and not on the firm's boundary-spanning relationships with external groups and organizations.

Brenner and Cochran (1991: 453–5), arguing primarily against the neoclassical model, have begun to articulate a more formal stakeholder theory of the firm. Their four initial propositions, below, begin to address the role of stakeholder needs and values in managerial decision making:

(1) Firms/organizations must fulfill some set of their various stakeholders' needs in order to continue to exist.

(2) Firms/organizations can understand the relevant needs of their stakeholders by examining the values and interests of their organization's stakeholders.

(3) Management of firms/organizations involves structuring and implementing choice processes among various stakeholders.

(4) The identification of an organization's stakeholders, their various values and interests, the relative importance of each stakeholder's value position, and the nature of the value trade-off processes used provides information useful for understanding the behavior of and within the firm/organization.

Brenner and Cochran (1991) suggest that each of a firm's stakeholders (for example, owners, employees, customers, suppliers, community, government) can be rated according to the strength with which that stakeholder maintains certain key values (for example, values for dividends, stock price, worker safety, job security, product safety, product quality). They suggest that a "value matrix can be used to predict that when stakeholders whose economic values dominate their concerns have a strong relative impact on organizational decisions, a more rational, economic value-laden [choice] process will be used" (p. 457). Similarly, other choice processes, such as bargaining or moral decision making, would be used when stakeholders with noneconomic values are relatively more influential.

Although stakeholder theory is still in its infancy, there are certain things we know about business–stakeholder relationships that can be useful to managers. These factors – stakeholder interests and power bases – are discussed below.

STAKEHOLDERS AND INTERESTS

The simple truth about stakeholders is that each of them has a *stake* in the company's activities, objectives, policies, and outputs. There is something of direct interest to them about the company – they hope to gain from it, they fear to lose or be harmed because of it, they are concerned about someone else's gain or loss, they want to change something or to have something remain stable. In this section we take a look at six categories of interests that stakeholders may have in the company, and two types of stakeholders (primary and secondary).

Stakeholder interests

Stakeholder interests are as broad and intricate as human interests in general. Freeman and Reed (1983) distinguish three types of stakeholder interests as equity (ownership), economic (financial or material), and influencer (political). We feel these categories are not comprehensive enough for more sophisticated stakeholder analysis, so we will distinguish six basic types of interests: material, political, affiliative, informational, symbolic, and spiritual.

Material interests are those interests in which something tangible or fungible is desired or at risk. Material interests of stakeholders may be financial, as in desires for wealth accumulation or fears of lost employment income. Material interests may also be non-financial, as in desire for access to good health care or fear of physical danger on the job. Table 5.1 provides a number of examples of stakeholders' material interests, classified according to whether they are desires for gain or fears of loss, and whether they are financial or non-financial.

Political interests are those having to do with the distribution and uses of power and influence. Oftentimes, stakeholders' political interests

Table 5.1 Financial and material interests of stakeholders: some examples

	Hopes of gain	*Fears of loss*
Financial interests	Wealth accumulation Stock dividends Stock price appreciation Income and benefits Cost reductions Increasing property values near a proposed shopping mall	Declines in retirement fund values Loss of income Loss of employment Declining property values near a proposed industrial waste dump
Non-financial material interests	Access to good, affordable health care Cleaner air and water	Workplace health or safety risks Adverse health effects of pollution

concern public policy, including legislation, regulation, legal rights, judicial decisions – that is, the allocation and uses of official government power. These interests may have to do with shaping public policy, finding and using routes of access and power to influence public policy makers in order to accomplish stakeholders' objectives. Stakeholders may also have political interests in the allocation of power and influence within the firm itself, or between the firm and external groups. A hostile raider seeking to control a majority of board members would be an example of the former; an external organization trying to influence a firm's charitable contributions policy exemplifies the latter.

Affiliative interests are those human needs to belong to a group, to feel part of a larger social network, to connect with other human beings. Stakeholders with primarily affiliative interests in a company will be concerned about issues such as how the company fits in with the values and social organization of the local community, the opportunities available for employees to network with peers, or desires to "belong" to the same social group as do people in the company.

Informational interests have to do with news, facts, opinions, data, research findings, and so on. Knowledge may be sought to aid stakeholders in understanding their other interests in the firm and in making decisions about their own courses of action, or to allow them to monitor relevant aspects of the organization's behavior. Opinions may be sought for the same reason, but in this case it may be that the nature of social networks is a more important consideration than are the factual aspects of the issue at hand. Stakeholders with informational interests will try to obtain greater transparency from the company.

Symbolic interests, drawing upon the work of Murray Edelman (1964: 6), are interests in symbols that evoke "an attitude, a set of impressions, or a pattern of events associated through time, through space, through logic, or through imagination with the symbol." Edelman distinguishes two types of symbols as *referential symbols*, shorthand terms that call up a body of facts, an event, an issue, or a situation; and *condensation symbols*, those that "evoke the emotions associated with the situation" (1964: 6). Edelman contends that citizen participation in US public policy decisions is largely symbolic, that is, it does not significantly affect the fundamental allocation of financial or material resources. Once citizens are reassured symbolically that the government is working properly, that the protection or gain they demand is on the way, they become once again quiescent.

This idea is easily extended into the realm of business–stakeholder relations. Some stakeholders may have little or no interest in how the firm allocates its financial, material, or human resources, but are very concerned about the firm's image in the community, its good will to customers, its appearance as a safe place to work, or even its conformity with nationalistic or dominant-culture or religious values. Such symbolic interests may be relatively easily satisfied by improved public relations, assuming, of course, that the firm has a solid record of performance to back up the PR.

Spiritual interests involve deep meanings, religious or philosophical values, beliefs about the divine, feelings of connection to nature or the universe, and so on. Stakeholders' spiritual interests often underlie conflicts that are based on perceived ethical problems. Issues that involve deeply-felt definitions of right and wrong often have a spiritual or religious foundation. Spiritual issues involving business often involve life and death: organ transplants and "harvesting," technological prolonging of life, and modern reproductive technologies are examples of such issues; many people, both pro and con, derive their positions on these issues from their religious beliefs.

Stakeholder power bases

Brenner and Cochran (1991) have implied that traditional classifications of stakeholders (for example, owners, employees, or customers) might eventually give way to reclassifications of stakeholders according to the values and interests they hold. This appealing insight does not go far enough, however; it would be necessary also to map stakeholders according to the type of power or influence they wield vis-à-vis the firm. Freeman and Reed (1983) moved toward this position with their preliminary analysis of how the historical configuration of stakeholder power and stakes has shifted with the emergence of more complex business environments.

Freeman and Reed discuss three types of power normally held by stakeholders over the focal company. First, *formal* or voting power is held by those stakeholders having an official role in corporate governance. In stock companies, these would be stockholders and their representatives on the board of directors; in codetermined companies, they would be stockholders, executive managers, employee representatives, and directors. Second, *economic* power is held by those stakeholders who can affect the company's cost and revenue structure, including customers, suppliers, creditors, and employees. Third, *political* power is held by those stakeholders who can influence the conditions under which the firm does business through their access to the public policy process.

The source of a stakeholder's power has implications for how the focal company and its managers can best handle the stakeholder relationship. For example, Freeman and Reed point out that the lines of power are now blurred; activists own stock so they can exercise the rights of those with voting power, stockholders can form grassroots lobbying networks to exercise political power, and political influencers can change the economic conditions of a business organization.

For some business managers, diagnosing stakeholder relations using multiple stakes becomes even more complicated because stakeholder groups take on multiple roles. Under employee stock ownership plans (ESOPs), for example, employees are also owners. If the employee/owners also buy the products they produce (for example, Mitsubishi or Volvo or Ford assembly line workers buy Mitsubishi or Volvo or Ford automobiles), then they become employee/owner/customers. If this group also lives around the plant, they become employee/owner/customer/ community members. Those who are environmental activists and those who get elected to local government councils add those roles. Sometimes stakeholder power becomes a function of cumulative powers acquired through multiple roles.

Primary stakeholders

Max Clarkson's contribution to stakeholder theory includes an expanded definition of what a stakeholder is, as well as practical definitions of primary and secondary stakeholders. He defines stakeholders as follows (1995: 106):

> Stakeholders are persons or groups that have, or claim, ownership, rights, or interests in a corporation and its activities, past, present, or future. Such claimed rights or interests are the result of transactions with, or actions taken by, the corporation, and may be legal or moral, individual or collective. Stakeholders with similar interests, claims, or rights can be classified as belonging to the same group: employees, shareholders, customers, and so on.

Primary stakeholders, then, are those "without whose continuing participation the corporation cannot survive as a going concern" (Clarkson, 1995: 106). At a minimum they include owners, employees, customers, and suppliers. Some authors (for example, Freeman and Gilbert, 1987) include competitors as primary stakeholders; we choose instead to include governments, because competitors are not a necessary part of a firm's environment (there are both monopolies and niche players in business), but government is always present and active in setting the social control rules and redistribution policies under which businesses function.

Owners of a corporation are those holding stock in it or otherwise supplying capital to it. Formerly in some capitalist economies, stockholders were often the *only* stakeholder group explicitly recognized by management. Their interests were assumed to be almost exclusively financial – stock price appreciation, dividends, corporate profits. In recent years, however, not only has the business–stakeholder map expanded to include numerous other groups, but the interests of owners have also undergone changes. So-called dissident shareholders, for example, buy stock in order to have access to management and a voice at the company's annual meeting, where they produce resolutions for stockholders to vote upon, attempting to force the management to change some aspect of company procedures or policy. In the US, dissident stockholders can also include institutional investors who have such large holdings of stock in a company that when they are dissatisfied they can't sell off their stock without substantial losses. These investors have increasingly taken an activist role toward management, making frequent visits and insisting on management actions that the investors believe will benefit their clients.

Employees of a firm have stakes in their jobs, benefits, and income – all material interests. They also have affiliative interests to the extent that they are tied to social networks on the job, informational interests of various sorts (for example, health and safety conditions, job-related knowledge), and symbolic interests in the personal and social meaning of their occupation and how they fulfill its responsibilities. Additionally, employees may have political interests in how the firm is governed as well as desires to influence public policy and external stakeholder actions as they affect the firm.

Customers, likewise, may have virtually any sort of interest in a firm's operations, though their needs are likely to be primarily material and informational. Symbolic interests, however, appear to be gaining importance as consumers learn to choose products according to the firm's environmental impacts. For example, business writer Leigh Bruce (1989: 25) notes, "For better or for worse, consumers are increasingly likely to ask, 'How green is your company?' before buying a product." Guides such as *Rating America's Corporate Conscience* (Lydenberg, et al. 1986) and *Shopping for a Better World* (Lydenberg, et al. 1988, 1989, and 1991.) also show the increasing relevance of symbolic values to consumers; these guides provide information, by brand name, on companies' "social responsibility" dimensions such as women and minority employees and directors, company participation in weapons production and nuclear power, product safety, employee safety and health, and environmental protection records.

Suppliers certainly hold material and informational interests in firms, and they may develop other interests. In the international environment, local suppliers may not always do business exactly the way one would like; there are innumerable cultural differences in business styles. But cultivating and using local suppliers may be essential, either because the national government has local content laws, or because the technological and market conditions of the host country may be such that foreign suppliers cannot service it. Highbarger (1988: 48) points out, for example, a problem facing companies desiring to establish good communications and management information systems in many countries: "Without local MIS personnel who know the local market, vendors, language and traditions, the job of purchasing and installing hardware, software and telecommunications facilities can overwhelm a company."

Governments have interests in companies for a variety of reasons. Firms provide the economic basis of the society and are both nourished and regulated by government with the intent of keeping the economy healthy enough to sustain the society and, of course, the government. Government may attempt to control the harms of business activity to other members of society. In some societies, government runs the economy via central planning mechanisms and state ownership of enterprise. The role of government is so important, in fact, that we have already devoted chapter 3 to it.

Secondary stakeholders

Secondary stakeholders are "those that are not directly engaged in the firm's economic activities but that nonetheless can exercise . . . influence over it or can be . . . affected by its operations" (Wood, 1990: 85). They can include virtually any kind of group or organization. In the US, they typically include such groups as the media, environmental activists, consumer protection activists, competitors, financial analysts and brokers, creditors, communities, and nonprofit (voluntary) organizations. Elsewhere in the world, secondary stakeholders can include a wide variety of groups and organizations. As we mentioned in chapter 4, companies doing business in certain parts of Central America, Africa, the Middle East, or Southeast Asia, might include as stakeholders any of the following: terrorists, religious activists, healthcare workers, customs officials, various political parties, revolutionary governments, diplomats, spies, military factions, gun-runners, and so on. Companies doing business in Ireland are likely to count both Catholic and Protestant churches and affiliated organizations among their stakeholders. Companies doing business in Japan would have the *kereitsu,* or industry councils, as important stakeholders. Companies operating in Central and Eastern Europe include research institutes and academies of science, labor councils, various green parties, NATO, and the European Parliament and Commission among their stakeholders.

One interesting characteristic of secondary stakeholders is that the power they hold in influencing corporations is also viewed as secondary to direct negotiations with companies. When a primary stakeholder group is dissatisfied with management, who do they turn to? The media? Activists? Competitors? Voluntary associations? No, they go straight to management or to the board of directors. Secondary stakeholders might have some direct way of influencing corporate decisions, but they are often have only indirect access to decision making processes. This does not make them less powerful or influential – consider the power of the media or of terrorist groups, for example – but it means that managers' relationships with secondary stakeholders need to be viewed and structured to account for their "once-removed" status with respect to business decision processes.

MAPPING INTERNATIONAL STAKEHOLDER RELATIONSHIPS

In the international context, stakeholder identification and management is exceedingly complex. One reason is that managers operating in foreign cultures may encounter stakeholder groups undreamed-of and sometimes unimaginable in the home environment. Imagine the shock, for example, of a Saudi Arabian firm setting up shop in Montréal and experiencing for the first time the impact of politically active feminist stakeholder groups! Additionally, global stakeholders and intercultural differences in stakeholder environments complicate the international picture. Here we explore these issues and outline the process of international stakeholder identification and mapping.

Global stakeholders

Just as business firms may be global in outlook and market reach, so too may certain stakeholders be worldwide in their membership, interests, and actions. A *global stakeholder* is defined as a group or organization having crossnational membership and crossnational interests in business activities.

Global *environmental* stakeholders are perhaps the best-known form of global stakeholder. The worldwide activities of groups such as Greenpeace and the World Wildlife Federation have been amply reported in the news media, and many multinational companies now routinely monitor the activities of such groups. As general awareness of the effects of pollution on the global ecology increases, environmental stakeholders are likely to become even more important to international business than they presently are. To see the point, just look at some of the current issues involving business: overseas and transborder toxic materials transport; multinational environmental disasters such as oil spills and nuclear accidents; the export of hazardous wastes by developed nations to developing ones; pollution of underground aquifers and freshwater reservoirs; third-world trade-offs between economic growth and pollution controls; and international action to stop destruction of rain forests, wetlands, and other important natural habitats.

Speth (1987: 21) observes that environmentalism, once a phenomenon only of the industrialized nations, has now spread worldwide:

> The environmental activism that gained momentum in the United States during the late 1960s is now catching on in third-world countries, spurred both by isolated events, such as the accident at Bhopal in 1984, and by chronic problems, such as urban pollution and the destruction of soil and forests. Today, the governments of these countries are more determined to protect their resources. Government regulation is increasing, and any informed discussion by corporate management of investment opportunities in the third world includes an assessment of environmental risks.

This view is confirmed by Maurice Strong, Secretary-General of the United Nations Conference on Environment and Development (UNCED), who believes that:

> We have already begun the transition to a new era in which environmental issues will increasingly drive our economic life. The transition to economically sound and sustainable development is as imperative for the continued viability of our economy as it is for our environmental security. Every business that impacts on the environment must accommodate the fact that the environment will have an impact on its business (United Nations, 1993: 1).

Global *political* stakeholders may be of various types. Political bodies such as the International Communist party can be considered global stakeholders. Their interests are not narrowly focused on a single country, but may span entire regions or continents. International military coalitions such as NATO can impact corporate decision making, even for non-defense-related businesses. International political bodies such as the World Court and the United Nations, as well as regional groups such as the European Union, the NAFTA, and the several economic communities of Latin America, can affect a multinational firm's operations, policies, and outputs.

International *terrorist* groups who strike in any number of countries and who are based in more than one country might be considered by some as political stakeholders, but we prefer to isolate them as a distinct category and not grant legitimacy to the use of violence to achieve political ends. Despite intense worldwide efforts to break up terrorist networks and to train business and government representatives in self-protection, terrorism does not appear to be abating, and thus demands attention from all international managers. The 1993 bombing of New York's World Trade Center first expanded the scope of terrorism to the United States, and the 1995 bombing in Oklahoma City brought terrorism home in a way never before experienced in that country, but all too familiar in others.

Global *religious* stakeholders are perhaps the constituency most likely to be overlooked by US managers and scholars. Elsewhere in the world, however, the influence of the major organized religions on public policy, social organization, and government activity – and thus on economic activity – is quite clear. A striking example was the global death warrant placed by Islamic fundamentalist groups on author Salman Rushdie, his publishers, and distributors. Rushdie's work was said to be blasphemous. The threat was taken seriously by publishers and retail booksellers, who had to make a choice about whether to carry the book or not. Other authors have since been "sentenced to death" for their words and ideas, including writer Taslima Nasrin of Bangladesh, whose works about Hindu attacks on Muslim temples in India, and on the treatment of women, have aroused the violent ire of religious fundamentalists. Another example of the influence of global religious stakeholders is the social and political resistance to birth control technology encountered by pharmaceutical companies selling contraceptive devices and drugs in predominantly Catholic countries.

When operating in specific settings, global stakeholders may be represented by local people, by foreigners, or by some combination. This can make it rather difficult at times to identify them and deal with them. In Hungary, for example, when environmental and political protests focused on a large hydroelectric project were mounting in the late 1980s, Hungarian environmentalists were assisted by Austrian and West German Greens. In some of the early demonstrations along the Danube River construction site, in fact, the Austrians were the *only* visible protesters, agreeing to shield their Hungarian colleagues from the political consequences of opposing the government (Wood, 1992).

Intercultural differences in stakeholder environments

In figure 5.1 we see a simple hypothetical example of a multinational corporation doing business in two foreign countries. Stakeholder maps for the three countries (home plus two host nations) will not look the same. Observe that customers and owners are boxed for the home country, employees for host country B, and suppliers for host country C. This suggests that the firm's capital is provided primarily by domestic owners, and that it supplies primarily domestic markets. However, the firm obtains critical raw materials from suppliers in host country C, and actually produces and packages its goods in host country B.

Now let's examine why the stakeholder maps look different for each of the three countries. In the home country, our firm is subject to *owner* demands for dividends, stock appreciation, and financial and organizational well-being of the company; *customer* demands concerning product characteristics, quality, price, packaging, and safety; *national government* constraints including regulation, taxation, and monetary policy; and so on through the list of stakeholders and their various interests. These are probably familiar stakeholders, with familiar interests.

Figure 5.1   Mapping international stakeholders

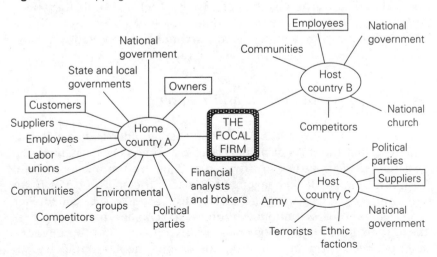

But in host country B, the situation is a bit different. Here the firm has factories, and therefore has both employee and local community stakeholders. The national government operates in conjunction with a national religion, and this means specific constraints on employee and community relations that the firm does not experience in its home country. The firm has no customers or owners in country B, but there are several competitors, also with production facilities. In this country, the firm's competitive situation has to do with how well it handles government and employee relations, not with how well it satisfies customers and product-service markets.

Finally, the focal firm maintains a small purchasing office in host country C, which has an abundant supply of a crucial natural resource the firm needs. Here the firm has a tiny number of employees and a very low profile in the community, although its purchasing volume means that it represents substantial economic value to country C. There are no domestic customers or owners to worry about, and no challenges yet from environmental or consumer protection groups. On the other hand, country C provides our focal firm with stakeholder relationships it has nowhere else. Country C's government is unstable, constantly threatened by militant politics, feuding ethnic factions, and power-hungry military officers. Some of these factions contain terrorist branches, and some terrorist groups based in other nations use country C as a "home" for their regional operations. Our focal firm is always unsure whether or not it will be welcome in country C. How to deal with these stakeholder relations is probably not something the firm's managers learned in business school!

Figure 5.2 shows clearly the mistake managers make if they assume that a domestic stakeholder map will tell them all they need to know about international stakeholder relations. Not only will the map itself differ from country to country, but the importance of various stakeholders to the firm will also vary by country.

Stakeholder identification and mapping

Freeman and Gilbert (1987: 397) define stakeholder management as "the idea that the tasks of managers in a business are to manage the stakeholder relationships in a way that achieves the purpose of the business. Stakeholder management provides the tools by which we can connect strategy to social and ethical issues." The stakeholder management process cannot begin unless stakeholders have been identified, their interests and power bases are assessed, and the relationships between them and the firm, and among them, are understood.

In this section we investigate the process of identifying and mapping a firm's stakeholders.

(1) Identifying stakeholder groups. Stakeholder management begins with understanding as precisely as possible *who* the company's stakeholders are, whether in international or domestic business. Categories such as customers or employees are useful starting points, but they must be expanded as much as possible to include the names and key subsets of actual stakeholders (for example, unions by name and non-organized labor; or local, regional, national, and supranational government agencies). Managers must be careful that their preselected categories do not permit them to overlook unexpected but important stakeholders. The supplier category, for example, might be thought of as suppliers of goods and raw materials, but it could also include key stakeholders such as banks (suppliers of financing) and insurance companies (suppliers of risk management). Also, it is important to think of potential stakeholders, those which may burst onto the scene, given particular organizational actions. The anti-abortion forces in the United States, for example, have suddenly become irritant stakeholders to large companies giving charitable donations to Planned Parenthood.

(2) What are the stakes? The next step is to relate stakeholders' various interests to the company's mission, operations, and objectives. Some stakeholder interests can be identified by inference, merely by knowing what type of stakeholder one is dealing with. Customers, for example, are normally going to be interested in product or service issues such as quality, price, durability, availability, environmental impact, and so on. For other stakeholder groups, however, it may be necessary to talk with local people about what is happening in the country, what people are concerned about, how the government operates, what political parties and religious groups are important, and so on. Local informants can identify stakeholder interests that would not be apparent to outsiders.

(3) Stakeholder power bases. In Freeman and Reed's (1983) terms, does the stakeholder have formal (voting), economic, or political power, or some combination of the three? Stakeholders with voting power normally need to be informed about what the company is doing and be brought into the company's decision making processes. Stakeholders with economic power need to be further investigated to discover exactly what their interests are and how it is possible for them to use their economic clout to meet those interests. Stakeholders with political power normally can't be won with information or with economic benefits; they respond best to channels of formal and informal influence.

(4) Stakeholder characteristics. Aside from interests and power bases, there are other useful things to know about a company's stakeholders. What is the stakeholder's mission or reason for being? Is the stakeholder a single, well-organized group, or is it a diffuse "public" whose members hold similar interests but are not organized to meet them? Is it local, regional, national, multinational, or global? How large is the group? Who are its members? Are they well-connected to the society's power structure? What are the stakeholder's financial resources, and where do they come from? How does the group use its money? Is the stakeholder primarily interested in a single issue, or does it have a multiple-issue agenda? Answers to these questions will tell managers a great deal about which stakeholder management strategies are likely to be the wisest choices.

(5) Relations among stakeholders. Stakeholder maps normally begin and end with a picture of groups and organizations surrounding a focal company in the center. But this is actually only the starting point of stakeholder analysis. Think about it – such a picture represents a world where the company is central, and all other relevant groups are oriented only toward that company. Is this realistic? Of course not. Stakeholder groups are also related to *each other*, and to other groups and organizations in the environment that may not be directly involved in a company's stakeholder map but that could be influential when operating through a company's stakeholders. Remember that the chief advantage of a stakeholder theory of the firm is that such a theory can accommodate the complex social organization in which firms actually exist. Companies and their stakeholders are intricately networked, and actions along one network dimension can affect remote corners of the social web.

A provocative exercise for managers is to conceptualize themselves as a key stakeholder group for one of their own stakeholders. For example, as illustrated in figure 5.2, put a government regulator in the center of a stakeholder map and consider the role managers might play as a stakeholder's stakeholder.

(6) Changes in stakeholder relationships over time. Finally, the fourth dimension – time – needs to be incorporated into a company's stakeholder map. Stakeholder groups, like other aspects of the environment, do not remain stable over time. Stakeholders are born and disappear; their interests may change; they may grow or shrink they form or abandon coalitions with others; they change their sources of economic and political support; their membership characteristics change and so do their stakes and power bases. Stakeholder configurations are therefore time-specific as well as culture-specific and need to be updated as social and political conditions within a country change.

Figure 5.2   Imagine managers as stakeholders

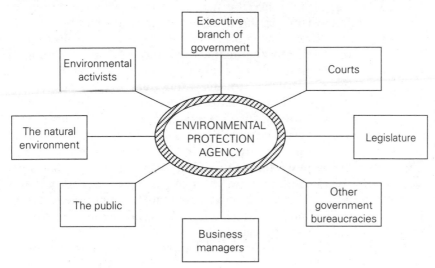

PREDICTING STAKEHOLDER ACTIVITY

Research by Mitchell, Agle, and Wood (1997) presents a powerful model for understanding and predicting stakeholder activity, based upon their possession or lack of three basic characteristics: legitimacy, urgency, and power. This section explains the model and shows how it can be useful to managers.

Figure 5.3 presents the basic model of stakeholder attributes, showing the logical categories of active stakeholders that result from various combinations of three key attributes: the *legitimacy* of the group's

Figure 5.3   Stakeholder typology: two or three attributes present

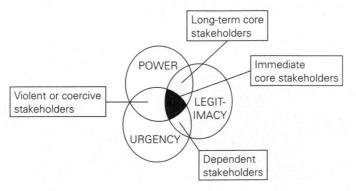

standing as a stakeholder or of its claim on the firm, the *power* of the stakeholder to influence the firm's behavior, and the *urgency* of the stakeholder's claim on the firm and its management.

Long-term core stakeholders are those with power and legitimacy, but no urgent claim. Most companies will recognize the standing of these stakeholders and will have some processes in place to handle their interests and concerns. However, they may or may not receive much management attention unless they acquire urgent interests or claims, and so move into the *immediate core* stakeholder group. *Dependent* stakeholders have legitimate standing and urgent claims, but no power to influence the firm independently of building alliances with other, powerful stakeholders. We can predict that such stakeholders will indeed try to make such alliances to get their claims met. Finally, stakeholders with power over the firm and urgent claims, but no legitimate standing, are likely to become *violent or coercive* in seeking to fulfill their interests.

Figure 5.4 shows the remaining stakeholder types, those possessing only one of the three key attributes. *Demanding* stakeholders possess urgent claims, but no power or legitimacy. A lone millenarian protestor at the corporate gates might be an example of such an irritant. *Discretionary* stakeholders have legitimate standing, but no power to influence the firm or urgent claims. Such groups – say, a local symphony orchestra or various charitable organizations – might be the beneficiaries of management choices to support them financially or undertake joint projects, but these stakeholder relationships are purely voluntary. *Dormant* stakeholders, finally, are the sleeping giants of the stakeholder world. With power to influence the firm's behavior,

Figure 5.4   Latent stakeholders: only one attribute present

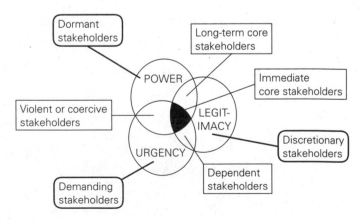

but no legitimacy or urgent claim, they deserve an occasional look because, should they acquire an urgent claim at any time, they would move into the violent/coercive stakeholder category and become a threat to the firm.

The model predicts that stakeholders with two of the three attributes are likely to try to acquire the missing attribute, except in the case of long-term core stakeholders who feel their interests in the firm are being met. So, we would expect violent or coercive stakeholders to try to acquire legitimacy through political processes, perhaps, or through aligning with an existing core stakeholder. Likewise, dependent stakeholders are predicted to try to gain power to influence the firm's behavior. Predictions among latent stakeholders are inherently less stable. If a latent stakeholder acquires a second attribute, that stakeholder is propelled into the active stakeholder group, but it makes a difference to the firm and its managers whether the formerly latent stakeholder becomes violent (possessing urgent claims and acquiring power but not legitimacy) or dependent (possessing urgent claims and acquiring legitimacy but not power) or long-term core (acquiring both power and legitimacy, but without urgent claims).

This predictive model of stakeholder attributes shows how important it is for managers to know something more about their stakeholders than just a general category such as "customers" or "government." Relationship management processes and strategies will vary for different types of stakeholders.

CONCLUSION

In this chapter we examined the emerging stakeholder theory of the firm, showing its potential for serving as a more realistic and useful basis than either the neoclassical or the behavioral theory for understanding business relationships with groups and organizations in the external environment. For both primary and secondary stakeholders, we investigated six basic types of stakeholder interests: material, political, affiliative, informational, symbolic, and spiritual. We considered also the power bases of stakeholders: formal (voting), economic, or political power.

The idea of global stakeholders was introduced, as was the fact that stakeholder maps and the relationships they represent are culture-specific as well as business organization-specific. We outlined the process of stakeholder identification and mapping, showing how managers can begin to systematically assess the nature and impact of the groups and organizations in their environment. Finally, we explained a predictive stakeholder model based on possession of three core attributes: power to influence the firm's behavior, legitimate standing, and urgency of claims on the firm.

The knowledge that firms operate in a dense and complicated network of stakeholder relationships is perhaps one of the most important developments of 20th century management thinking. Stakeholder theory is still evolving and has numerous problems of measurement and conceptualization. For international managers, nevertheless, understanding stakeholder relationships can make the vital difference between successful business ventures and dismal intercultural failures.

REFERENCES

Ackoff, Russell. 1970. *A Concept of Corporate Planning.* New York: Wiley.

Brenner, Steven N., and Philip Cochran. 1991. "The stakeholder theory of the firm: Implications for business and society theory and research." *International Association for Business and Society Proceedings* (Sundance, Utah): 449–67.

Bruce, Leigh. 1989. "How green is your company?" *International Management* (Jan.): 24–7.

Clarkson, Max B. E. 1995. "A stakeholder framework for analysing and evaluating corporate social performance." *Academy of Management Review* 20:1 (January): 92–117.

Cyert, Richard M., and James G. March. 1963. *Behavioral Theory of the Firm.* Englewood Cliffs, NJ: Prentice-Hall, Inc.

Edelman, Murray. 1964. *The Symbolic Uses of Politics.* Urbana, IL: University of Illinois Press.

Freeman, R. Edward. 1984. *Strategic Management: A Stakeholder Approach.* Boston: Ballinger (currently New York: HarperCollins).

Freeman, R. Edward, and Daniel R. Gilbert, Jr. 1987. "Managing stakeholder relationships." Pp. 397–422 in S. Prakash Sethi and Cecilia M. Falbe (eds.), *Business and Society: Dimensions of Conflict and Cooperation.* Lexington, MA: D. C. Heath.

Freeman, R. Edward, and David L. Reed. 1983. "Stockholders and stakeholders: A new perspective on corporate governance." In C. J. Huizenga (ed.), *Proceedings of Corporate Governance: A Definitive Exploration of Issues.* Los Angeles: UCLA Extension, 1983.

Friedman, Milton. 1962. *Capitalism and Freedom.* Chicago: Univ. of Chicago Press.

Galbraith, John Kenneth. 1975. *Economics and the Public Purpose.* New York: New American Library.

Highbarger, John. 1988. "Diplomatic ties: Managing a global network." *Computer World* 22:18 (May 4): 46–8.

Lydenberg, Steven D., Alice Tepper Marlin, Sean O'Brien Strub, and the Council on Economic Priorities. 1986. *Rating America's Corporate Conscience.* Reading, MA: Addison-Wesley.

Mitchell, Ronald K., Bradley R. Agle, and Donna J. Wood. 1997. "Toward a theory of stakeholder identification and salience: Defining the principle of who and what really counts." *Academy of Management Review* 22 (October).

Lydenberg, Martin, Alice Tipper, Jonathon Schorsch, Emily Swaab, and Rosalyn Will. 1991. *Shopping for a Better World*. New York: Random House. Council on Economic Priorities, Ballantine Books.

Speth, James Gustave. 1987. "An environmental agenda for world business." *Across the Board* 24 (March): 21–6.

Thurow, Lester. 1983. *Dangerous Currents: The State of Economics*. New York: Random House.

United Nations Conference on Trade and Development Programme on Transnational Corporations. 1993. *Environmental Management in Transnational Corporations: Report on the Benchmann Corporate Environmental Survey*. New York: United Nations.

Wood, Donna J. 1990. *Business and Society*. New York: HarperCollins.

Wood, Donna J. 1992. "'Dams or democracy?': Stakeholders and issues in the Hungarian–Czechoslovakian hydroelectric controversy." Proceedings of the International Association for Business and Society, Leuven, Belgium, pp. 139–48.

6

Micro-Level Issues: Ethics and Values

> The minister of a foreign nation where extraordinary payments to lubricate the decision-making machinery are common asks you as a company marketing director for a $200,000 consulting fee. In return, he promises special assistance in obtaining a $100 million contract which should provide at least $5 million profit for your company. What would you do?
> (a) *Pay the fee*, feeling it was ethical in the moral climate of the foreign nation.
> (b) *Pay the fee*, feeling it was unethical but necessary to ensure the sale.
> (c) *Refuse to pay*, even if the sale is thereby lost.

This vignette is one of several used in a widely cited study of business ethics (Brenner and Mollander, 1977). The vignettes were presented to 5,000 *Harvard Business Review* readers (1,227 responded), and when each respondent was asked what they personally would do:

- 36 percent chose "a"
- 22 percent chose "b"
- 42 percent chose "c."

Those individuals believing that they would "refuse to pay" nearly equalled those who would pay whether they thought it ethical or not. However, when each respondent was asked what they believed that the average executive would do:

- 45 percent chose "a"
- 46 percent chose "b"
- 9 percent chose "c."

Almost half of the respondents believed that their peers would make the payment, even when those peers thought that the payment was unethical.

Then, as now, many (perhaps most) business executives see themselves as generally more ethical than their peers. They see themselves as making the difficult sacrifices which often accompany "doing the right thing," and they see others as engaging in questionable practices while pursuing narrowly focused personal or organizational gain: "while executives see themselves as being faced with ethical dilemmas and as handling them correctly, they are not so confident about their peers' reactions" (Brenner and Mollander, 1977). A recent study of CPAs' evaluations of the ethical acceptability of CPA behavior found that "CPAs tend to picture themselves as more ethically oriented than their peers" (Ward, Ward and Deck, 1993: 601).

Later in this chapter, we will return to this "I'm more ethical than they are" conviction implied by the responses to the vignette. For now, think about some other factors raised in the vignette that are helpful for understanding microlevel issues about ethics and values in the international arena.

For example, the vignette shows that whether unisocietal or international, *all ethical issues are ultimately matters of individual choices and the consequences of those choices*. A person, not a government, requests a payment. An individual, not a business organization, must make the decision about the payment. The organizational context ("we really need the sale") and the societal context ("payments are part of the system, and if we don't make them our competitors will") can influence the decision. But, a person must ultimately decide whether the payment will be made.

As well, the vignette shows that *ethical conflicts are the underlying triggers to matters of business ethics*. The individual must decide between two or more courses of action, each of which may appear to have elements of correctness or may involve undesired harms to others. Shouldn't managers take actions that enhance the profitability of their companies? But, shouldn't sales be based on the product's value rather than on the availability or amount of a questionable payment? Shouldn't managers abide by the laws and customs of the country in which they are operating? But, what if the payment is illegal or unethical in either the home or the host country – is the law or custom wrong and are managers justified in violating it?

The vignette also implies that *ethical conflicts are only resolved through some process of individual ethical reasoning*. Multiple standards for evaluating different decisions exist because of the multiple influences on the individual's reasoning. Questions like these normally arise: "What are my alternatives? What are the consequences? How was I taught to view and solve the problem? What do I believe? What would my family say if they knew that I decided to make the payment? What would my family do if I lost my job because I refused to make the payment?"

This chapter focuses on individual decision making – the central problem in all issues of ethics and values in international business contexts. Chapter 7 will explore *organizational* issues relating to managing business ethics within multinational corporations.

ETHICS AS INTERACTIONS

Philosophers define ethics as the formal study of principles of right and wrong. From a more practical perspective, ethics can be simply understood as *the principles of right and wrong that motivate individual behavior and underlie evaluations of the appropriateness of one's own and others' behavior.* Most people easily recognize the first role of ethics (as a motivator of behavior). However, the second role of ethics (as an underlying factor in evaluating the correctness of behavior) is often overlooked. To understand ethics and ethical issues on the individual level, *interactions*, not stand-alone actions, must be the unit of analysis. Ethics exist in a social world, and only the mythical individual stranded forever on a desert island can ignore the interactive quality of ethics. "Right" and "wrong" do not apply to objects or persons; they apply to ideas about human behavior in relationships. Ethical rules govern and provide guidelines for interactions between and among people. The interaction between actor and evaluator is especially pertinent when international business ethics are the focus, because there are simply more actors, more evaluators and more standards at work.

To see this point, consider the question "Is it ethical?" This is a question asked by people as they consider various courses of action, and it is also a question asked by evaluators as they consider the correctness of others' behaviors. Yet, "Is it ethical?" is a loaded question because it assumes a standard underlying the motivation for an action or underlying the evaluation of the action, and rarely is that standard articulated as part of the question. The result is that the actor goes on a search for the appropriate standard to motivate behavior and the evaluator goes on a similar search for a standard against which the actor's behavior can or will be assessed.

In a single society, the search for a standard by both the actor and the evaluator might easily end with the same standard; common values and ethics are, after all, one of the factors that distinguish one society from another. However, in an international setting, the actor and the evaluator are less likely to arrive readily at the same standard with respect to a single behavior. Thus, in order for ethical reasoning processes to work properly at the international level, both the actor and the evaluator must consider multiple standards.

For example, is it ethical for multinational corporations to export pesticides which are banned (because of their negative, long-term health effects) in the home country, but are perfectly legal in the importing country? As actor or evaluator, this question can only be answered with any large-scale consensus if the standard is known and accepted. If the standard is self-determination of nations, then exporting the pesticide seems ethical. But, if the standard is the marketing of safe products, then the exporting practice seems unethical. If the standard is one of providing products which improve a society's ability to grow food and feed its people, then the exporting seems ethical. If the standard rests on balancing long-term consequences with short-term solutions, then the exporting seems unethical. The question "Is it ethical?" involves a search which often begins and ends in conflict.

ETHICAL CONFLICTS

Ethical conflicts are defined as dissonances among principles of right (do good) or among principles of wrong (cause no harm). That is, an ethical conflict exists when competing principles suggest different behaviors. There are situations in which a manager might feel that an ethical conflict exists, even though the manager is actually facing a problem, not a conflict. *An ethical problem may be defined as a situation with ethical content, requiring individual choices.* Ethical problems may involve choices between right and wrong actions, or choices where the ethical dimensions are not clear. But problems and conflicts are different and require different decision inputs.

One case of an ethical problem, but not an ethical conflict, would be the clearcut choice between a right action and a wrong one, as the manager understands these things. In this case the manager would be wrestling with conflicting personal motivations to gain from a wrong act or to take the right course of action by refraining, but lose something valued. For example, an international manager might be told that the Somalian government has agreed to accept the company's toxic waste and will build a disposal facility. However, the manager knows that there *is* no Somalian government and strongly suspects that a disposal plant will never be built. But, the manager's job and family security are on the line too. So, the problem is whether or not to ship toxics to Somalia where they are likely to be dumped near a village or in a drinking-water supply. There is an ethical *problem* here, but not an ethical *conflict* – in this case, the manager knows right from wrong and the choice is clear, although the manager may or may not make the right choice. Managers (like everyone) sometimes do make wrong choices, motivated by greed, arrogance, fear, denial, and so on, but this is an ethical problem, not an ethical conflict.

Another case of an ethical problem, but not a conflict, would be when a manager feels that something is wrong but is unable to articulate a principle on which to base a reasoning process or decision, or is unable to produce any convincing evidence that a problem exists. For example, a manager might sense that a new product has potentially hazardous design flaws even though it passed the company's and the government's standard tests. Or, a manager might feel that tying children's cartoon shows to toy lines is wrong, but be unable to articulate a reason that others could understand.

It is important to distinguish ethical conflicts from ethical problems because ethical conflicts represent the more difficult challenge for individuals in international business. The after-the-fact rhetoric of the actor or the evaluator might suggest that ethical conflict involves right versus wrong, but when right versus wrong is the choice, people normally choose right. To repeat, ethical conflict exists when there are competing principles of right or competing principles of wrong.

To illustrate, the exporting of pesticides example above creates a conflict not because it sets right against wrong, but because it poses tradeoffs among several right principles and courses of action. Self-determination of nations is right. Marketing products that do not harm consumers is right. Exporting products that permit societies to feed themselves is right. Balancing long-term consequences with short-term effects is right. If the exporting of pesticides involved a clear tradeoff between right and wrong (export the pesticide and the entire population of the importing country would die within a year), there would be no ethical conflict, although wrong choices might still be made.

The degree to which individuals experience ethical conflicts in business has not been (and perhaps, cannot be) well documented. In the study cited at the beginning of this chapter, over half of the respondents admitted to experiencing an ethical conflict in a business situation. However, this finding resulted from self-reporting, and those in the subgroup who, for whatever reasons, experienced ethical conflict but refused to admit it simply cannot be determined. Results of a recent survey of American employees on their exposure to ethical problems in business are summarized in exhibit 6.1. Another recent survey of managers found that only 36 percent of the sample worked for companies that had formal ethics training programs, but that these managers believed that their companies were more sensitive to ethical issues and more facilitative of ethical decision making (Delaney and Sockell, 1992).

One problem in determining the amount of individual ethical conflict is in distinguishing ethical conflict from simple disagreements. Not all disagreements are grounded in inconsistencies among ethical principles; many disagreements relate to the practical interpretation or application of a principle rather than to the principle itself. For example, some within Nestlé may have argued against marketing infant formula in developing countries. If their argument was based on whether developing countries needed and could properly use the product, then ethical conflict may have occurred. However, if their argument was based more on applying principles of new market development, then disagreement occurred, but not ethical conflict.

Many disagreements are over facts and not principles, and thus are not ethical conflicts. For example, the causes of infant mortality in the developing nations are very difficult to isolate. So, when activists produced data purporting to show that "Nestlé kills babies," Nestlé

Exhibit 6.1   How ethical is American business?

A survey of 4,035 American workers conducted by the Washington-based Ethics Resource Center found that nearly one-third of all employees said they feel pressured by their companies to violate official company policies in order to achieve business success.

The survey also found that one-third of all employees witnessed violations of company ethics policies, while only half of these blew the whistle.

The most common types of transgressions witnessed by employees were:

- lying to supervisors
- falsifying records
- stealing
- sexual harassment
- drug or alcohol abuse at work
- conflicts of interest

Source: "Ethics in the News," 1994 Business & Society Review 91 (Fall): 5

was able to produce data showing multiple causes of infant dehydration, malnutrition, and water-borne disease leading to death. The facts were complex enough to permit no single culprit to be identified.

Furthermore, not all disagreements over principles lead to ethical conflict. The disagreements must be sufficiently intense such that the prospect of losing the argument creates significant internal dissonance. For example, once the decision to market infant formula in developing countries was made, the question of how Nestlé would market the product had a number of possibilities for ethical conflict. For those who recognized that sanitation and literacy conditions in developing countries were inadequate to support infant formula as a safe and properly used consumer product, how to market the product could trigger significant conflict. Different strategies such as targeting individual consumers, offering free samples, working through government channels or through health care networks, all take on significant ethical features once it is determined that conditions in the target market cannot support a widespread proper use of the product. Should infant formula be marketed only through physicians who could control both how the product is used and who uses it? Should infant formula be mass-marketed to everyone? The answer to the marketing question would not simply be a possible "loss" in the "game" of business, but a matter of life and death for infants, one of those problems that "gnaw at the gut" and cause sleepless nights. Intensity as well as the source of the conflict distinguishes ethical conflicts from simple disagreements.

The difference between ethical conflicts and simple disagreements is probably most evident for personal preferences, tastes and minor customs. If you don't like my shirt, or I don't like your briefcase, or neither of us likes the way the other uses utensils while dining, we are not going to have an ethical conflict although we may have a disagreement. There is no principle at stake, no fundamental issue of right and wrong – in short, no source for an ethical conflict.

Thomas M. Jones (1991) has suggested that there are five major factors which contribute to the level of *intensity* of an ethical conflict. Assuming that an ethical conflict exists, the level of intensity will be influenced by:

(1) *The magnitude of the consequences* – the sum of the harm (or benefits) done to the victims (or beneficiaries) of the act. The more harm or benefit, the greater the intensity.

(2) *The degree of social consensus* – the strength of social agreement about applicable underlying principles. The less the consensus, the less the intensity.

(3) *The probability of the effect* – the likelihood that the act will actually take place and create the harm (or benefit). The higher the probability, the greater the intensity.

(4) *The temporal immediacy* – the length of time between the present and the onset of the consequences. The less the immediacy, the less the intensity.

(5) *The social, cultural and psychological proximity* – the feeling of nearness that the actor or evaluator has for the victims (or beneficiaries). Closer proximity yields greater intensity.

In the international arena, these factors take on much greater complexity and relevance. For example, during the initial decisions about whether and how to market infant formula in developing countries, Nestlé executives may have experienced negligible or low-intensity ethical conflict because: (a) they saw more benefit than harm, (b) there was no strong social consensus against the action, and (c) they were relatively detached from the developing countries. This does not justify their action; it merely helps explain it. Indeed, many other companies (for example, Abbott Labs, Borden and Bristol-Myers) were also marketing infant formula in developing companies. But, for Nestlé, the intensity of the ethical dilemma was heightened once the problem was clearly articulated and they chose to resist change. Once the magnitude of the consequences, the temporal immediacy and the probability of effect became clearer, a strong social consensus formed against the action, and the problem was brought closer to home, then Nestlé decision makers likely experienced an ethical conflict.

Ethical conflicts drive ethical issues for individuals. In an ethical conflict, either the actor or an evaluator sees some inconsistency among principles of right or principles of wrong; questions are then raised. The inconsistency must be of sufficient intensity that it leads to substantial internal dissonance in either the actor or the evaluator. Billions of business transactions take place each day where ethics is not an issue. This occurs not because ethics is unimportant in these transactions, but because either no inconsistency among principles of right or principles of wrong is involved, or because the inconsistency did not create sufficient dissonance for the actor or an evaluator.

Finally, it is important to keep in mind that when an ethical conflict develops, it may be one of two types. First, an *internal conflict* may occur within the thinking of an individual when there is an intense inconsistency among right or among wrong principles or actions. Second, an *external conflict* may occur between the individual taking the action and another party viewed as significant by the individual taking the action, when there is an intense inconsistency between views about what is right or what is wrong. Whether internal or external, ethical conflicts are always based on competing principles, and this competition is likely to be far greater in international settings than within societies.

THE BUSINESS CONTEXT OF ETHICAL CONFLICTS

How does the business context in general, and the international business context specifically, influence and structure ethical conflict for individuals? A good starting point is to examine the meaning of the phrase "business ethics." For some, "business ethics" is a classic oxymoron ranking alongside "jumbo shrimp," "military democracy," or "gourmet dogfood." The great social philosopher, Marx (Groucho, not Karl), once said that "the key to business ethics is honesty; once you learn to fake that, everything else is easy." But, such shattered idealism about the meaning of "business ethics" is based upon some normative concept about the way business *should* operate. The meaning attached to the term "business ethics" is therefore a critical underlying aspect of the whole question of ethical conflict.

Ethics in the business game

Some people believe that business ethics involves principles of right and wrong that are unique to the business setting. Advocates see business as somehow separate from the rest of society, and thus, acceptable behavior in a business setting need not be consistent with societal principles of right and wrong. It may be wrong from a societal perspective to be untruthful, but in a business situation lying (or "bluffing" as advocates of this position like to refer to lying) is not just acceptable, it is expected (see Carr, 1968): "Individuals who abhor lying in any other part of their lives accept it in the business context because lying is thought to be appropriate as long as it doesn't violate the law. So long as all parties understand that 'legal' lying is acceptable, then this questionable behavior is permitted within the business context." This view of business ethics often relies upon the "business is a game" metaphor. Once a person joins a business organization, that person is now part of a football team trying to win its game. Football (or business) has a unique set of rules, and there are referees (government and the public) to enforce the rules. If the rules are broken (laws or ethics are violated), then the team is penalized (sales go down, jobs are lost, fines are assessed). So the goal of the team is to compete (sell goods and services) as much as possible within the rules of the game (market behavior in capitalistic economies) in order to win the game (maximize profit). The team's coaches (senior management) devise game plans (strategies), evaluate player performance (appraisal systems), and take responsibility for the team's success. To this point, the metaphor seems apt.

However, as a foundation for understanding business ethics, the game metaphor quickly degenerates into shallowness. For example, when rules are broken the team is penalized only if it gets caught; should we conclude that anything goes so long as it is undetected by the government and the public? Indeed, many business crimes, particularly in the financial sector, seem to operate on this idea (for example, the insider trading scandals of the 1980s, routine padding of expense accounts, or the worldwide criminal operations of the Bank of Commerce and Credit International). Again, players must do what coaches tell them; does this mean that the boss is always right? This leads to denial of responsibility all of the way down the organizational hierarchy, and makes crises or disasters inevitable. A third aspect of the game is that once it is over, the consequences of winning or losing are borne only by the team; but does business operate in a vacuum with no third-party effects? In today's complex global business environment, this is never true. A final aspect is that each team (company) competes with only one other team (competitor) at a time and they are both playing by the same set of rules. This simply does not translate into international business, where there are many competitors and several sets of ethical and economic rules. *Overall, the shallowness of this game metaphor rests with minimizing the status of the individual in business ethics to nothing more than a computer waiting to be programmed by the organization, when in fact the individual is always the fundamental actor in matters of ethics.*

Ethics in business

The second school of thought on business ethics puts the individual at center stage: business ethics means the application of individual ethics within the business situation. Organizations do not dictate ethics; individuals contribute ethics to organizational activities. Rather than doing whatever it takes to win (so long as it goes undetected), doing whatever the boss says, and ignoring third party effects, the *interaction between individual ethics and perceived organizational objectives* gives meaning to the term "business ethics." The business situation is merely a context for decision making, and all decisions have an ethical dimension to them.

This school of thought sees individuals, not organizations, as ethical actors. Organizations can influence individuals' decisions, but the ethical actor is always an individual. As illustrated in figure 6.1, a person's ethics are grounded in *values* (judgments of good and bad), *morality* (approaches to resolving ethical conflicts) and *ideology* (constellations of values which describe ideals), further, ethics may be tempered by experience. The standards which we call "ethics" come from the individual's interactions with family, peers, religion, education, culture, and other value-forming institutions, and they all contribute to the formation of an actor's or evaluator's set of principles of right and wrong. Yet, it is always the individual who must take ethical responsibility within the business context.

The contrast between the two views relating to the meaning of "business ethics" can be illustrated by considering an individual who is just joining a business organization. At entry, the individual brings with her/him a host of standards of right and wrong (Kohlberg, 1981). The first school of thought says that the individual should forget all of these standards of right and wrong. The second school of thought says that these standards are part of the tools which the person brings to the business setting.

Upon entering the company, the individual is confronted with both the formal and informal ethics of the organization. The formal set of ethics is articulated in codes of conduct, ethics statements, and ethics programs, and perhaps in the company's mission statement and written policies. The informal set of ethics is communicated through interactions with organizational superiors, subordinates and peers, and

Figure 6.1   The relationship among ethics, values ideology and morality

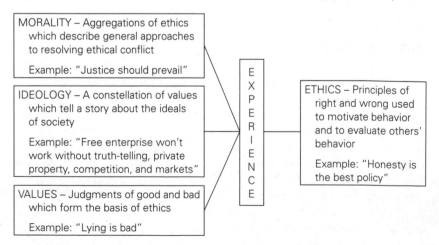

through observations of whether and how policies are actually followed and what happens to people who violate them. The "business game" school of thought says to adopt all standards laid out in the formal and informal organizational climates, whether they are internally consistent or not, and not worry about how they relate to one's own ethics. The "ethics in business" school of thought says to evaluate the company's standards for internal consistency – does the rhetoric match the reality? – and test them against one's personal standards of right and wrong.

As the individual invests time in the organization, decisions will arise where organizational interests will be inconsistent with either the general standards of right and wrong in the business community or with the general standards of right and wrong of the society within which the organization operates. The "business game" school of thought says to do what's best for the organization (just don't get caught!). The "ethics in business" school says that the individual must draw from personal standards of right and wrong in an attempt to reconcile organizational, business, and societal interests.

Hereafter, we use the second school of thought about business ethics. The "business game" school of thought may be more comfortable for some who do not want to face tough choices or who are not comfortable taking responsibility for their individual decisions. Yet, the first school of thought and its "Dallas/Dynasty" approach to business ethics is simply naive. The complexity of interactions among the individual and the various ethical climates which comprise the contexts of business decisions makes the second school of thought more meaningful and realistic.

The multiple contexts within which individuals experience ethical conflicts and make decisions can be illustrated as in figure 6.2. If, for example, the formal and informal organizational ethics are consistent, one is left merely to decide whether the organizational ethical climate is compatible with his/her individual ethics. If compatibility exists, then few if any ethical conflicts occur for that person at the organizational level. If compatibility does not exist, then the person must adjust standards, behaviors, or both. Alternatively, suppose that the formal and informal ethics of the organization are not consistent, that is, a "do as I say, not as I do" principle prevails. Then, the person must grapple not just with the inconsistency between formal and informal ethics in the organization, but also with an inconsistency between one of these sets and the individual's personal ethics. Such subtle yet difficult situations may lead to cynicism among employees who want to believe that they make right choices but who recognize that the workplace demands wrong choices. Multifaceted ethical conflict results.

Figure 6.2   Major influences on the ethics of decisions

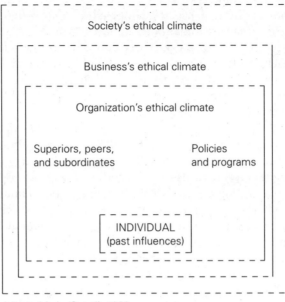

Society's ethical climate

Business's ethical climate

Organization's ethical climate

Superiors, peers,
and subordinates

Policies
and programs

INDIVIDUAL
(past influences)

Adapted from Carroll, 1989

To illustrate, return to the vignette at the beginning of this chapter. If the formal and informal organizational ethics clearly state that no questionable payments will be made to secure sales and the individual believes that this principle is right, then no ethical conflict would occur. Ethical conflict occurs only when one of these elements suggests that payments are acceptable. So suppose that the formal ethics statements and the individual believed that such payments were wrong, but the individual's organizational superior said she/he would look the other way if the payment were made because it would be wrong to pass up the contract, when without it people would be laid off and the organization would suffer. The ethics of the individual are not in conflict with the formal organization, but they are in conflict with the informal ethical climate as expressed by the organizational superior.

On another level, ethical conflicts may result from inconsistencies outside the organization. There may be total consistency between the individual's principles of right and wrong and the formal and informal ethical sets of the organization. Still, conflict may occur because of inconsistencies with the prevailing ethical climate of business or the prevailing ethical climate of the society (or societies) within which the business is operating.

Senior managers of US-headquartered companies which had sub-sidiaries operating in South Africa in the 1980s all professed to abhor the apartheid system in that country. Yet many subsidiaries continued to operate under justifications such as (a) "if we leave, then one of our competitors will simply replace us," or (b) "we can do more good by staying in South Africa than by leaving it." The ethical climates of global business and the ethical climates of the societies within which the companies operate were creating ethical conflict by countering arguments for divestment.

Figure 6.3 illustrates the different sources of ethical conflict under-lying business ethics issues. In the international arena, more societal and institutional contexts are involved. Depending on the degree to which subsidiaries are allowed to develop and adopt their own ethical climates, even more organizational contexts may come into play. These contexts create enormous complexity and influence for a person faced with an ethical issue. Yet the individual, not the organization, institution or society, must still decide, leading us to examine the individual process of resolving ethical conflict.

Figure 6.3 A typology for the sources of ethical conflict

	Formal organization	Informal organization	Business climate	Societal climate
Individual	One against policy	One against practice	One against industry	One against society
Formal organization		Organizational culture clash	Organization bucking trends	Wildcat organization
Informal organization			Organizational manipulation	Rogue organization
Business climate				Macro culture clash

ETHICAL REASONING: PROCESS AND SHORTCOMINGS

Resolving ethical conflicts would be simple if all individuals ranked their ethics and values in a neat hierarchy of "1 to 100," and all actors and evaluators had identical rankings. When confronting an ethical conflict, one could just go to the "ethics checklist" and make sure that the decision conformed to the highest ranked ethics. Any evaluator would check to see if the list was adhered to before judging a decision as "ethical" or "unethical." Say, for example, that the #1 ranked value was "truthfulness." To determine whether a decision was ethical, an actor would merely ask whether the decision involved truthfulness, and any evaluator would also apply the same criteria of truthfulness as her/his first assessment. Too bad that ethics and values do not come in such a neat package!

Ethics and values appear to be ordered in clusters rather than linear hierarchies. A person's core values could include, say, honesty, self respect, respect for others, family security, and responsibility. When these core values imply alternative actions or decisions, ethical conflicts result. To those who argue that honesty is *always* the most important criterion for judging the ethics of a decision, philosophers like to pose the question: suppose that you are in Nazi Germany and you are hiding a Jewish person in your attic; when the Gestapo knocks on your door and asks "are you hiding a Jewish person in your attic?", what is your response? Although this may be an extreme case, it illustrates the idea of core value clustering. It isn't that honesty is not important, but rather that in some situations another core value has higher priority.

The process of ethical decision making is much like any other decision making process. The model of decision making shown in figure 6.4 suggests that individuals: (1) gather data, (2) develop alternatives, (3) forecast outcomes from the developed alternatives, (4) apply criteria to the outcomes, and (5) select an action. The concept of "bounded rationality" suggests that no decision is ever based on total information, since acquiring all of the information involved in a decision is never possible; nor can an individual process all pertinent information relating to a decision. Nevertheless, one can still undertake an ethical reasoning process based on available information.

However, ethical decision making may differ from other kinds of decision making because of (1) the types of shortcomings individuals face in ethical reasoning, and (2) the types of criteria which individuals use to select a behavior.

For example, consider the problem of data gathering. Individuals feel less comfortable and more insecure about gathering data related to ethical issues. It is almost as if the person believes that he or she is supposed to know what is right in every situation and refuses to admit it when this is not the case. This leads to preempting data gathering before sufficient facts are obtained, or to acceptance of "facts" which may or may not be accurate. Imagine the US manager who begins a business activity in Mexico. The first Mexican who advises the American says that bribery of government officials is the way in which business is done in Mexico. Does the American seek to confirm this "fact" by seeking other information from other sources? Imagine

Figure 6.4 Ethical reasoning as rational/logical decision making

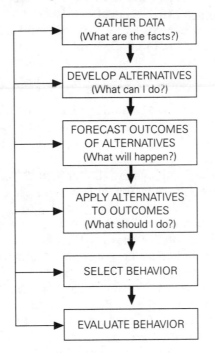

a Japanese manager who comes to the US and hears from a lobbyist at a cocktail party that the way to get things done in America is to "buy off" legislators with huge campaign contributions. Does the Japanese manager accept this proposition?

Consider also the shortcoming involved with developing alternatives for an individual's ethical conflict. People tend to set up alternatives as a dichotomy – "either I do A or B; after all, ethics are matters of right and wrong so alternatives must be set up as right versus wrong." We have already seen, however, that ethical conflicts do not relate to right versus wrong. More to the point, consider what would happen if other decisions were addressed with only dichotomous alternatives – either we charge $433 for this product or $627; either I hire Jane the accountant or Joe the engineer. Dichotomous alternatives simply don't work in many decision situations, but for some reason they are prevalent, though unnecessary and distracting, in ethical reasoning.

Dichotomous thinking is also a shortcoming in examining the consequences of alternatives because people tend to oversimplify and make poor assumptions: "If I don't bribe government officials in Indonesia, I won't get the business." This may or may not be true, but if this consequence is merely assumed and not verified, it is a shortcoming in ethical reasoning. Granted, it is simpler and easier to think of consequences as either/or propositions, but to do so can create major flaws in ethical reasoning. Suppose that an organizational superior tells an individual, "your future in this department is riding on this assignment." Should it be assumed that the individual will lose his or her job if the assignment is not completed satisfactorily? What does satisfactory completion mean – perfect, good enough, like the boss wants it? What does "your future" mean – promotion or demotion, continued employment, life or death? These are all matters relating to consequences which people may refuse to clarify, yet these are instrumental in making an ethical decision.

Also, there is the question of which criteria to apply as an actor or evaluator. Even if all of the relevant facts have been properly gathered, several alternatives have been developed, and a thorough analysis of the consequences of each alternative has been accomplished, there is still the question of which values should be applied – under what rationale should I export the pesticide, should I make the payment, should I market the unsafe product? It is at the stage of applying criteria that the individual actually resolves the ethical conflict.

The major shortcoming at this stage has been captured by Carroll (1987) in his "search for the moral manager." Carroll argues that the major problem in business is not the moral manager versus the immoral manager, but is the tendency toward *amorality*. Exhibit 6.2 catalogues Carroll's definition of the amoral manager. In essence, the amoral manager is the person who refuses to consider anything beyond bare-bones economic criteria when facing an ethical conflict. The amoral manager wants everything quantified financially and anything that will not meet this technique cannot be considered. Amorality, wherever it exists, is a debilitating shortcoming of the ethical reasoning process.

To illustrate, an historical example is instructive. Before the US became involved in World War II, ITT had created close ties with a number of industries in Germany. As the war developed in Europe, executives at ITT apparently experienced little ethical conflict about continuing to provide communications to Hitler's armies or, through a partially owned subsidiary called Focke-Wulf, bombers for Hitler's air force (see Sampson, 1973). After all, business was business, and it was especially profitable business given Hitler's increasing power. Even after the US entered the war, ITT for a time continued its business involvement with Nazi Germany. ITT played a game of hedging in

Exhibit 6.2   The amoral manager

(1) *Moral imagination*
Sees a web of competing economic claims as just that and nothing more; is insensitive to and unaware of the hidden dimensions
of where people are likely to be hurt.

(2) *Moral identification and ordering*
Sees moral claims as squishy, not definite enough to order into
hierarchies with other claims.

(3) *Moral evaluation*
Is erratic in the application of ethics, if it gets considered at all.

(4) *Tolerance of moral disagreement and ambiguity*
Cites ethical disagreement and ambiguity as reason for forgetting
ethics altogether.

(5) *Integration of managerial and moral competence*
Sees ethical decisions as isolated and independent of managerial
decisions and managerial competence.

(6) *A sense of moral obligation*
Has no sense of moral obligation and integrity that extends beyond normal managerial responsibility.

Source: Carroll, 1987

relation to which side would win the war; their amorality short-
circuited ethical reasoning.

RESOLVING ETHICAL CONFLICT

How individuals ultimately resolve ethical conflict rests with the degree of development of their process of ethical reasoning and especially with their choice of criteria which are applied to the situation.
A practical approach for improving ethical decision making is Laura
Nash's "twelve questions for examining the ethics of a business decision." In exhibit 6.3, the twelve questions have been arranged according to each of the phases of rational/logical ethical reasoning (see
figure 6.4). As with most other approaches for improving ethical decision making, Nash's emphasis is on the application of multiple principles of right and multiple principles of wrong.

Exhibit 6.3 Twelve questions for examining the ethics of a business decision

---

Gathering facts
Have you defined the problem accurately?
How did the situation occur?

Developing alternatives
How would you define the problem if you stood on the other side of the fence?
What is your intention in making the decision?
Can you discuss the problem with affected parties before you make the decision?

Forecasting outcomes
Whom would your decision or action harm?
What is the symbolic potential of your action if understood? If misunderstood?

Applying criteria
How does your intention compare with the probable results?
Could you disclose without qualm your decision or action to your boss, your CEO, the board of directors, your family, society as a whole?
To whom and to what do you give your loyalty as a person and as a member of the corporation?
Under what conditions would you allow exceptions to your stand?
Are you confident that your position will be as valid over a long period of time as it seems now?

Source: Adapted from Nash, 1981 (questions are quoted; organization is revised)

Another approach to resolving ethical conflict attempts to focus particularly on cross-cultural conflict (see Kohls and Buller, 1994). This approach suggests that there are seven strategies for dealing with cross-cultural conflict: (1) avoiding, (2) forcing, (3) educating, (4) infiltrating, (5) negotiating, (6) accommodating, and (7) collaborating. The available alternative strategies for resolving conflict rest with the "Yes / No" responses to the following three questions:

- Is this situation high in moral significance?
- Do I have a high level of influence over the outcome of the situation?
- Is there a high level of urgency to resolve the issue?

As illustrated in table 6.1, the recommended strategic alternatives are a matter of how these three questions are answered. Three "yes" answers implies a forcing or negotiating strategy, three "no" answers implies avoiding or accommodating, and other combinations imply different alternatives.

Cavanagh, Velasquez, and Moberg (1981) also used this "series of questions" approach in the general model of ethical decision making portrayed in figure 6.5. To illustrate the use of this model, return one last time to the vignette at the beginning of the chapter. Assume that the facts as given are correct and that no more information is available. The analysis begins with an attempt to apply the three criteria of utility, rights and justice.

Table 6.1 A decision tree approach to resolving cross-cultural ethical conflict

Is this situation high in moral significance?	Do I have a high level of influence over the outcome of the situation?	Is there a high level of urgency to resolve the situation?	Strategic alternatives
Yes	Yes	Yes	Forcing Negotiating
Yes	Yes	No	Educating Collaborating
Yes	No	Yes	Avoiding
Yes	No	No	Educating Infiltrating Collaborating
No	Yes	Yes	Avoiding Forcing Negotiating Accommodating
No	Yes	No	Educating Negotiating Accommodating Collaborating
No	No	Yes	Accommodating
No	No	No	Avoiding Accommodating

Source: Kohls and Buller, 1994

Figure 6.5   Resolving ethical conflict

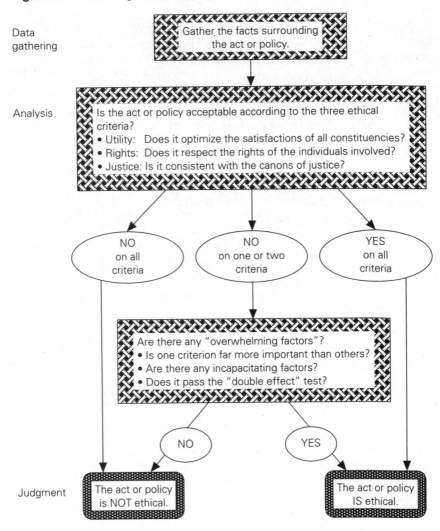

Source: Velasquez, Cavanagh and Moberg, as adapted in Cavanagh, 1984

Utility is a well-known criterion for business decision making, where it simply means the value or use of something by the business organization. As an ethical criterion for individuals, utility also means value, but the base of application is broader. The ethical criterion of utility derives from utilitarian moral philosophy, seeking the greatest good for the greatest number, and is expressed as follows: *"Does the act or policy under consideration optimize the satisfactions of all constituencies?"*

That is, does it create acceptable value, in an appropriate mix, for all relevant stakeholders?

Applied to the question of payments, the utility criterion might be assessed this way. Shareholders, employees, suppliers, and management would benefit in the short run from making the payment and obtaining the contract. In the longer run, however, there could be unforeseen costs for these stakeholders, such as rapidly escalating payment demands or seizure of assets by an incoming government that sees the company as a tool of the old regime. Customers and communities would bear the cost of payments in higher prices, and could suffer from lower product quality if the paying company obtains unfair advantage over competitors that offer high-quality products. So it appears that making the payment does not satisfy the utility criterion, but this conclusion is not particularly strong.

Rights, both legal and moral, are often at stake in ethical conflicts:

> The concept of a "right" implies the existence of some condition to which persons are entitled simply because they are human beings or citizens of a nation. The existence of rights implies the existence of duties. In the theory of rights, first developed by Immanuel Kant, the giant of 18th century philosophy, a person's rights are seen as irreducible, that is, they may not be traded or abridged arbitrarily. Each person is viewed as an end, never merely as a means. (Wood, 1994.)

The rights criterion is expressed as follows: "*Does the act or policy under consideration respect the rights of the individuals involved?*" Because every individual has rights, it is inevitable that legal and/or moral rights will sometimes be in conflict. Legal rights are those guaranteed by law (for example, the right to vote or to own property); moral rights are those that should apply to every human being (for example, the rights to dignity, privacy, free speech, freedom from torture).

Returning to the payments example, assume that making the payment is not illegal. (This may be a poor assumption, since most countries have laws against such payments, and the US Foreign Corrupt Practices Act of 1977 would cast a shadow over the payment's legality for a US-based MNE.) This could be read that the official has a legal right to demand a payment and the company has a legal right to pay; at least, payments are not prohibited by law. But what about the moral rights involved in making the payment? Does the company violate anyone's privacy, dignity, or freedoms? Is anyone's right to a livelihood threatened? Is any torture or undue physical harm involved? The answers depend to a large extent on how such payments are seen in the host culture. Some countries tacitly or openly support such payments as a kind of social welfare system, as a way of keeping elderly relatives or less efficient workers employed. Some countries view payments as a token of respect for an official's position; some see payments as a sign of good faith in cementing a relationship. In such cases, the company could be violating people's rights in the host country by *not* making the payment. On the other hand, the host culture might view such payments as a violation of people's rights to be free from extortion, and the extorting official might hold his or her position through corrupt or coercive means. In such case, a company might conclude that making the payment violated human rights by supporting coercion and corruption. We are reaching stronger conclusions.

Justice, finally, has to do with fairness in a social system, or, as one ethicist puts it, with "the comparative treatment given to the members of a group when benefits and burdens are distributed, when rules and laws are administered, when members of a group cooperate or compete with each other, and when people are punished for the wrongs they have done or compensated for the wrongs they will suffer" (Velasquez, 1992: 75). If one takes the position that justice is defined only within cultures, then any prevailing distribution system may be viewed as fair. But this view will not solve ethical conflicts that arise when the prevailing system is seen as being dramatically different from, and in conflict with, the manager's beliefs about just distribution. For example, it is one thing to say that a culture's prevailing distribution system will be considered just for a company's dealings with that culture. It is quite another thing to actually visit the culture and see, for example, a tiny cadre of very rich elites and a huge underclass that suffers disease, malnutrition, and early death to support the elites. Ethical benedictions which only support the status quo are always worth examining further. Managers are better off referring to some fundamental principles of justice rather than making the assumption that every culture is "right" in the way it distributes benefits and burdens.

John Rawls, the leading justice theorist, asserts that one can arrive at fundamental rules for fair distribution by imagining what rules a group of people would invent if they were building a society from scratch and *did not know what position they would have in that society.* Rawls says that people "behind the veil of ignorance" will develop rules of justice that include these principles:

(1)   each person has an equal right to the most extensive basic liberties compatible with similar liberties for all, and

(2)   social and economic equalities are arranged so that they are both

(a)   to the greatest benefit of the least advantaged persons, and

(b)   attached to offices and positions open to all under conditions
of fair equality of opportunity. (Paraphrased in Velasquez,
1992: 85.)

These principles support personal freedom in the context of other
people's rights to freedom, equal opportunity to achieve any position
in society, and a bottom-rung standard of living that would be minimally acceptable to any member of society. Any distribution system
from pure capitalism to utopian communism could be supported as
just, as long as these fundamental conditions were met.

Returning to the payment situation, here are some questions to ask
about the host culture to see whether the payment can be viewed as
just or not:

- Does the payment support people's rights to equal freedom? Does
  it infringe on anyone's personal rights?
- Does anyone in the society have the opportunity to reach a position
  where he or she can demand payments from foreign companies?
- Does the payment contribute to a bottom-rung quality of life that
  would be minimally acceptable to anyone in the society?

A manager in an MNE might conclude, based on such a Rawlsian
analysis, that the payment *is* consistent with equal rights and does not
infringe on anyone's personal freedom, but that it is *not* true that
anyone in the society could have access to a payment-demanding
position. Even so, the culture appears to support such payments as a
way of creating a minimally acceptable lifestyle for an underclass of
minor officials. Overall, from this analysis, the conclusion may be that
the payment is consistent with two principles of just distribution of
the society's benefits and burdens, fails on the equal access principle,
but may be acceptable anyway because equal access has to do with
obtaining a fair share of society's overall benefits, not with the access-
ibility of every particular resource.

At this point in the application of the model in figure 6.5, we are
left with mixed results. The payment situation is neither entirely
ethical nor entirely unethical. Thus, we turn to "overwhelming factors." The relative importance of each criterion, any incapacitating
factors, and the "double effect" test are noted as possible "overwhelming factors" in the model. Do any of these come in to play here?

When Carl Kotchian, former President of Lockheed, was faced with
the "relative importance" question in the early 1970s, he concluded
that the interests of the employees, shareholders, suppliers and management of Lockheed far outweighed all other matters of ethics in

making demanded payments to Japanese officials. Lockheed was fighting for survival, ultimately ending up with a bailout from the US government, so he decided to make the payments to obtain the Japanese contracts. At the time, no US law made the act illegal, but Kotchian soon found that no Lockheed stakeholders' interests were served by the decision to overvalue the utility criterion, because the decision led to an upwardly spiraling system of extortion. Thus the principle of one dominating criterion was found wanting.

What if Kotchian had seen the existence of the system of payments which dominated the world aerospace industry at the time to be an incapacitating factor? This was also the time in which Prince Bernhard in the Netherlands was forced to abdicate as a result of accepting illegal payments related to aircraft sales. Whether the Kotchian payments were ethical or unethical may be argued as a function of the context of the incapacitating factor of worldwide industry conditions.

A final "overwhelming factor" is the double-effect test, applied to acts or policies that have both good *and* bad (beneficial and harmful) effects. Cavanagh (1990: 146) suggests that the act or policy can be morally chosen if the actor does not intend the bad effect to happen, if the bad effect is simply a side effect and not a necessary path to the good effect, and if the good effect outweighs the bad effect. Although moving in the right direction, the problem with this view of the double-effect is that the first of these criterion is too easily manipulated to reach one's preconceived desired conclusion. Also, it overlooks the rights and justice aspects of good and bad effects. Therefore, the following points need to be added to the double-effect test:

- What is the tradeoff between beneficial and harmful effects, and what is the certainty that the harmful effect will happen? (For example, one might accept a high risk of baldness in a cancer-curing drug but be unwilling to accept a high risk of cancer in a baldness-curing drug.)
- Does the harmful effect violate any person's legal or human rights?
- Is the harmful effect only a violation of a person's or stakeholder's wants? (If the harmful effect is that a competitor loses a sale, that by itself does not make a transaction unethical.)
- Does the harmful effect violate any rule of justice?

In the example of Kotchian's payment, from the company's perspective, the good effect of Lockheed's continuing business and the bad effect of escalating extortion passes some parts of the double-effect test but fails other parts. Kotchian almost certainly did not intend to initiate an extortion spiral; it is unlikely that anyone's rights were violated; and in the beginning the tradeoff between good and bad effects seemed weighted toward making the payments. But the payments fail on other double-effect criteria: (a) the bad effect was a certain route to the good effect, that is, bribery had to be consciously chosen in order to maintain the contracts and (b) the spiraling violated rules of justice in terms of equal access and fair distribution.

As another example, William Kalmbach (1987: 812), in an analysis of issues concerning labeling of hazardous materials for export, points out that developing countries depend on imports such as pesticides and herbicides to fuel their agricultural production and feed their populations and to reduce the number of disease-bearing insects. Labeling of such materials, however, is a major problem:

> The form and content of the label, the language or languages of the label, the exact item to be labeled, and the unit to be labeled – all are issues which must be resolved in order to insure developing nations are importing dangerous chemicals only with full knowledge and awareness of the products' risks. (Kalmbach, 1987: 812.)

In addition, Kalmbach observes that any international regulation of hazardous materials labeling would have to include liability and enforcement mechanisms as well as precise labeling requirements if it was to provide meaningful protection for developing nations.

In the absence of international regulation, companies have three choices: "they can simply comply with the laws and regulations of the host countries; they can comply with the standards in their own countries; or they can ask, 'Does the product or service comply with environmental and human protection standards and standards of freedom from false or misleading advertising or directions *when used by the final purchasers?*'" (Kalmbach, 1987: 823–4). MNEs can apply an ethical standard on their own, in conjunction with their understanding of regulations but independent of those regulations. Host-country rules may not be geared toward protecting users or the environment; home-country rules may not be transferrable technologically or may not be culturally or ecologically appropriate. In such cases, ethical standards need to be applied: (1) protect human life, health, and safety; (2) protect the environment; and (3) provide full, accurate, understandable, useable information to end-users.

So what can we conclude? Resolving ethical conflict is an individual task which requires thought and reflection in order to effectively analyze complex situations. Multiple standards and multiple contexts attendant to operating in the international arena make resolving ethical conflict especially complicated. Unlike quantitative problems which dictate specific methods to answer specific questions, the luxury of mathematical manipulation is not available for resolving ethical conflict.

ADDITIONAL CAVEATS RELATED TO RESOLVING ETHICAL CONFLICT IN THE INTERNATIONAL ARENA

Resolving ethical conflict has partly to do with how the person feels after the decision is made (Blanchard and Peale, 1988), but this is not the end of it. The actor must also consider how *others* (evaluators) feel about his or her choice. Remember that ethics is about interactions, and that the standards chosen by evaluators for assessing the ethicality of an action or policy are important. In the international domain, this evaluative function of ethics raises some caveats.

For example, recall from the beginning of this chapter the notion that both actors and evaluators (but especially evaluators) tend to believe that they are more ethical than their peers – "I wouldn't make that payment, but they would." Study after study shows this "I'm more ethical than they are" mind set of evaluators (see Victor, Trevino and Shapiro, 1993; O'Clock and Okleshen, 1993; Trevino and Victor, 1992; Posner and Schmidt, 1992, 1987). Now, in a unisocietal situation, reconciling differences between actors' and evaluators' concepts of the appropriate standard against which a decision should be judged can be based on appeals to law, to ideology, or to values which differentiate one's own society from another. In international business, these socialization mechanisms simply don't exist with the same sort of authoritative underpinnings. The negotiated institutional aspects of law, ideology and culture are more apparent at the international level. Thus, the actor who is attempting to resolve an ethical conflict by considering the expectations of evaluators is left with a variety of home country and host country stakeholders, all of whom believe that they are more ethical than the actor.

This condition underlies a major debate emerging among those who study international business ethics. Donaldson (1989) argues that there are global ethics which exist across all societies and can be used as standards for both actors and evaluators. These common ethics include: core human rights including those related to human freedom, physical security and well-being, informed consent and ownership of property, and the obligation to accord equal dignity to every person. Freeman (1994) contends that resolving ethical conflict across societies rests with a pragmatic negotiation among actors and evaluators. Negotiation centers around the question, "upon what standards can actors and evaluators agree?" Both sides in this debate are seeking consensus, but they come at it in very different ways. Both sides emphasize commonality rather than differences among actors and evaluators, but the legitimacy of the results rest on substantially different foundations. This debate about the universal principles versus negotiated ethics is quite different from the idea of ethical relativity, which suggests that it is impossible to evaluate one person or culture as ethically better or worse than another. The debate is over *how* such evaluation shall occur, not whether it occurs.

In chapter 7, we will take a closer look at whether values are converging or diverging as business globalization increases. But, it does seem fundamentally true that it is not possible to take an ethically neutral stance in the arena of international business. Multinational corporations doing business in South Africa in the 1980s – Japanese companies as well as US companies – found out that home country global stakeholders would simply not allow ethical neutrality (Paul, 1992).

But, before moving on to chapter 7 and considerations of organizational efforts to deal with business ethics, one final caveat concerns the phenomenon of "the gullible manager." Americans are vulnerable here, so they will be used as examples. Americans believe in cultural and ethical relativity, or, if they don't, at least they are willing to act as if they do when first entering a host country. So, the "rookie" American manager first landing in, say, Banglanesia, meets someone at the dock who says, "Oh, it is very hot today and no one wants to work. How unfortunate that your medicines will be ruined in the heat. But perhaps I can help. To process your shipment expeditiously will not be easy, however. It will require some cash, say $5,000?" The gullible manager doesn't like paying bribes, thinks it is unethical, knows it's not in line with company policy, but is versed in the idea of cultural relativity and tolerance. So, he/she says, "Oh, this is the way you do business in Banglanesia! Okay, here's $5,000." What the manager doesn't know is that he/she has run into a crook or an opportunist, not a Banglanese official. Dock processors are indeed paid something for their troubles, but in dollars the amount is more like $5 than $5,000. This "official" saw the gullible manager coming. Hooked again by ethical relativity and the desire to be tolerant of cultural differences!

Gullibility is only laughable – and somewhat excusable – the first time it happens. From an ethical point of view, it is more important what a manager does the second time. The gullible manager was caught off guard the first time. Now the real test is whether he or she leaves the matter there (or even worse, puts it into a policy statement for future managers coming to Banglanesia), and continues to assume that paying $5,000 bribes is simply "the way they do business in Banglanesia." Do the large bribes continue blindly, or does the manager check around to see what norms actually prevail or try to figure out an alternate route around the bribery?

The "gullible manager" is an example of *overgeneralizing* about another culture – "assuming that all members of the culture share some attribute, history, or attitude" (Wood, 1994), and it is a naive effort at overcoming ethnocentricity – believing that own's own culture is superior. Ethnocentricity raises dangers for international ethical behavior:

- *Contempt* – making derogatory or disgusted statements about another culture or its people. This violates people's right to dignity and respect and is certain to lead to practical difficulties in doing business.
- *Blind assumptions* – making incorrect attributions about culture based on minimal or no information. An example would be the manager who assumes that all developing countries extort questionable payments from foreign multinationals or, even worse, the manager who assumes that members of certain cultures (or religions) do not value human life so much and therefore do not need the same attention to product and workplace safety that the home culture residents do.
- *Same-as-self attributions* – making incorrect assumptions that the other culture is just like your own. This can lead managers to avoid considering that ethical standards may be different in host countries. (Adapted from Pasquero and Wood, 1992.)

The cure for finding the proper balance between gullibility and ethnocentricity comes only through sound application of ethical reasoning.

CONCLUSION

Dealing with international business ethics is largely a matter of wrestling through the ethical issues, conflicts, and problems created by clashing principles and complex situations. It seems easier to do financial cost/benefit analysis and choose alternatives on that basis without integrating ethical decision processes, but the result of this narrow focus is certain disaster for stakeholders and the company. In the short term, unethical acts may create personal or organizational competitive advantages in either a unisocietal or multisocietal context, but in the long term everyone has to look in a mirror. What you see in that mirror is a matter of your own choosing.

REFERENCES

Blanchard, Kenneth H., and Norman Vincent Peale. 1988. *The Power of Ethical Management.* New York: W. Morrow.

Brenner, Steven N. and Earl Mollander. 1977. "Is the ethics of business changing?" *Harvard Business Review* 55:1 (Jan./Feb.): 57–71.

Carr, A. Z. 1968. "Is business bluffing ethical?" *Harvard Business Review,* 46:1 (Jan.–Feb.), 143–53.

Carroll, Archie B. 1987. "In Search of the Moral Manager." *Business Horizons* 30:2 (March/April): 7–15.

Carroll, Archie B. 1989. *Business and Society: Ethics and Stakeholder Management.* Cincinnati, OH: Southwestern Publishing.

Cavanagh, Gerald. 1984. *American Business Values in Transition,* 2nd ed. Englewood Cliffs, NJ: Prentice-Hall.

Cavanagh, Gerald F. 1990. *American Business Values in Transition,* 3rd ed. Englewood Cliffs, NJ: Prentice-Hall.

Cavanagh, Gerald F., Manuel Velasquez, and Dennis J. Moberg. 1981. "The ethics of organizational politics." *Academy of Management Review* 6: 363–74.

Delaney, John Thomas, and Donna Sockell. 1992. "Do company ethics training programs make a difference? An empirical analysis." *Journal of Business Ethics* 11:9, pp. 719–27.

Donaldson, Thomas. 1989. *The Ethics of International Business.* New York: Oxford Univ. Press.

"Ethics in the news." 1994. *Business & Society Review* 91 (Fall): 5.

Freeman, R. Edward. 1994. Presentation at the 2nd Toronto Conference on Stakeholder Theory, University of Toronto.

Jones, Thomas M. 1991. "Ethical decision making by individuals in organizations: An issue-contingent model." *Academy of Management Review* 16(2): 366–95.

Kalmbach, William C., III. 1987. "International labeling requirements for the export of hazardous chemicals: A developing nation's perspective." *Law and Policy in International Business* 19:4, 811–49.

Kohlberg, Lawrence. 1981. *The Philosophy of Moral Development: Moral Stages and the Idea of Justice.* San Francisco: Harper & Row.

Kohls, John, and Paul Buller. 1994. "A decision tree for strategy selection in cases of cross-cultural ethical conflict." *International Association for Business and Society: 1994 Proceedings,* Steven L. Wartick and Denis Collins (eds.), pp. 38–43.

Nash, Laura. 1981. "Ethics Without the Sermon." *Harvard Business Review* 59:6 (Nov.–Dec.), 70–90.

O'Clock, P. and M. Okleshen. 1993. "A comparison of ethical perceptions of business and engineering majors." *Journal of Business Ethics* 12:9, pp. 677–87.

Pasquero, Jean, and Donna J. Wood. 1992. "International Business and Society: A Research Agenda for Social Issues in Management." *Proceedings* of the Conference on Perspectives on International Business: Theory, Research, and Institutional Arrangements. Columbia, SC: University of South Carolina, Center for International Business Education and Research.

Paul, Karen. 1992. "The impact of US sanctions on Japanese business in South Africa: Further developments in the internationalization of social activism." *Business & Society* 31:1, 51–8.

Posner, Barry Z., and Warren H. Schmidt. 1992. "Values and the American manager." *California Management Review* 34:3, pp. 80–94.

Posner, Barry Z., and Warren H. Schmidt. 1987. "Ethics and American companies." *Journal of Business Ethics* 6:5, pp. 383–91.

Sampson, Anthony. 1973. *The Sovereign State of ITT.* New York: Stein and Day.

Trevino, Linda K., and Bart Victor. 1992. "Peer reporting of unethical behavior." *Academy of Management Journal* 35:1, pp. 38–64.

Velasquez, Manuel. 1992. *Business Ethics: Concepts and Cases.* 3rd ed. Englewood Cliffs, NJ: Prentice-Hall.

Victor, Bart, Linda K. Trevino, and D. L. Shapiro. 1993. "Peer reporting of unethical behavior." *Journal of Business Ethics* 12:4, pp. 253–63.

Ward, Suzanne P., Dan R. Ward, and Alan B. Deck. 1993. "Certified public accountants." *Journal of Business Ethics* 12:8, pp. 601–10.

Wood, Donna J. 1994. *Business and Society,* 2nd ed. New York: HarperCollins.

7

Managing Business Ethics in Diverse Societal Environments

Exhibit 7.1 Ethics quiz

If it was your decision to make, what would you do?

(1) *Country A*
It is explained to you by a government official that it is customary to do business in his country by hiring a representative who arranges meetings and otherwise serves as a middleman between your company and the government. He says he has an uncle who is very well connected who might be persuaded to do this. His fee is low – only 1 percent of business transacted, with a minimum of $5,000. Is it okay to hire the uncle?

(2) *Country B*
You are working in the Washington office of a company head-quartered in Europe. Through a friend you are invited to a party being given by a well known Korean rice merchant who has admitted "paying off" a number of congressmen and officials. Is it okay to go to the party?

(3) *Country C*
You are visited by the tax assessor, who reports that your company is scheduled for a heavy tax increase. However, if you were to contribute privately to help with his personal expenses, which are heavy, in the amount of, perhaps, $1,000, he will guarantee that your tax increase will be just as light as it can possibly be. Is it okay to save money for the company in this fashion?

(4) *Country D*
You're transferred to country D, and one of the first things you need to do is get a driver's license. You go to the office where

licenses are issued and discover that it will take three to six months to process your request for a driver's license; your application disappears at the bottom of the pile. However, if you pay the license clerk what amounts to about $10, your license application will, as if by magic, make its way to the top of the pile. Do you pay?

(5)   *Country E*
You are in a country E office and plans are being drawn up for a chemical complex located in this host country. You are working directly with the government, yet a local group of businessmen in the vicinity of the proposed location are acting as "sponsors" and have been telling the country E government that your company should be selected to build the complex. These local promoters come to you and ask how much of a fee they are going to be able to collect from you for their services. You don't really feel they've done enough to earn a fee, but without their support, the project will die. Do you pay the fee?

(6)   *Country F*
You receive a wedding invitation involving the daughter of a high official of government, whom you have met once (the official, not the daughter) on business. It is customary in this country to give quite lavish wedding presents; in fact, it is an insult not to give one if you are invited to the wedding. You learn that the competitor firms, especially the Germans, are giving generously. Do you give a wedding gift?

These situations are adapted from an ethics quiz used in the mid-1980s by the transportation division of a large MNE. The quiz was intended to deal with the controversial question of making payments in international business. Managers would take the quiz upon being assigned for the first time to a position abroad, and their answers serve as a discussion tool to communicate the division's expectations about when it is OK to make payments. Whenever the manager's answer differed from senior management's answer, the vignette would be examined and discussed by the manager and his or her organizational superior. A policy statement or code of ethics could have been used for the same purpose, but executives believed that the principles underlying their approach to making payments were enhanced through discussion of examples instead of statements of "do's and don'ts." For this division in this company, it was thought acceptable to make the payments in the case of Country D only, and in no other cases.

The ethics quiz introduces the fundamental conflict of managing business ethics in diverse societal environments. Societal differences in ethics may cause confusion for individual employees, and confused employees may take actions which can damage the company's viability. All ethical decisions are ultimately individual decisions, and individuals are influenced by their culture, its institutions and organizations. The problem of managing business ethics within diverse societies is, therefore, *how to create and maintain an ethical climate within an organization or unit which allows for individual ethical diversity yet promotes organizational integrity and goal attainment.*

GENERAL APPROACHES TO MANAGING BUSINESS ETHICS IN DIVERSE SOCIETAL ENVIRONMENTS

When MNEs develop general approaches to managing business ethics in diverse societies, there are three major variables in the equation. Historically, MNEs have emphasized each of these variables in attempts to manage business ethics.

(1) The *individual* and all of the influences incorporated into individual ethical sets and decision making processes.
(2) The *host society* within which the individual is operating, especially its expectations of individuals' ethics and how people should conduct themselves.
(3) The ethical expectations of the *home society* of the MNE for which the individual works.

The earliest approach MNEs took for managing business ethics in diverse societies could be unflatteringly called *"ethical imperialism."* This approach demands that host societies change their ethical expectations in order to meet the home society's ethical expectations. So, when a US-based MNE set up a subsidiary in Honduras, managers and employees were expected to behave as US citizens and to abide by US standards of right and wrong, regardless of local custom or Honduran societal norms. The "ugly American" was more than a caricature. But, by the mid-1970s, such widely read books as Barnet and Mhuller's (1974) *Global Reach* or Servan-Schreiber's (1969) *The American Challenge* questioned the cultural dominance assumed by American MNEs. Although vestiges remain, ethical imperialism quickly waned as a general approach.

The decline of ethical imperialism could be attributed to a new respect for cultural heritages and traditions or to more sophisticated worldwide communication. Yet, probably most instrumental was simply the increasing globalization of business. Ethical imperialism is predicated on an imbalance in the power relationship between MNEs and host societies; when MNEs had more to give to host countries (for example, jobs, technology, or products) than host societies had to give in return, "ethical imperialism" could prevail. But with increasing globalization, the power relationship changed in favor of the host society. More MNEs were available to compete for host country resources and markets. And, the longer an MNE stays within a host society, the greater the consequences of expropriation, nationalization and other forms of political or social rejection in the host society. Yet, from a managerial perspective, ethical imperialism was a simple way to deal with business ethics in diverse societal environments; it was easy to say, "be like us or we'll go elsewhere."

A second general approach, *ethical relativism,* seemed to be the exact opposite of ethical imperialism. This approach is captured in the adage, "when in Rome, do as the Romans do." The "when in Rome" approach is based on the idea that whatever the host society's ethical standards might be, they are the standards of right and wrong for business operations within that society. Managers within MNEs must simply abide by local custom, and individual ethical decision making will not be an issue. As MNEs employed more individuals from host societies and as the weaknesses of "ethical imperialism" became more apparent, the appeal of the "when in Rome" approach was great. Here again was an easy solution to managing international business ethics – simply adjust to the ethical expectations of all host societies.

This "when in Rome" approach is still popular today, but it is falling out of favor. Host societies might favor its appropriateness because it allows them to always "set the rules." It is not uncommon that self-appointed "interpreters" of local ethics will inform naive managers in MNEs (the "gullible managers" discussed in chapter 6) that certain activities which coincidentally enhance the interpreter's position are perfectly normal business practices and entirely ethical in the host country even when they may not be legal. Also as mentioned in chapter 6, Carl Kotchian's experience with payments in Japan was hardly as accepted a local custom as his "interpreter" suggested. Kotchian adopted the "when in Rome" approach and, besides losing the sales of the aircraft, his actions triggered a worldwide scandal within the aerospace industry. The "when in Rome" approach can be extremely unreliable except in the most benign of customs such as the proper exchange of business cards with Japanese colleagues.

The "when in Rome" approach is also becoming less prevalent because of a faulty assumption that if expatriate managers "go native" by adopting local ethics as their own, they will by some magic be treated no differently than managers from the host society. Increasingly this assumption is found to be inaccurate; foreign managers are always foreigners. For example, a recent study on negotiation activities showed that Americans who attempt to adapt to Japanese or Korean negotiating norms and values are not likely to be treated like "native" Japanese or Koreans (Francis, 1991). Instead, "the results caution against wholesale adoption of strategies that work for natives. They suggest that the advice, 'When in Rome do as the Romans do', should be applied with due caution" (p. 425).

Also, the "when in Rome" approach ignores home society expectations, and home societies are increasingly more activist about articulating their ethical expectations. The US Foreign Corrupt Practices Act of 1977 (discussed in chapter 3) was one clear beginning point in this effort. The "when in Rome" approach carried little weight in congressional debate about that legislation. Also by the 1980s, US companies operating in South Africa had to finally acknowledge the ethical demands of home society stakeholders who first insisted that the companies adhere to the Sullivan principles[1] and then demanded that companies withdraw entirely. Japanese companies in South Africa experienced similar pressures (Paul, 1992). The "when in Rome" argument holds little status in that continuing encounter. More recently, French, German and US companies which sold war materials to Iraq's Saddam Hussein or Libya's Moamar Khaddafi were challenged by home society stakeholders to explain the ethics of those transactions. The "when in Rome" approach was again impotent.

Finally, the "when in Rome" approach completely overlooks the emergence of global stakeholders along with giant MNEs. Home and host country expectations are likely to become less relevant to MNEs as they shift their own perspectives toward "equidistance from markets" (Ohmae, 1989), and as crossnational stakeholders such as environmental activists, human rights organizations, terrorists, and promoters of various international regimes increase their influence.

Although they appear to be simple methods for addressing international business ethics, neither the ethical imperialism approach nor the "when in Rome" approach are effective. Progressive companies have therefore turned to a third approach – more complex and riskier. It can be labeled the *transnational approach*, since it is premised on the idea that MNEs must examine their fundamental stances on values, develop principles to support those stances, and then enforce the applications of those principles. The result is an ethics position which may draw from many societies and which defines what the company will be in the international arena.

This transnational approach is more complicated than the ethical imperialism or "when in Rome" approaches because the ethics are not given as a set, and they may not be totally consistent with home or host society expectations. This approach is also riskier in the sense that senior management must exercise choice and expose the values which underlie their collective sense of appropriate business actions. Gone is the excuse that unethical practices result from coercion from home or host societies. The process of examining and enforcing adopted ethical principles becomes open and accountable.

The ethics quiz at the beginning of this chapter is an example of how the transnational approach is appearing in corporate practice. Must all companies accept only the country D situation as being acceptable and reject all other cases as being inappropriate? Isn't it an invasion of privacy to tell a manager that he/she should not attend a party thrown by the Korean businessman (country B)? If the dollar value of the payment in country D were higher (say, $1,000), is it still acceptable? How can you conclude that the "sponsors" (country E) haven't done enough to earn a fee when without their support "the project will die"? These are legitimate questions to be asked and answered under the "transnational" approach. The ethicality of the final position rests on principles chosen by senior management, providing a standard against which the corporation chooses to be held accountable.

CREATING AND MAINTAINING AN ETHICAL CLIMATE: STRUCTURAL MATTERS

As with unisocietal corporations, creating and maintaining an ethical climate in MNEs requires setting up a supportive structure. Unethical decisions and practices within organizations may be the result of "bad apples," but they could also result from a bad apple barrel (Trevino and Youngblood, 1990). The transnational approach to ethics makes the issue of structure even more significant.

There are several structural elements relating to ethics available to any corporation. One summary of these elements (Gellerman, 1990) includes: (1) establishing a code of conduct, (2) reducing the inducements for misdeeds, and (3) raising the risk of exposure. Exhibit 7.2 provides more detail on these structural elements. For example, establishing a codes of ethics does clarify expectations and shift the focus back to individual responsibility. As well, reducing the incentives for misdeeds does make organizational rewards and punishments consistent with an organization's ethical interests. And, raising the risk of

Exhibit 7.2 Major structural factors for managing business ethics

Establish a code of ethics.
Standards which may have been unstated or unclear are made explicit.
Misdeeds due to ignorance or false assumptions are minimized.
The individual (not the organization) is back in the forefront of ethical decision making.

Reduce the inducements for misdeeds.
Be careful about unusually high rewards for performance and unusually severe punishments for low performance.
Beware of implicit sanctioning of questionable behaviors.

Raise the risk of exposure.
Draw clear lines between acceptable and unacceptable behavior.
Emphasize and discuss ethics.
Establish disclosure mechanisms.

Source: Gellerman, 1990

exposure enhances ethical reasoning processes. It is, however, worthwhile to also look at each element as it relates specifically to MNE operations.

Establishing codes of conduct

Codes of conduct have become familiar to managers in many US firms. The 1980s saw unsurpassed growth in the number of US-based MNEs adopting codes. European, Japanese, and developing country multinationals have lagged behind American companies in the development of codes of conduct, but the gap appears to be closing.

Part of the impetus for non-US multinationals to adopt codes has come from international bodies such as the United Nations Commission on Transnational Corporations (CTC), the Organization for Economic Cooperation and Development (OECD), and the International Chamber of Commerce (ICC). Each has offered its code of conduct for multinational enterprises. In general, these codes address big concerns such as national sovereignty, market integrity, social equity, organizational autonomy, and human rights. More specific codes have been formulated by the European Union for companies with interests in South Africa, and by the World Health Organization for companies marketing infant formula throughout the world (Paul, 1989). None of these codes have the force of law. Yet, their influence should not be ignored because: (a) they provide reference points and standards for influential MNE stakeholders, and (b) they may be precursors to future international regulations.

Company codes offer more counsel for managing ethical climates within MNEs. Development of multinational codes are subject to the same issues as within unisocietal companies. For example, balance is still an issue. A code cannot be so broad and lacking in substance that it is merely public relations fluff; nor can a code be so exhaustive that it becomes a quasi-legal document that employees scrutinize for loopholes. Also, the code must be strong enough so that employees may use it to refuse to do certain acts, and it must be reasonably, fairly, and consistently enforced.

The key issue in developing company codes for multinationals is subject matter, the critical question of what to include, which resurrects the contrast between ethical imperialism, "when in Rome," and transnational approaches discussed earlier. MNEs that emphasize ethical imperialism will include applications of home country standards in host country situations. Those emphasizing "when in Rome" will focus on complying with host country standards. And those taking a transnational approach will provide a blend of standards.

Table 7.1 shows the results of a study of the topics actually covered in codes of ethics for MNEs based in different countries. The most interesting contrast is between US and European multinational corporations. Note the relatively stronger emphasis which European corporations place on employee conduct and innovation/technology, and

Table 7.1 Topics addressed in multinational codes of ethics

	UK n = 33 %	France n = 15 %	Germany n = 30 %	Europe n = 75 %	US n = 118 %
Employee conduct	100	100	100	100	55*
Community and environment	64	73	63	65	42
Customers	39	93	67	96	81
Shareholders	39	73	60	54	NA
Suppliers and contractors	21	13	20	19	86*
Political interests	12	20	17	15	96*
Innovation and technology	6	20	60	33	15*

* = statistically significant differences between Europe and the US.
Source: Langlois and Schlegelmilch, 1990

the relatively stronger emphasis among US multinationals on suppliers, contractors, and political interests. One wonders how effective the typical US-based multinational code of ethics would be if applied wholesale in Europe, or vice versa. Regardless of topical content, the most important aspect of a corporate code of ethics is that it be built upon a strong base of underlying principles.

The importance of considering multiple stakeholders in codes of ethics (even if stakeholders are given varying levels of emphasis or importance) cannot be overstated. In a recent discussion in an Executive MBA class, the focus was identifying practices which are both legal and ethical. Many suggestions were shot down on the grounds of unethical manufacturing or labor practices of partners – even the child's lemonade stand lost out on the grounds that illegal migrant workers were probably used to harvest the lemons! Supplier and partner relationships in international business provide a level of complexity in managing business ethics that far exceeds day-to-day concerns such as inflating expense accounts or exaggerating a product's merits. A portion of Levi Strauss & Co.'s code of conduct, shown in exhibit 7.3, illustrates how one company uses a structured approach to try to address complex partner relationships worldwide.

Exhibit 7.3   Levi Strauss & Company, business partner terms of engagement

Our concerns include the practices of individual business partners as well as the political and social issues in those countries where we might consider sourcing.

This defines Terms of Engagements which addresses issues that are substantially controllable by our individual business partners. . . .

(1) Environmental Requirements: We will only do business with partners who share our commitment to the environment.

(2) Ethical Standards: We will seek to identify and utilize business partners who aspire as individuals and in the conduct of their business to a set of ethical standards not incompatible with our own.

(3) Health and Safety: We will only utilize business partners who provide workers with a safe and healthy work environment. Business partners who provide residential facilities for their workers must provide safe and healthy facilities.

(4) Legal Requirements: We expect our business partners to be law abiding as individuals and to comply with legal requirements relevant to the conduct of their business.

(5) Employment Practices: We will only do business with partners whose workers are in all cases present voluntarily, not put at risk of physical harm, fairly compensated, allowed the right of free association and not exploited in any way. In addition, the following specific guidelines will be followed.

- Wages and Benefits: We will only do business with partners who provide wages and benefits that comply with any applicable law or match the prevailing local manufacturing or finishing industry practices. We will also favor business partners who share our commitment to contribute to the betterment of community conditions.
- Working Hours: While permitting flexibility in scheduling, we will identify prevailing local work hours and seek business partners who do not exceed them except for appropriately compensated overtime. While we favor partners who utilize less than sixty-hour work weeks, we will not use contractors who, on a regularly scheduled basis, require in excess of a sixty-hour week. Employees should be allowed one day off in seven days.
- Child Labor: Use of child labor is not permissible. "Child" is defined as less than 14 years of age or younger than the compulsory age to be in school. We will not utilize partners who use child labor in any of their facilities. We support the development of legitimate workplace apprenticeship programs for the educational benefit of younger people.
- Prison Labor/Forced Labor: We will not knowingly utilize prison or forced labor in contracting or subcontracting relationhips in the manufacture of our products. We will not knowingly utilize or purchase materials from a business partner utilizing prison or forced labor.
- Discrimination: While we recognize and respect cultural differences, we believe that workers should be employed on the basis of their ability to do the job, rather than on the basis of personal characteristics or beliefs. We will favor business partners who share this value.
- Disciplinary Practices: We will not utilize business partners who use corporal punishment or other forms of mental or physical coercion.

Source: Levi Strauss & Co., Worldwide Policy. Levi Strauss & Co., P. O. Box 7215, San Francisco, CA 94120

Reducing the incentives for misdeeds

The organizational context of individual ethical decision making can be very influential in terms of final actions. The organizational context, after all, does provide rewards and punishments, or consequences, relating to ethical conduct.

Consider the country C situation presented in the opening ethics quiz. The ultimate decision about whether to contribute $1,000 to the country C tax official will rest with the individual, but part of that decision will be a function of organizational consequences. If the contribution is made and reported honestly to organizational superiors, and the manager is somehow rewarded for reducing the overall tax burden in country C, the message is clear. If the contribution is not made and the manager is removed from his/her position because of the heavy tax burden, that message is also clear.

How do organizational consequences get factored into individual ethical decision making? Recall from chapter 6, that Jones (1991) suggested that there are five factors which contribute to the intensity of an ethical conflict: magnitude of the consequences, social consensus, probability of effect, temporal immediacy, and proximity. Organizationally, all five of these factors can be brought down to the individual level to serve as the basis for a system of rewards and punishments. For example, swift and fair application of clearly articulated *consequences* for ethical deeds or misdeeds will influence individual perceptions of the *probability of effects* and the *temporal immediacy* of their ethical decision making. Holding people accountable for deeds and misdeeds will enhance *proximity* and magnify the important ethical factors within the organization's *social consensus*. Reward and punishment systems will therefore yield yet another piece to the puzzle of creating and maintaining an ethical climate.

One final caveat relates to the extremes of organizational rewards and punishments. Behavioral science tells us that if you want a certain behavior you should reward the occurrence of the behavior. But, this principle creates an organizational dilemma in the overlap of ethical and economic performance. In figure 7.1, this overlap is illustrated.

It would be a wonderful world if only situations 1 and 4 existed – high economic and ethical performance, and low economic and ethical performance, were always coupled. These situations create no incentive problem: 1 gets rewarded, 4 gets fired. The dilemmas come with situations 2 and 3. For example, in situation 3, to what extent do you reward the individual who is doing the right thing but not producing economically, as William Norris of Control Data Corporation

Figure 7.1   Systems of rewards and punishments

Economic contribution	Ethical contribution	
	HIGH	LOW
HIGH	(1) This person makes money and does the right thing	(2) This person makes money unethically
LOW	(3) This person does the right thing, but doesn't make money	(4) This person neither makes money nor does right

has been accused? In situation 2, what do you do with the person who is producing economically, but doing so in an unethical manner, as seen in the Beech-Nut fraudulent apple juice case? Either situation could result in reward or punishment for the individual, depending on the organization's culture and values.

To the extent that either ethical or economic performance is largely ignored in an organization, the reward and punishment system is flawed. For example, if ethical performance is ignored, then situations 1 and 2 get rewarded and situations 3 and 4 are punished. This can create deception and cynicism within the organization as it is clear than ethics are not valued. On the other hand, if economic performance is ignored, then situations 1 and 3 get rewarded and situations 2 and 4 are punished. This type of incentive system can lead to economic complacency or lack of competitiveness. Ethics and economics have to be full partners in organizational reward systems, and rewards and punishment should be consistent with the act.

Now, return once again to the MNE. Economic performance is transnational; how a business is permitted to earn profits may differ from nation to nation, but earning profit, if that is an organizational goal, seems to transcend societal boundaries. Only the most progressive companies, on the other hand, have moved to a transnational approach to organizational ethics. For an MNE, the dilemma of reward and punishment systems is heightened, unless a principled approach is taken so that the company's incentive systems are closely matched to its ethical values and norms.

Raising the risk of exposure

With a code in place and incentives for misdeeds minimized, the third structural dimension of managing an ethical climate relates to creating ways to expose both ethical and unethical acts. Mechanisms such as "hotlines," ethics ombudsmen, or "ethics games" come to mind. The jury is still out on the long-term effectiveness of these mechanisms; they are potentially costly and may yield false accusations. Nevertheless, ethics must be brought more into the open within organizations.

Structure and ethical issues

The attempt to address ethical issues in organizations through structural responses is intriguing. To illustrate, consider the following three important concerns associated with organizational ethics:

- *Ethical climate is a top-down process:* organizational superiors are the major source of ethical conflict within organizations, and creating or maintaining an ethical climate is therefore a "top-down" process.
- *Honesty is the biggest problem:* the major topic of ethical conflict is honesty in communications.
- *Ethical conflicts abound at lower levels:* the lower the level in the organization, the more likely is ethical conflict.

Dealing with these conditions is difficult enough for the single-society business enterprise, but for the MNE, these conditions present an enormous hurdle. How can structural responses, especially within an MNE, address such concerns?

Ethical climate is a top-down process. The "top-down" principle of organizational ethics raises issues of ethnocentricity. How can senior management of an MNE understand the impact of multicultural standards when the senior management group is dominated by individuals from the home society? For example, in a 1991 listing of the CEOs of the 1,000 most valuable publicly-held US companies (Bremner, Ivey, and Grover, 1991), only 30 of the CEOs were both born and university-educated outside the United States. This group contained one each from Argentina, Japan, China, and Palestine; the other 26 were from Canada, Western Europe, South Africa, and Australia. Most of the 1,000 companies consider themselves to be multinational, and the dearth of non-Americans in top leadership roles is striking. Of course, American executives in Japanese firms, or Chinese executives in European firms, are also more the exception than the norm. An MNE whose senior management is all home-country may be able to develop and maintain an internally consistent ethical structure, but there is a risk of ethical imperialism, or even worse, an amoral "anything goes" approach to ethics.

Honesty. Given the well-known difficulties with crosscultural communications, how can the problem of honesty in communication be minimized in MNEs? For example, because of their unions and societal culture, it is assumed that French factory workers know what they are doing, know how to do it, and will self-manage. Job descriptions are therefore relatively uncommon. The American manager who insists upon job descriptions in a French subsidiary is asking for communications problems which may be interpreted as mistrust. Likewise, a Swiss multinational corporation operating a plant in Altoona, Pennsylvania, may find that communicating Swiss standards of community involvement (where social services are largely provided by government) leads to ethical issues regarding a perceived lack of social responsibility and even dishonesty in the host country.

The problem of honesty in communication applies to outside as well as inside communications. For example, recall from chapter 6, Kalmbach's (1987) discussion of the ethical issues involved in labeling hazardous materials for export. Developing countries depend on imported pesticides and herbicides to fuel agricultural production and feed their people. In the absence of international regulations, companies have three choices: "they can simply comply with the laws or regulations of the host countries; they can comply with the standards in their own countries; or they can ask, 'Does the product or service comply with environmental and human protection standards of freedom from false or misleading advertising or directions when used by the final purchasers'?" (Kalmbach, 1987: 823–4). Errors of omission in communications can be just as important as errors of commission.

Rampant ethical conflicts below. Ethical conflict is more likely at lower levels in an organization for several reasons:

- Incentives are likely to be pegged to very specific performance measures without regard to the means for meeting goals.
- Lower-level employees may respond to non-organizational incentives and objectives more than organizational ones, broadening the chances of ethical conflicts.
- Lower-level employees may not be sufficiently socialized into the values and norms of the company.
- Lower-level employees may have less at stake and may simply not care about the organizational implications of their ethical choices.

So, to the extent that hiring of host country natives occurs mostly at the lower levels of the organization, are MNEs creating through their hiring and relocation practices an increased vulnerability to ethical risk? Many multinationals move senior and middle management people throughout their world operations. Yet, these same MNEs may view human resources at the lower levels of the organization to be societally fixed and in cost competition with one another. Suppose that boards of directors decided to take the same approach with CEOs and promoted cost competition among Japanese CEOs working for 10 times the pay of the lowest paid organizational employee versus American CEOs working for 200 (two million dollars annually versus $5 per hour) times the lowest pay in the organization. Or, suppose that American workers (rather than senior managers) were transferred to plants throughout the world in order to gain valuable international experience. Although far-fetched given the reality of multinational organizational life, structural change could deal with the issue of lower-level employees experiencing more ethical conflict.

Structure is clearly an important part of creating and maintaining an organizational climate that allows for individual ethical diversity yet promotes organizational integrity and goal attainment. Yet, it is not enough. A code of ethics, a well-developed system of organizational rewards and punishments, and mechanisms for raising the likelihood of exposing unethical practices must complement informal organizational processes which influence the ethical climate within multinational organizations. Structural responses may be necessary, but they are not sufficient.

CREATING AND MAINTAINING AN ETHICAL CLIMATE: PROCESS MATTERS

Within any organizational structure, the informal interaction between and among organizational superiors, subordinates and peers is the key to determining ethical climate. All of the structures discussed above may be present, but without ethical interactions supporting it, the structure won't matter. Clearly developed informal processes relating to human interactions are the necessary condition for effectively managing a company's ethical climate. Two of these informal processes that are particularly important in MNEs are (1) *emphasizing shared values instead of value differences* and (2) *building organizational cultures*.

Emphasizing shared values instead of value differences

It is clear that individuals possess different values and that these varying values come into play as underpinnings to ethical decision making. The development of individual values is a function of family, education, peers, religion, culture and other value-forming institutions and experiences. For single-society companies, the variability among individual values is obviously less than for MNEs. For multinationals, value diversity among individuals is an important fact of life.

It is very common among managers and scholars alike to focus on *value differences* when analyzing intercultural or global ethics. Because the "when in Rome" idea has been so popular, a norm of respect and tolerance for host country values can be observed in many MNEs. So, the Japanese manager running a plant in the US may be expected to respect and tolerate the individualism which is an integral part of American culture. The American manager operating a subsidiary in the Middle East may be expected to respect and tolerate the extreme gender segregation within Moslem cultures. Most often, the emphasis on value diversity is justified with a broad axiom of acceptance of differences. Within firms, the notion of acceptance becomes equated with effective management of value diversity, even though it often fosters ethical conflict as well as general frustration among MNE managers.

From comparative studies of crosscultural value differences, we learn that:

- When groups of Asian and American managers were presented with the question, "If you were on a sinking ship with your wife, your child and your mother who could not swim, which one would you save if you could rescue only one?", 60 percent of the Americans chose their child, 40 percent of the Americans chose their wife, and all of the Asians chose their mother (McCaffrey and Hafner, 1985, in Daniels and Radebaugh, 1989: 86).
- Given the results of questionnaires completed by 116,000 people employed throughout 50 different countries by the same multinational, people in the Netherlands and Scandinavia "place more importance on social needs and less on self-actualization" (Hofstede, 1983, in Daniels and Radebaugh, 1989: 92).

In the popular business press, comparative studies of attitudes which reflect differing underlying values are also common. From these works (see table 7.2 for one example), we again learn of differences among individuals in various societies. Values, ethics, attitudes, language, perception, decision making, and so on all have important intercultural implications, and MNE managers are usually taught that these differences must somehow be recognized, respected and tolerated.

However, the other side of the coin can be more significant in managing value diversity. Firms should try to determine *common values* around which interpersonal interactions among organizational superiors, subordinates and peers can be promoted. Without a doubt, it is important to recognize, respect and tolerate individual value differences; but by ignoring common values, MNE managers miss an

Table 7.2   Office workers rate their jobs

Percent of those who . . .	US %	EC %	Japan %
are very satisfied with their work	43	28	17
are proud of the company's products and services	65	37	35
believe management is honest and ethical	44	26	15
say the pay is good	40	26	16
feel that they can contribute significantly to the company	60	33	27
believe doing a good job greatly helps them achieve their life goals	53	65	31
think management is sensitive to family needs	35	19	21
try to do it right the first time	67	40	30
work too many hours	21	31	33
feel safe from layoffs	56	56	50

important opportunity for creating and maintaining ethical climates in their organizational units. *Industry Week*'s 1993 International Workplace Values Survey ("US global value, compared") showed that individual values around the globe have continued to evolve, but organizational value development lags behind. Respondents recommended, for example, that their organizations should exhibit more openness and less secrecy in their operations ("US global values compared," *Industry Week*, 1994). This finding corresponds to the observation, revisited in Chapter 10 of this book, that global ethical values are evolving in the direction of greater human rights protection, including the right to free speech and to adequate, accurate information needed for individual decision making.

The obvious question is where to look for common values. Most MNE managers can sort out value differences, but the question of identifying common values remains underdeveloped.

One place to look for common values is among groups rather than individuals. Although individuals differ in value orientations, they also belong to groups that may exhibit common values. Frederick and Weber (1987) showed that this principle is true when they used the Rokeach Value Survey to look at group commonalities (and differences) among a sample of American corporate managers, union members and social activists. It is possible that attendant to globalization of business there is also an evolution toward global managerial values. This value set would contain values common across the group but not necessarily common to each and every individual in the group. The evolution of such a "business management value set" extending across societies reflects support for what some call the "convergence" (as opposed to "divergence") of values.

Empirical support for the convergence theory of managerial values is especially strong in studies conducted during the 1980s and 1990s. Most recently, Wartick (1995) completed a study similar to the Frederick and Weber work, but focusing on American versus non-American managers' value preferences. The data in table 7.3 show the aggregated responses to the Rokeach Value Survey for the 147 senior managers in the sample. The 87 American managers come from several industries (for example telecommunications, automobiles, and chemicals) and range in age from 29 to 57 years. The 60 non-American managers have similar industrial diversity and a similar age range; they represent countries as diverse as Kenya, Japan, the United Kingdom, and Brazil.

The Rokeach Value Survey asks individuals to rank the 18 final (meaning fundamental or ultimate) values and the 18 instrumental values (ties are not permitted). None of the 147 individuals provided identical rankings, but when the rankings were aggregated into group rankings, certain commonalities become apparent. For example, among final values, "family security," "self respect," "freedom," "happiness," and "sense of accomplishment" are the five highest ranked values for both groups, and the rankings at the bottom of the 18 are similarly clustered. For instrumental values, "honesty," "responsibility," "ambitious," and "capable" head both rankings, and "polite," "clean," and (is this a surprise?) "obedient" show up at the bottom of both.

The traditional approach to managing value diversity would be to focus on the big differences in the two groups. It is not difficult to imagine American management seminars for those going overseas for the first time where the basic messages are: "don't be concerned if your subordinates seem to place less value on being cheerful and happy, but more value on accomplishment, broadmindedness and social recognition." Conversely, these seminars, if they were to focus on commonalities, would tell the participants that in interpersonal relations throughout the organization, emphasizing family, self-respect, honesty, responsibility, ambition and capability will be accepted. The argument becomes this: "what's more important for achieving organizational objectives in an MNE, changing managerial values to become more consistent with different host country values or showing

Table 7.3 Common values among American and non-American senior managers

Americans: Final values		Non-Americans: Final values	
Family security	4.25 (3.29)	Family security	4.25 (3.29)
Self-respect	6.81 (3.86)	Sense of accomplishment	6.50 (4.52)
Freedom	6.83 (4.67)	Self respect	6.81 (3.86)
Happiness	6.95 (4.32)	Freedom	6.83 (4.67)
Sense of accomplishment	7.40 (4.82)	Happiness	6.95 (4.32)
Mature love	7.88 (4.23)	Inner harmony	8.16 (4.36)
Inner harmony	8.16 (4.36)	A comfortable life	8.26 (5.49)
True friendship	8.81 (4.49)	Mature love	8.55 (3.76)
Wisdom	8.94 (4.85)	Wisdom	9.61 (4.85)
A comfortable life	10.36 (4.76)	An exciting life	9.68 (5.59)
An exciting life	10.55 (5.00)	True friendship	10.18 (3.95)
Salvation	10.88 (6.72)	Pleasure	11.30 (4.54)
Pleasure	11.30 (4.54)	A world of peace	11.38 (4.36)
A world of peace	11.38 (4.36)	Equality	11.63 (4.07)
Equality	11.63 (4.07)	Social recognition	11.63 (4.40)
National security	12.80 (4.59)	Salvation	12.57 (6.42)
A world of beauty	13.61 (3.74)	National security	13.06 (4.63)
Social recognition	13.80 (4.23)	A world of beauty	13.61 (3.74)

Americans: Instrumental values		Non-Americans: Instrumental values	
Honest	3.04 (2.74)	Honest	4.53 (3.86)
Responsible	4.83 (3.63)	Responsible	5.88 (3.47)
Capable	6.85 (4.26)	Capable	6.38 (4.65)
Ambitious	7.47 (5.28)	Broadminded	7.63 (4.38)
Independent	7.71 (4.28)	Ambitious	7.91 (5.36)
Logical	8.90 (4.06)	Courageous	8.45 (4.06)
Loving	8.96 (4.80)	Logical	8.80 (4.44)
Courageous	9.00 (4.16)	Independent	9.00 (5.13)
Broadminded	9.43 (4.38)	Intellectual	9.15 (4.76)
Cheerful	9.75 (4.55)	Loving	9.45 (4.81)
Intellectual	9.98 (5.09)	Self-controlled	10.00 (4.81)
Helpful	10.44 (4.39)	Imaginative	10.10 (5.37)
Imaginative	10.49 (5.59)	Helpful	10.53 (4.30)
Forgiving	10.59 (4.54)	Forgiving	11.55 (4.90)
Self-controlled	11.47 (4.31)	Cheerful	12.03 (4.36)
Polite	12.29 (3.80)	Polite	12.10 (4.01)
Clean	14.52 (3.38)	Clean	13.15 (4.87)
Obedient	15.08 (3.60)	Obedient	14.31 (4.54)

(N = 87 Americans and 60 non-Americans; parenthetical numbers are standard deviations)
Source: Wartick, 1995

managers where the starting points are in terms of common values?" Without a doubt, both sides should be emphasized, but just because value differences may be more intriguing or curious, common values should not be overlooked. They are the starting point for an effective approach to multinational ethical behavior.

Another place to look for common values is within ideology. As discussed in chapter 2, ideology provides the ideals of society, a blueprint for its operation, and a "story" about the way things ought to be. To the extent that different societies profess to adopt similar ideologies, another source of common values useful in managing cultural diversity is revealed.

For example, the world appears to be turning toward free enterprise capitalism as its prevailing economic ideology. But, what does the "story" or "blueprint" of free enterprise capitalism mean? Is it merely private property, markets and minimal government? Cavanagh (1990) has defined ideology as "a constellation of values" which interrelate rather than stand alone. Thus, any single value is meaningless except as it relates to the other values of an ideology. Figure 7.2 provides one explanation of free enterprise capitalism which shows the interrelationship of values which underlie ideology. This ideological statement tells a story, it paints a picture, and it provides a blueprint for what ought to be. Further, to understand and appreciate free enterprise capitalism, the whole story must be told and adopted. Ideology can reinforce shared values (rather than differences) among culturally diverse individuals and groups.

Building organizational cultures

In addition to emphasizing shared values in interpersonal relations, building strong ethical climates within organizations must be addressed as part of managing organizational ethics. In the simplest terms, ethical climates are institutionalized shared values which can promote or obstruct certain decisions. More specifically, corporate culture has been defined as:

> The customary or traditional ways of thinking and doing things, which are *shared* to a greater or lesser extent by all members of the organization and which new members must *learn* and at least partially accept in order to be accepted into the service of the firm [emphasis added]. (Jacques, 1951.)

This forty-plus year old definition suggests that corporate culture is more than just a fad of the 1980s and 1990s, and that the question of institutionalizing shared values is fundamental to creating effective

Figure 7.2 The values within free enterprise capitalism ideology

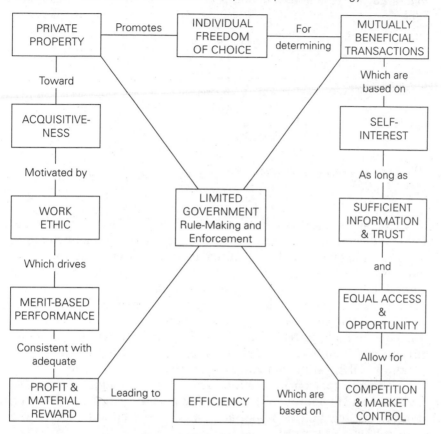

Source: Adapted from Davis, Keith, William C. Frederick, and Robert Blomstrom. 1975.
Business and Society: Environment and Responsibility. New York: McGraw-Hill.
Reproduced with the permission of The McGraw-Hill Companies.

ethical climates. The ethical climate within a corporate culture can be
very supportive – Johnson & Johnson's support of its credo may be
the best-known illustration of this assertion – or it can be very harsh.
One researcher (Kamata, 1982: 31) has reported that within Toyota
there were 20 suicides in one year during the 1980s. One of these
suicides occurred when a man at the plant in Tsutsumi overdosed on
pills because he had been berated in front of his fellow workers for
tardiness and was forced to publicly apologize.

The study of ethical climates is just beginning, but one promising
work centers around a typology of ethical climates as presented in
figure 7.3.

Figure 7.3 Types of ethical climates

TYPE OF CRITERIA	LEVELS OF ANALYSIS		
	Individual	Local	Cosmopolitan
Egoistic	Self interest	Company interest	Efficiency
Utilitarian	Friendship	Team play	Social responsibility
Principled	Personal morality	Rules and regulations	The law or professional codes

Source: Victor, Bart and John Cullen. 1988. "The organizational bases of ethical work climates." *Administrative Science Quarterly* 33:1 (March): 101–25.

Victor and Cullen (1988) combine levels of analysis (individual, local, and cosmopolitan) with types of ethical decision making criteria (egoistic, utilitarian, and principled) in order to create nine different types of ethical climates. In turn, each type of climate has some central focus (self-interest, team play, social responsibility) which becomes a dominant theme in the organization's decision making. In their empirical analysis, Victor and Cullen detected only six of the nine theoretically possible cultures. These six were (1) professional, (2) caring (a combination of friendship, company interest, and team play), (3) rules, (4) instrumental (self-interest), (5) efficiency, and (6) independence (personal morality). These types of climates may give us a convenient shorthand for identifying, classifying and discussing ethical climates, but the important point is that ethical climates are both shared and learned.

Like corporate cultures, ethical climates of organizations start with shared values and extend to assumptions ("where should we begin our thinking about ethical issues?") and operational meanings ("how do we go about getting things done?"). Like corporate cultures, ethical climates are learned not just through the structural activities noted earlier in this chapter, but also through stories, sagas, and myths about organizational "heroes" and "villains," and through day-to-day actions and decisions of organizational superiors, subordinates and peers. As Schein (1985) has suggested about corporate culture, ethical climates are influenced not just by structural factors, but also by informal matters such as what organizational leaders pay attention to, measure, and control, and how organizational leaders react to critical incidents and organizational crises. Finally, like corporate cultures, ethical climates help to provide company identities, support mission and strategic change, help to resolve crises, and provide guidance in routine decisions.

In terms of MNEs particularly, the fundamental question relating to ethical climates is "upon what principles are we going to base our international transactions – what are we going to stand for?" As noted in chapter 6, Thomas Donaldson at the University of Pennsylvania suggests that from a global perspective there are hypernorms which extend across societies and are logical candidates for emphasis within an MNE's ethical climate. The earlier identified "common values" might also be considered as important components of the ethical climates for MNEs. Most importantly, the company must decide how to handle the issue of multinationality of its operations. Do executives wish to emphasize host country ethics, home country ethics, some combinations, or some set of ethics which transcend the ethics of any single society? With this idea, we have come full circle in the question of managing organizational ethics in multinational environments.

CONCLUSION

Managing organizational ethics in diverse societal environments is a difficult task faced by the senior management of MNEs. What often appears to be inconsequential turns out to be a major obstacle to achieving corporate performance. This chapter focused on many of the key issues relating to underlying philosophies as well as to fundamental structure and process concerns within MNEs. The basic lesson of this chapter is simple. The companies who learn to effectively manage the philosophy, structure and process of organizational ethics are those who will gain competitive advantages by minimizing ethical conflict and ethical disaster.

NOTE

1 The Sullivan Principles, promulgated by the Rev. Leon Sullivan, a US activist for South African rights, were a set of guidelines for multinational companies operating in South Africa. For a time, compliance with the Sullivan Principles was monitored by Arthur Andersen, the accounting firm, until Rev. Sullivan declared in 1983 that stronger measures were needed to force social and political changes in South Africa.

REFERENCES

Barnet, Richard J., and Ronald E. Mhuller, 1974. *Global Reach: The Power of the Multinational Corporations.* New York: Simon & Schuster.
Bremner, Bryan, Mark Ivey, and Ronald Grover. 1991. "The corporate elite." *Business Week* (November 25): 174–216.

Cavanagh, Gerald F. 1990. *American Business Values in Transition*, 3rd edition. Englewood Cliffs, NJ: Prentice-Hall.

Daniels, John D., and Lee H. Radebaugh. 1989. *International Business: Environments and Operations*. 4th ed. Reading, MA: Addison-Wesley.

Davis, Keith, William C. Frederick, and Robert Blomstrom. 1975. *Business and Society: Environment and Responsibility*. New York: McGraw-Hill.

Francis, J. N. P. 1991. "When in Rome? The effects of cultural adaptation on intercultural business negotiations." *Journal of International Business Studies*, 22: 403–28.

Frederick, William C., and James Weber. 1987. "The values of corporate managers and their critics: An empirical decription and normative implications." Pp. 131–52 in William C. Frederick (ed.), *Research in Corporate Social Policy and Performance*, vol. 7. Greenwich, CT: JAI Press.

Gellerman, William. 1990. *Values and Ethics in Organization and Human Systems Development: Responding to Dilemmas in Professional Life*. San Francisco: Jossey-Bass.

Jacques, Elliott. 1951. *The Changing Culture of a Factory*. London: Tavistock Publications.

Jones, Thomas M. 1991. "Ethical decision making by individuals in organizations." *Academy of Management Review* 16:2 (March/April): 366–95.

Kalmbach, William C., III. 1987. "International labeling requirements for the export of hazardous chemicals: A developing nation's perspective." *Law and Policy in International Business* 19:4, 811–49.

Kamata, Satoshi. 1982. *Japan in the Passing Lane: An Insider's Account of Life in a Japanese Auto Factory*. New York: Pantheon Books.

Langlois, Catherine C., and Bodo B. Schlegelmilch. 1990. "Do corporate codes of ethics reflect national character? Evidence from Europe and the United States." *Journal of International Business Studies* 21:4: 519–39.

"Office woes East and West." 1991. *Fortune* (November 4): 14.

Ohmae, Kenichi. 1989. "Managing in a borderless world." *Harvard Business Review* 67:3 (May–June), 152–61.

Paul, Karen. 1989. "Corporate social monitoring in South Africa: A decade of achievement, an uncertain future." *Journal of Business Ethics* 8:6 (June): 463–70.

Paul, Karen. 1992. "The impact of US sanctions on Japanese business in South Africa: Further developments in the internationalization of social activism." *Business & Society* 31:1, 51–8.

Schein, Edgar H. 1985. *Organizational Culture and Leadership*. San Francisco: Jossey-Bass.

Servan-Schreiber, Jean Jacques. 1969. *The American Challenge*. New York: Avon Books.

Trevino, Linda K., and Stewart A. Youngblood. 1990. "Bad apples in bad barrels – A causal analysis of ethical decision making behavior." *Journal of Applied Psychology* 75:4, 378–85.

"US, global values compared." 1994. *Industry Week* 243:10 (May 16): 26.

Victor, Bart, and John B. Cullen. 1988. "The organizational bases of ethical work climates." *Administrative Science Quarterly* 33:1 (March): 101–25.

Wartick, Steven L. 1995. "Organizational cultures in transnational companies: An empirical analysis of shared managerial values." Paper presented at the Annual Meeting of the Academy of Management, Social Issues in Management Division, Vancouver, British Columbia, Canada.

8

Tying it Together: International Issues Management and Public Affairs

So far we have focused on trying to understand the major components of the international dimensions of business and society. The institutional–ideological model, business–government relations, corporate social performance, stakeholder management, and ethical analysis are all tools for looking at the same phenomena from different angles. In this chapter, we pull these components together into a cohesive whole through the tools of international issues management and public affairs.

DEFINING INTERNATIONAL ISSUES MANAGEMENT AND PUBLIC AFFAIRS

Issues management is defined as "the process by which the corporation can identify, evaluate, and respond to those social and political issues which may impact significantly upon it" (Johnson, 1983: 22). The key terms in this definition are *"process"* (involving the three stages: identify, evaluate, and respond) and *"impact significantly."*

Process is important because, in issues management, it is not so much that one is managing an issue as that one is managing responses to an issue (Dutton and Ottensmeyer, 1987). The three stages – identify, evaluate, and respond – describe simply the process of response development. There are other issues management models with ten stages, or seven stages, but these three are both elegant and sufficient.

"Impact significantly" is important because it is organizational impact that ultimately differentiates issues from non-issues. Issues, of course, can exist whether or not they have impact for a particular organization; but without an impact, the issue doesn't exist *for that organization.* For example, unless the social issue of abortion rights has an impact on a business firm, that firm will not consider abortion rights to be an issue.

Within this general issues management framework, many types of issues can be addressed. Social and political issues, strategic issues, "public" issues – the only real difference in these categorizations is the question of where and how they impact the organization (Dutton and Jackson, 1987). Different organizations will focus on different issues in their issues management process. Thus, the process may be referred to as "strategic issues management" or "public issues management" or "social issues management," but the type of issue is less important than the organization's process for handling issues (Ansoff, 1980).

The question of where issues management belongs in the organizational structure has been widely debated over the past decade. Some companies have a separate staff: some include issues management as part of their line managers' duties. Some believe that hiring consulting firms is the most effective approach. Commonly, issues management is located within the public affairs function.

Public affairs has been defined as "the management function responsible for monitoring and interpreting the corporation's noncommercial environment and managing the firm's response to those factors" (Bergner, 1983). The major categories of public affairs responsibility include: "environmental assessment, issue identification and management, government relations activities, community action/involvement, corporate public affairs training and constituency development, and corporate policy and strategy development" (Bergner, 1983: 3). Public affairs has emerged as an important function within corporations because of the complex, dynamic business environments of the past three decades. As is true of most functional areas of business, public affairs became a designated function when CEOs found they were spending an inordinate amount of time handling external "noncommercial" relations. Specialists in public affairs thus arose to take the burden off the CEOs. Public affairs is a broader area than issues management, even though the underlying process is much the same. Yet public affairs is neither public relations, government relations, nor philanthropy. Public affairs takes seriously the questions relating to operating in a dynamic business environment.

With globalization, both public affairs and issues management have achieved a new scope (Nigh and Cochran, 1987). Take, for example, the issue of waste management. The MNE will have to deal with multiple economic, political, and social ideologies concerning the role of business, government, and public institutions with respect to pollution control. The MNE's relations with multiple national governments, compliance with various national laws, and participation in developing international environmental law will be very complex. The social performance and ethical aspects of waste management will be magnified many times over as MNEs wrestle with questions such as the ethics of selling toxic wastes to developing countries or of developing "earth-friendly" or less-polluting technologies or packaging. The number of key stakeholders may reach mammoth proportions. A domestic company may be able to handle waste management by contracting with a local government or by shipping wastes to a commercial disposal facility; a multinational company does not have it so easy. Public affairs and issues management in such cases help MNE managers understand what problems and opportunities they face with respect to waste management, and how to develop appropriate responses.

Global complexity and dynamism can make the task of international issues management and public affairs seem impossible. For example, one popular device for coding countries on political risk lists 22 areas, each with as many as eight components, including patent law, environmental regulations, tax law, contracts, visas, permits, local content rules, nationalization risk, foreign exchange considerations, local ownership rules, joint venture restrictions, wage and price controls, GNP, inflation, recession, government policies to deal with economic climate, unemployment rate and policies, interest rates, money supply, human rights violations, censorship, property confiscation, government power struggles, clarity of leadership succession, bloodless and violent military coups, civil wars, elections, public opinion, strikes, slowdowns, boycotts, protests, assassinations, riots, ethnic or religious conflicts, embargoes, sanctions, diplomatic arrests, espionage, border disputes, immigration, balance of payments, natural disasters, and a whole lot more. (Rogers, 1983: 103–5) This kind of approach is certainly rational, but practically impossible. Imagine an MNE asking all its local general managers to keep an eye on all these factors! If IM/PAM is held responsible for monitoring, interpreting, and responding to *all* of these events and conditions in *every* country in which the firm operates, the function is bound to fail.

So, what MNE managers need is a way of monitoring change so that when an issue arises, someone in the company knows it, and knows how to start doing something about it. Volumes of statistics and extensive political risk assessments aren't much help if no one knows what to do with the information. Issues management provides a process for making sense out of nonsense.

In the remainder of this chapter we are going to focus most heavily on issues management rather than the more diffuse function of public affairs. According to the National Association of Manufacturers (1978: 1), "issues management is an advanced process of strategic public affairs planning and action that goes beyond the conventional public affairs function." Accordingly, we view issues management as the prime strategic tool for implementing corporate public affairs.

UNDERSTANDING ISSUES

One approach to making sense out of the nonsense of statistics is to focus on what issues are, and where they come from. It is not too helpful to define an issue as "a problem, question, or choice being faced" (Tombari, 1984: 353), or to take a passive approach, as many managers do: "We'll just know an issue when we see it." Such vague definitions never let managers leave the starting gate. For effective issues management, two questions must be answered: What is an issue? What is not an issue? The concept of an "expectational gap" is a useful tool for answering these questions.[1]

Expectational gaps

Expectational gaps occur when there are inconsistencies in views of *what is* and/or *what ought to be*. Issues managers should be primarily concerned with expectational gaps which relate to the facts of and society's expectations about business performance. An issue arises when expectations about what is happening and/or what should happen get out of kilter. For example, many analysts refer to the Bhopal disaster as an issue, but it isn't. It is an event that triggered an issue – the inconsistency between Union Carbide's plant safety performance and societal (and global) expectations about what that performance should be. As another example, Nestlé's marketing of infant formula in developing countries is not itself an issue. The issue results from an expectational gap between what Nestlé thought it ought to be doing and what various stakeholders thought the company ought to be doing.

These examples illustrate that issues come in different forms, and issues relate to different topics, but underlying all issues are expectational gaps. Therefore, issues managers need not be confused because some issues look like ecological problems, and some look like ethical or cultural problems, and some look like technological problems, and so on. The content itself doesn't tell us whether or not there is an issue. Similarly, the mere existence of an expectational gap also does not tell us whether an issue exists. Two additional factors must be considered: the *controversy* generated by the expectational gap, and the *impact* or potential impact of the controversy on the organization.

Controversy

Controversy, or intensity, is necessary in order for an issue to exist. In chapter 6 we saw the role of intensity in ethical dilemmas. Similarly, an expectational gap must have a certain degree of intensity, or controversy, in order to be an issue. Controversy is generated by stakeholder groups exercising voice through:

- their willingness and ability to *confront the relevant parties* in an expectational gap; or
- their willingness and ability to *push their concerns into a broader public forum*.

For example, in some cultures, nepotism represents an expectational gap between societal ideals of equal opportunity and rewards for individual merit, and the occasional reality of preferential employment practices. Stakeholders in the US have been willing to voice their concerns over nepotism and preferential employment in the public forums of the courts as well as corporate offices and boardrooms. An issue results. In other cultures, nepotism may be the accepted and expected practice, so that an expectational gap does *not* exist until perhaps an MNE comes in and refuses to hire preferentially. Even then, until some stakeholder group voices concerns either with the management or in the public forum, there is no issue.

Impact

Impact is necessary for an issue to exist, because expectational gaps can develop and be controversial, but unless there is some identifiable present or future impact on the organization, there is no issue for that organization. There might be a public or social issue, in the sense that controversy is going on about gaps in expectations, but unless there is an impact on the firm, the issues management and public affairs units should not be concerned. For example, there could be a controversy about exchange rate controls among several countries, but unless you are doing business in one or more of those countries, or plan to be doing business there in the future, this is not an issue for your company.

Types of issues

The MNE manager can watch for three types of expectational gaps, resulting in issues that are controversial and have impact on the firm:

- *A factual gap: an inconsistency between what is and what is.* For example, an MNE might face the issue of whether a pesticide it produces is as harmful to human health and the natural environment in Pakistan as it is in the United States.
- *A conformance gap: an inconsistency between what is and what ought to be.* To continue the pesticide example, the MNE could face a conformance gap if it continued to market the pesticide in Pakistan, over stakeholder objections.
- *An ideals gap: an inconsistency between what ought to be and what ought to be.* The MNE would experience this kind of issue in asking the question, "Should the criteria for determining and handling hazardous products in one country be applied worldwide?"

We return to these types later in the chapter, when we consider development of responses to issues, because the type of issue a company faces has dramatic consequences for which responses are appropriate and effective.

Organizational issues, then, arise from expectational gaps in facts, conformance, or ideals. They are controversial and have an impact on the organization. Issues, however, are not static. They emerge, develop, are or are not resolved, sometimes disappear, and sometimes reemerge. In short, there is a life cycle – a recognizable pattern of development – to organizational issues.

The issue life cycle

Figure 8.1 represents a generalized model of the issue life cycle. The fundamental relationship in any issue life cycle is changing public attention over time. Life cycles are made up of three stages separated by discrete events.

Nascent stage. In the earlier, or nascent, stage, expectational gaps are opening and closing, becoming controversial, and implying impact, but public attention doesn't rise until some dramatic event or "trigger" moves the issue into its middle, or developing, stage. For example, international chemical plant safety was an issue for many years, but the event of the Bhopal disaster triggered a rise in public attention and propelled this issue into the middle life-cycle stage. However, triggers that move issues from the early to the middle stages need not be catastrophes. They can be government reports, media attention, lawsuits, boycotts, a worldwide conference, or the establishment of a new stakeholder group focused on the issue.

Developing stage. In the middle, or developing, stage, the issue goes through a period of public debate and, frequently, redefinition. The debate occurs in public forums such as government hearings,

Figure 8.1   The issues life cycle

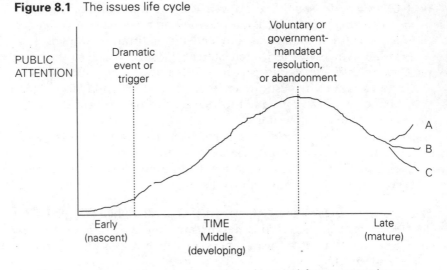

A = The issue re-emerges because the resolution is not satisfactory or new issues emerge from the resolution (or abandonment).
B = The issue is satisfactorily resolved as long as a resolution mechanism remains in place.
C = The issue dies because of further social, political, technological, economic or ecological change.

Source: Adapted from Tombari, 1984.

media reports, educational activities, religious organizations, clubs, political parties, and so on. The stakeholder groups choose sides, build their coalitions, and debate not only alternative resolutions to the issue, but also basic definitions of the issue and rules about what information and ideas are allowable in the debate. As a result, public attention rises.

Resolution. The middle stage ends with the discrete event of a resolution, either voluntary or government-mandated. A voluntary resolution suggests that some stakeholders change their perspective or their expectations so that the expectational gap closes. This may happen because some key stakeholders unilaterally change, or because all stakeholders change through compromise, or because all agree to abandon the issue. If a voluntary resolution cannot be found, or is not explored, an option is to demand or request that a third-party authority – say, an influential national government or a United Nations organization – mediate or impose a resolution.

Mature stage. The discrete event of reaching a resolution moves the issue into the third, mature, stage of the life cycle, where public attention begins to fall off because only the most ardent and interested of stakeholders are monitoring the effectiveness of the resolution. Three outcomes are possible:

(1) *Reemergence:* the issue may reemerge because the resolution is not satisfactory or stable, or because new expectational gaps open up from the resolution itself, and a new cycle begins.
(2) *Equilibrium:* a kind of equilibrium may be reached, so that as long as the resolution is in place, the expectational gap remains closed and the issue remains quiescent.
(3) *Disappearance:* the issue may permanently disappear, and its resolution can be removed (that is, no one needs to pay further attention to it), because underlying social, political, technological, or economic changes eliminate the underlying gap or make the issue irrelevant.

There are obvious problems with this conceptualization of an issue life cycle. To begin with, we do not know, and cannot predict, the time dimension for each stage. Likewise, discrete events that separate the stages are better known with 20/20 hindsight, but the future doesn't always reflect the past. Also, within any "issue area," there may be a number of expectational gaps that make up the issue area (think, for example, of "women's rights" or "pollution"), making it difficult to focus specifically enough to come to a resolution (Mahon and Waddock, 1992). And, levels of public attention (*not* public opinion) are not truly amenable to quantitative tracking.

Nevertheless, as a conceptual tool for managers in multinational enterprises, the issue life cycle improves understanding of the relationship between environmental change and issues. It is a powerful heuristic device for tracking issues over time. Some public affairs managers have even used the issue life cycle as a means of reporting periodically to senior executives or boards of directors, to help them understand how issues affecting the company are developing.

Example: tracing an issue through its development

To illustrate the issue life cycle, let's consider the example of illegal trade in prescription drugs across the Mexican–US border. This is a good example of the need to surface a variety of expectational gaps in what the media and other stakeholders consider to be a single issue. We could review this case from the perspective of individuals using the drugs, or in terms of government efforts to control the trade, but we will focus instead on the business implications.

The fundamental expectational gap in this issue-area is based on a "what is–what is" difference: specifically, pharmaceuticals in the US cost about four to eight times more than they do in Mexico. Zantac, for example, a popular ulcer treatment, costs $102 in the US but less than $23 in Mexico (see Solis, 1993). This factual gap is *not* an issue, however, because it is not controversial as a set of facts. No one disagrees that the price differential exists.

There is another factual "what is–what is" expectational gap concerning the *reason* for pharmaceutical prices, and this gap underlies the issue that exists. Pharmaceutical companies argue that they must recover their extraordinarily high research, development, and certification costs in those countries where they can, because it would be unethical to withhold beneficial drugs from countries with severe price controls, but their costs must be recovered for them to stay in business, and prices only reflect costs. For the companies, the "what is" situation regarding prices is no more than sound business practice and cannot be factually disputed. Some stakeholders, however, see the price differentials – and indeed the high prices themselves – as unethical gouging, completely unrelated to costs and depending instead on what the companies can get away with. This "what is–what is" gap is directly related to a disagreement about the facts of pharmaceutical costs and prices.

There is also a conformance gap in this issue-area based on a "what is–what ought to be" difference: some stakeholders believe that the higher US prices represent corporate greed and should be lower. A controversy exists over this expectational gap because these stakeholders can and do exercise voice to move the issue into the public policy domain. Therefore, there are potential implications for business, and this issue-area should be of concern to pharmaceutical issues managers.

A complicating factor is that Mexico has price controls on pharmaceuticals and the US does not. This leads to an ideals gap: "what ought to be–what ought to be." The Mexican price controls have been "temporary" since World War II. The "ought–ought" gap relates to the question of whether these controls should be dropped. Some believe they should be dropped, and others do not. This ideals gap is also controversial, with implications for pharmaceutical companies.

The further one gets into the issue, the more expectational gaps can be surfaced. But the examples above are sufficient to illustrate the value of a "gap check" in clarifying what "an issue" is really about. With an analysis of gaps complete, attention can turn to exploring how the issues and gaps within this broad issue-area might develop through their life cycles.

Early/nascent stage. At this point, all of the issues identified above are in the early stage of their life cycles (Bigelow, Fahey, and Mahon, 1993). Media reports and stakeholder actions so far have not been sufficient to trigger a movement of the issues into the developing stage. But an important issues management question is, "what might trigger such movement?" Here are some examples of possible triggers:

- A "preponderance of evidence" might develop as more media or stakeholder attention is paid to drug pricing, price controls, border issues, and so on, leading to congressional hearings and perhaps further public policy shifts.
- The detailed implementation of NAFTA (North American Free Trade Agreement) might trigger increased attention to the pharmaceutical costs, prices, markets, and controls.
- Large-scale illegal importing of drugs from Mexico might develop, eventually causing manufacturers to go out of business or drop a particular drug. Then the drug is no longer available to anyone at any price.
- Studies might find that the drugs being shipped to Mexico are inferior quality and have side effects not observed in the US versions.
- A German pharmaceutical firm might enter the Mexican market with aggressive pricing, eventually driving out the US firms, who must now rely even more heavily on the US market to recover their research costs.

Issues managers will develop many such possibilities and try to anticipate their likelihood and impacts on the company. NAFTA implementation negotiations, for example, have a high probability of occurring and are certain to have impacts on pharmaceutical companies, so this possible trigger will be high on the issues manager's list of things to consider when analyzing the development of the issue.

Middle/developing stage. Assume that a trigger does occur, and that the issue-area moves into the developing stage. In the development stage there will be much discussion and debate about "what is *really* the problem," and about what alternatives exist for resolving it. For example, some will focus on the "temporary" Mexican price controls and argue that they should be removed: some will focus on the companies' costs of research, development, and certification of drugs and recommend that verification or adjustment is needed. Some will focus on the apparently high prices of US drugs and be critical of pharmaceutical company management, asking them to "open the books" (ultimately increased regulation may be suggested). Some will even want to focus on the question of market access to the drug and argue that everything is fine, since those who want to bear the costs of going to Mexico for the drugs are doing so, and those who don't want to go are paying higher prices in the US. As suggested, all these interpretations of what is going on carry an implied resolution.

In addition to the clarifications, redefinitions, and implied resolutions of this stage, the developing stage also involves a great deal of coalition formation. Stakeholders compromise on their positions and the different sides of the issue-area firm up. What side of the issue will consumers be on, for example? Much depends on how the issue is framed and how consumers perceive their own interests.

Debate, redefinition, implied resolutions, and coalition-building in the middle stage of the issue life cycle eventually lead to a second trigger in the issue life cycle. This second trigger is an actual resolution to the issue, which moves the issue-area into its late or mature stage. The trigger may be one of the resolutions implied by the various definitions, it may be a compromise resolution, or it may be some unpredicted event that happens because other parties enter the controversy later on, or because world events change in a way that affect the issue's definition, development, or possible resolution.

Late/mature stage. With resolution of the issue, much of the public attention previously devoted to the issue falls away. (This may suggest a response strategy for issues managers in some circumstances.) The key question is, which stakeholders will continue to monitor the resolution's effectiveness? One stakeholder we can count on is the pharmaceutical companies themselves and, in all likelihood, the pharmaceuticals trade association. Sometimes a new "watchdog" coalition will form for the specific purpose of monitoring the resolution on behalf of some stakeholders such as consumers. Sometimes an existing stakeholder group, say, one of Ralph Nader's consumer groups, will take on the monitoring task. Government agencies might monitor the resolution. Once the resolution is reached, someone will be watching, but not everyone.

Will the issue reemerge? It all depends on whether the resolution closed the fundamental gaps that existed. If yes, the issue will not reemerge. If no, the issue is almost certain to reemerge, and it will be the watchdog stakeholders who reintroduce the issue into public consciousness.

Will secondary issues emerge as a result of the resolution? Let's say the resolution is the elimination of price controls in Mexico. Mexican pharmaceutical prices skyrocket. Now the Americans won't cross the border because there is price parity. Health care in Mexico suffers because the country and its people can no longer afford to buy US drugs. So, the issue may reemerge as a national health care issue, bringing in new stakeholders (for example, the World Health Organization) and new definitions of the issue.

Will fundamental change occur, making the issue irrelevant? For example, say a one-time cure for ulcers or high cholesterol is discovered – maybe an innoculation or a genetic manipulation. The market for ulcer drugs and cholesterol-reducing drugs disappears when the one-time cure becomes widely available. So, the prices of these drugs are no longer relevant because the drugs themselves are no longer relevant. (Who worries these days about the price of cod liver oil?)

Wrapping up. So, issues reflect expectational gaps (factual, conformance, or ideal), are controversial, and have impact on the company. The expectational gaps, degrees of controversy, and types of impact can change as the issue moves through the stages of its life cycle. But fundamentally, these factors – gaps, controversy, impact, and life cycle development – are the keys to understanding what an issue is and how companies that use issues management may think about responding to it.

TECHNIQUES OF ISSUES MANAGEMENT

One popular guidebook (J. F. Coates, 1986) lists the following issues management techniques: networking, precursor events/bellwethers, media analysis (column/inch counting), polls/surveys, executive jury, expert panel, scanning and monitoring, content analysis, legislative tracking, Delphi, conversational Delphi, consensor, cross-impact, decision support systems, computer-assisted techniques, small group process, scenario building, trend extrapolation, technological forecasting, decision analysis, factor analysis, sensitivity analysis, trigger event identification, key player analysis, and correlation and regression. Such lists are common in treatments of issues management, but they do not tell us what we really want to know. Nor is there any help on which techniques are most useful, or whether issues managers are supposed to apply all of them to, say, that list of issues earlier in this chapter! It's easy to see why managers sometimes believe that issues management is overwhelming and absurd.

But the process need not be overcomplicated. The key question in choosing techniques of issues management is this: What are you trying to accomplish? In this section we discuss techniques oriented toward three different objectives:

- issues identification and environmental scanning to find expectational gaps;

- issues analysis to assess controversies and impacts; and
- response development to help close expectational gaps.

Issues identification and environmental scanning

The goal of issues identification and environmental scanning is to be able to see (and to a certain extent, predict) expectational gaps opening (Ansoff, 1975). Gaps will open when there are changes in corporate performance and policies, when societal expectations or beliefs change, or when both corporate performance and policies *and* societal expectations and beliefs change at the same time. The relevant techniques for issues identification are those that monitor change in corporate behavior or in societal perceptions and expectations.

Exhibit 8.1 shows some of the sources an issues manager might use to identify present and potential expectational gaps. Moving from top to bottom in exhibit 8.1, the more the issues manager relies on visionary sources for identifying possible expectational gaps, the more trouble he or she might have with presenting a credible argument to organizational decision makers. On the other hand, by the time an issue appears in the mass media, the gap is clearly open and is more difficult to "nip in the bud." Therefore it makes sense that issues managers track what is happening in earlier stages even though this information might be kept "close to the vest" until a response appears appropriate and defensible. In other words, the visionaries can show that a gap is opening, but they may not be so helpful on the dimensions of controversy and impact. Sources further down the list may show clear gaps, and be more helpful on how much controversy is likely to erupt and what impacts the company might expect. So, issues management is more than just reading science fiction.

Here's an example. Suppose that through reading visionary literature in Spanish, an MNE issues manager picks up the idea that Argentina may be likely to disintegrate into several smaller countries. Because the MNE has substantial investments and interests in Argentina, a gap opens between what is currently and what is the future of Argentina. Lively discussion about the possibilities may be provocative, stimulating, and fun, but it is unlikely to reveal whether a controversy over splitting up Argentina will *actually* develop, or what impacts such a split might have on the company. Until issues managers can present the entire coherent argument, from gap to controversy to impact, it is unlikely that the splintering of Argentina will be viewed by decision makers as a credible organizational issue.

Finding potential issues through a source list such as that in exhibit 8.1 is a way of identifying changes in stakeholder expectations. In

Exhibit 8.1   Finding out what's happening

Visionary ideas	Art, poetry, drama, science fiction
Ideas are applied	Underground/radical/fringe press, unpublished speeches and notes, working papers, monographs, posters
Details are developed	Scientific, professional, and technical journals; specialized, narrow-viewpoint journals; statistical documents, social indicators; abstracting services
Idea diffusion	Prestigious journals (*Science*), insider bulletins (e.g., product safety or environmental bulletins), popular intellectual magazines (*Harper's, New Republic*),
Institutional response	Network communications (bulletins, newsletters), stakeholder-related journals (consumer reports)
Mass media attention	General interest magazines (*Time, Newsweek, The Economist*), condensations (*Reader's Digest*, executive summaries)
Politicizing the idea	Public opinion data, attitude and behavior studies, UN agency and government hearings and reports
Mass consumption	Fiction and non-fiction books, national and international newspapers (*Financial Times, New York Times, Christian Science Monitor*), radio and television commentary
Idea becomes a norm	Textbooks, almanacs, school materials, university courses
Historical analysis	Traditional doctoral theses, historical scholarly works

Source: Molitor, 1978

addition, issues managers need to be alert for changes in their own company's performance, changes that may be motivated by specific company conditions, industry conditions, or general business conditions, but changes which lead to the opening of expectational gaps.

The process of corporate social reporting is one tool which can be used for internal monitoring to assess changes in company performance and the relationship between those changes and stakeholder expectations. (Chapter 9 deals more explicitly with this tool.)

There are many good sources detailing specific issues identification techniques (for example, Fahey and Narayanan, 1986; Molitor, 1978). In addition, there are a few studies of how multinational corporations handle issues identification and environmental scanning. To get a feel for how MNEs use different techniques in issues identification, two studies are described below.

Preble, Rau and Reichel (1988: 5) surveyed almost 100 large US-based multinationals on their environmental scanning practices in the late 1980s. They found a variety of practices, summarized in table 8.1.

Table 8.1 Summary: US MNC environmental scanning practices

Practice	firms utilizing %
Overall nature of scanning system	
ES is tied to planning, uses computer data banks, involves most countries in which the firm operates, integrates information worldwide	5
Firm uses at least one executive to monitor developments in countries of operation	48
Use of consultants and/or external services to monitor conditions and political risk in countries of operation	15
Little or no environmental information sought except upon entry into a country or in a crisis	27
Use of computers in scanning	
Little or no use	51
Some use, mainly at world/regional headquarters	28
Central computers linked to branches	12
Highly integrated and sophisticated computer use	5
Percent giving "high importance" to environmental sectors	
Economic	49
Competitive	39
Legal	24
Political	24
Technological	13
Cultural	6

Source: Adapted from Preble, Rau, and Reichel, 1988

Scanners in these firms got information from a variety of sources, including in-house executives, publications, bankers, government officials, lawyers, accountants, customers, distributors, and even competitors. The authors were encouraged by their results; earlier studies had shown very little use of environmental scanning practices by MNEs, so there had been growth in this area. However, their data also show that the sophistication in scanning is relatively low; most companies rely on published news sources and the information of their own host-country executives, and most have no high-powered or systematic way of analyzing the data once it is obtained. The authors conclude (1988: 13) that "for the MNCs that haven't done so, setting up or upgrading a systematic and sophisticated environmental scanning process in their firms represents an opportunity to stay abreast of the rapidly changing international environment in which they operate."

Beyond the authors' concerns, a notable finding of this study is that *very* little attention was paid to cultural/social scanning, and only slightly more to legal and political environments. Yet world events have demonstrated over and over again that these are the very environments most likely to affect businesses seriously. These are the environments that underlie changes in economic variables such as inflation rates, currency exchange rates, and balances of payments (McCann and Gomez-Mejia, 1986). A recent study of executive political awareness concluded that many international firms are "operating unresponsively from unrealistically safe views of reality" (Richardson, 1995). In a study of international hotel chain environmental scanning practices, it appeared that these practices surfaced the most obvious and visible of issues, such as the need to be more ecologically conscious, but did not yield more sophisticated information about the social and political environments of business (Olsen, Murthy, and Teare, 1994).

Another study of international environmental scanning practices compared new data on six large South Korean firms with previous studies of US MNE practices. Using interview and questionnaire data, the author obtained information on the following scanning categories. (Ghoshal, 1988: 72.)

- *Kind of information acquired:* "competitive, market, technology, regulatory, resource-related, broad issues, and others."
- *Sources:* (1) *internal:* "personnel in the same office, personnel in other (including foreign) offices of the same company, in-house meetings, internal reports, computer databases, and others." (2)

external: "customers, suppliers, bankers, advertising agents, agents and distributors, consultants, general publications, trade publications, trade shows, and others."
- *Scanning modes:* "viewing, monitoring, investigation and research."

Concerning types of information gathered, the Korean firms were similar among themselves in their emphasis on competitive and market data. Prior studies of US multinationals had shown similar findings, but US industry-specific studies showed considerable variation in the attention firms paid to various issues. In terms of sources of information, the six Korean firms relied heavily on a common group of sources, but US firms showed a broad diversity in their sources. Finally, on scanning modes, Korean firms used "all four scanning modes more or less equally" (p. 77), whereas US studies showed similar findings for farm equipment manufacturers and meatpackers, but much heavier emphasis on viewing and monitoring for financial services firms and multinationals. The author concludes that Korean firms' environmental scanning practices are remarkably similar among themselves, but not very similar to US firms' practices. He suggests that, because they are so much alike, Korean firms may not be sufficiently adaptable to continue to be competitive in global markets, to respond quickly to changing conditions.

How did all this conformity occur? The author points out that Korean society is very tradition-bound, but beyond this, he traced a very specific source of Korean similarity in scanning practices:

> The primary reason for the remarkable similarities in the formal scanning units in the Korean firms was found to lie in the role played by a small consulting firm – Business Intelligence and Research Institute (BIRI) – and by its owner, Mr. Eun Key Yoon. An ex-intelligence officer of the Korean Army, Mr. Yoon had entered the business world in the early 1970s as an executive in the Samsung group of companies. . . . He had set up a scanning unit in the . . . flagship unit of the group, and the same model was later adopted by other firms within the group. The model, in essence, was a miniature version of the intelligence unit in the Korean Army.
>
> In 1981, Mr. Yoon resigned from Samsung to form BIRI. . . . The principal activity of the company was to train managers in client firms both on how to scan for external intelligence and also on how the scanning function should be organized within the company. Mr. Yoon had a blueprint of how a scanning unit should be structured – basically, the Korean Army model that he had institutionalized in Samsung – and in three years time, he had spread this blueprint to over thirty of the largest Korean firms. (Ghoshal, 1988: 81–2.)

Issues identification and environmental scanning continue to evolve. Given the enormous changes that take place month to month, sometimes day to day, in the global business environment, the issues identification process must serve as the foundation for effective issues analysis and response development.

Issues analysis

The goal of issues analysis is to be able to assess *degrees* of controversy and impact so that resources can be allocated efficiently and effectively. The issues identification process will identify issues with controversy and impact. Now the question becomes how the organization should use its limited resources in responding to those issues. The relevant factors to consider are depth and breadth of controversy, salience of impact, and urgency of impact.

Depth and breadth of controversy. Among the issues identified as relevant to the company, which are likely to be most and least controversial? Here are seven factors to consider in making these judgments. (Eyestone, 1978.)

- Support: Is there a critical mass of interested stakeholders?
- Knowledge: What degree and type of information is available on the issue? Is there a logic that explains the importance of the issue?
- Communications: Is there a pressworthy story? Do interested stakeholders have access to relevant media channels?
- Results: Do the interested stakeholders see a reasonable probability of success for their efforts?
- Targets: Are there powerful symbols at stake, such as causes, or villains?
- Triggers: What events are moving the issue from one stage of development to another?
- Leadership: Who is making an effort, or perhaps sacrifices, to move the issue along? Who is financing the stakeholders? Who are the champions?

The issues manager, when assessing the degree of controversy over an issue, must analyze the presence and degree of these seven factors for the relevant stakeholders of the issue. If all seven of these factors are present, there is a high probability of great controversy, especially if there are two or more competing stakeholders, each having all seven factors present. When one or more factors are missing, the controversy is likely to be smaller, more contained, more benign.

For example, consider the issue of Japanese trade barriers. Some US business leaders have been working to raise the level of controversy over this issue:

- by trying to bring in more interested stakeholders such as affected industries and labor unions;
- by bolstering the available knowledge and logic about the domestic costs of Japanese trade policy ("Japan-bashing");
- by keeping the story current in the media through legislative initiatives and special-interest stories;
- by experiencing some successes and choosing activities with a higher probability of success;
- by targeting MITI as the "bad-guy villain" that interferes with free trade;
- by using legal triggers such as trade-deficit reports and dumping complaints;
- by exercising leadership for a variety of stakeholders who have interests in the issue but are unwilling or unable to exercise leadership themselves.

In this example, all seven factors are present – support, knowledge, communications, results, targets, triggers, and leadership – indicating a high degree of controversy.

On the other hand, the US–Japanese controversy is only part of the story. What if China and Korea object to the Japanese opening their borders to US goods? Then the controversy achieves new complexity, new breadth and depth, as more stakeholders are drawn in, more "bad guys" emerge, more logics are developed, more media attention is paid, and so on. The point is that MNE issues managers need to consider both the present and future of powerful stakeholder involvements.

Salience of impact. Simply defined, salience of impact means how important the impact will be for the organization. A US company that exports beef products might consider Japanese trade barriers to be a relevant issue, but the impact of even a complete breakdown of barriers would be relatively insignificant, as the Japanese do not eat much beef and already import what they do eat from Australia. On the other hand, a US auto company might consider the fall of Japanese trade barriers to have a highly significant impact, not only because more Japanese might prefer American cars, but also because of the possibility of competing for Japan's extensive mass transit contracts.

However, there is an important twist: an issue's salience must necessarily rest not only with those dimensions of importance that are identified by issues management, but also with those that *add value* to what senior executives already know. For example, if the issues manager can only say, "Japanese trade barriers are really hurt-ing our company financially," no one is likely to be impressed with the value of issues management. However, if the issues manager can say, "Japanese trade barriers are an important issue for us because they are damaging our trade with *Europe*, interfering with our labor negotiations *at home*, and causing problems with our *South American expansion plans*," now everyone is paying attention.

Urgency of impact. The probability that an impact will occur within a given time frame tells us how urgent it is for the company to respond to the issue. Even if an issue has enormous impact on the company, the question of when that impact will occur can change the priority given to the issue. For example, if Japan completely dropped its trade barriers, there would be enormous impacts on many multi-national enterprises. However, although Japanese trade barriers do seem to be changing, the change is happening so slowly that import-ant impacts for most enterprises appear to be far in the future. Thus, for some companies, this issue may not be ranked as highly as issues relating to NAFTA, which have slightly lower impact but much higher immediacy.

Issues analysis techniques. Issues analysis can employ a variety of techniques, only some of which will be mentioned. Cross-impact analysis is a headquarters-level technique that looks at the internal trade-offs of various resource allocations with respect to salient issues. Key player analysis helps issues managers to identify and assess the degree of controversy surrounding the issue by surfacing the relevant stakeholders, their interests, and their power bases. Developing altern-ative scenarios, based on several possible streams of events, can help to identify the impacts of an issue and their salience and urgency. Game-theory applications can show some of the trade-offs among alternative views of an issue. Whatever techniques are chosen, issues analysis should arrive at some ranking of issues, and it therefore sets the stage for the last part of issues management – effective response development. (See Lusterman, 1985; Blake, 1977; De George, 1993; Business International, 1991, for more details on international issues management.)

Response development

The goal of response development is to move toward closing expecta-tional gaps, and a company's response to an issue must first and foremost be consistent with the type of gap the issue represents. To illustrate the need to match responses with the type of gap, return to the earlier example of drug prices across the US–Mexican border. Three expectational gaps were identified:

- A "what is–what is" factual gap related to a disagreement about the facts of pharmaceutical costs and prices – necessary cost recovery versus greed and gouging.
- A "what is–what ought to be" conformance gap wherein some stakeholders believe that drug prices should be lowered.
- A "what ought to be–what ought to be" ideals gap concerning whether the Mexican price controls should or should not be dropped.

A *factual gap* (what is–what is) calls for responses such as objective studies to clarify the facts, and not debates with stakeholder groups over what ought to be the company's operations or policies. As noted earlier, one response of a pharmaceutical company would be to open its books to stakeholder inspection, but this may not be seen as reasonable by senior management. So, an alternative would be to hire a credible external auditor to verify the company's costs. Other options would be to sponsor industry-wide studies of drug development costs or to request that an international body or a national government – and not just the home country government – conduct such studies. The point is that responses should deal with the type of gap being faced.

Conversely, an *ideals* gap (ought–ought) calls for debates and discussions over the values and ideals at stake; no amount of fact-based studying will move any of the stakeholders an inch because facts are not the issue. In the example, studying pharmaceutical costs will not close the gap on the issue of whether Mexican price controls should be dropped. Studies may be used to support speculative results about what might happen if the controls were dropped, but closing the gap still rests with the ideals underlying the resulting conditions. For such a gap, encouraging a public debate is the right response. Some possible company responses might be advocacy advertising, sending people to testify before government and international hearings, arranging for a television exposé of the harms done to pharmaceutical producers and consumers by the price controls, sponsoring a conference, contributing to think-tanks that think the way the company does, using the trade association to escalate the debate, and getting "think pieces" published in popular and intellectual news magazines. All these responses are oriented toward closing the ideals gap by debating the values or ideals that are at stake over the issue of Mexican price controls.

If the gap is one of *conformance*, what is versus what ought to be, appropriate responses will rest with the possibility of adjusting the positions of one or both or all conflicting parties. These are the tough ones. Although it may be true in some cases, few conformance issues will be resolved by unilateral change in one party because parties are generally not willing to give up their own interests if no one else has to lose. Imagine, for example, that our pharmaceutical company responds to pricing complaints with, "Gee, prices *are* too high! We'll lower them by 500 percent and close that expectational gap."

Negotiated responses are more likely to be effective. These gaps are best closed by techniques such as legislative and regulatory public policy processes, arbitration, mediation, collaborative social problem solving (Gray, 1988, Gray and Wood, 1991), and conflict resolution procedures – that is, stakeholder management. In the drug price example, the gap is represented by the belief of some stakeholders that drug prices are high (what is) and should be lowered (what ought to be). The company will probably want to make sure that the issue of Mexican price controls and cross-border pricing, with respect to pharmaceuticals, is dealt with in NAFTA implementation negotiations, and that the company is regularly consulted by negotiators on this issue.

Response development follows no standard pattern, but will vary depending on the type of issue being faced, the degree of controversy, the salience and urgency of impact, and the company's resources for responding. A realistic response is targeted, implementable, fits within the company's resource capabilities, and fits within the organization's strategy. If a realistic response is not forthcoming, the issue might be one for the industry or trade association to handle, or even the government, but not the company. Especially in the international arena, the appropriate response to some issues may be to try to pass the resolution off to governments or international bodies such as regional economic communities or United Nations agencies (Austrom and Lad, 1989).

Response development is the phase of issues management where creative managers can have their biggest influence on organizational decision making, because of the chance that they can break up the "group think" of senior executives by introducing nonobvious, but highly salient, impacts and by suggesting appropriate responses. They can challenge the assumptions of the organizational culture and open new paths for constructive change (Mitroff, 1987).

CONCLUSION: THE IMPORTANCE OF STRATEGIC ISSUES MANAGEMENT SYSTEMS

In this chapter we have illustrated how many of the concepts and tools discussed in earlier chapters hold together through the vehicle of issues management and particularly the development of appropriate responses to issues. Response development will be a function of the institutional–ideological situations in countries where the firm does business. The nature of business–government relations can be crucial in whether or not issues arise, what impacts they can have on businesses, and what responses might be most appropriate. Similarly, as illustrated in table 8.2, the concepts of corporate social performance, stakeholder management, and ethical analysis have something to offer issues management, and thus corporate performance.

The single most important contribution of issues management, as illustrated in the corporate social performance model of Robert Miles, 1987 (see figure 8.2), is how it enhances strategic decision making. Miles identifies two types of strategy in business organizations – corporate strategy and external affairs strategy. Both are influenced

Table 8.2 Business and society concepts and issues management

	Issues identification	Issues analysis	Response development
Institutional–ideological model	Frames of reference for issue emergence and definition	Frames alternative ranking systems	Frames reasonable responses
Business–government relations	Sources of issues Sources of data Stakeholders	Influences issue rankings	Provides response alternatives
Corporate social performance	Knowledge of stakeholder expectations	Frames internal trade-offs	Provides criteria for response selection
Stakeholder management	Patterns of interaction with stakeholders	Identifies key players	Provides avenues for negotiated responses
Ethical analysis	Source of underlying conflicts and gaps	Weighs competing values and ideals	Weighs the moral rightness of responses

Figure 8.2   Miles's model of corporate social performance

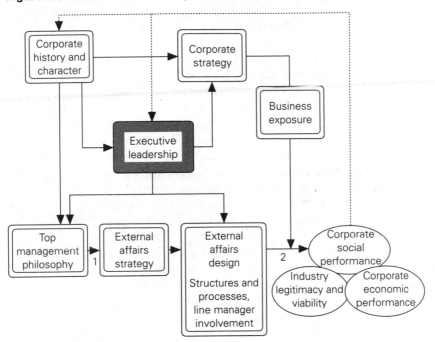

Explanation
1 = The Philosophy-Strategy Connection
2 = The Exposure-Design Contingency
—— direct influence
······ indirect influence

Source: Robert H. Miles, *Managing the Corporate Social Environment: A Grounded Theory.* (c) 1987, p. 274. Reprinted by permission of Prentice Hall, Upper Saddle River, New Jersey.

by corporate history and character, and both have consequences on organizational performance. Corporate strategy influences the business's exposure to threats and opportunities in the environment. Issues management is found in both external affairs strategy and design. Organizations that employ corporate strategy without an external affairs strategy may yield effective economic performance but will remain vulnerable to challenges of social legitimacy. The contribution of issues management is to broaden the framework of business exposure to include threats and opportunities in social and political environments, and to contribute to better social performance outcomes and more stable legitimacy, consequently enhancing economic performance as well. In short, corporate strategy is targeted only to economic performance within "given" environments; corporate plus external affairs strategy recognizes the interrelated nature of economic and social performance within the dynamic environments of international business.

Issues management, contrary to what many believe, is not crisis management. Crisis management, because it is almost purely reactive to some event, centers around tactics. Issues management, which seeks responses rather than reactions, centers around planning and strategy. In many cases, a crisis occurs because no one in the company has paid attention to an emerging issue, or because the crisis was so improbable that the company probably shouldn't have paid any attention to it. In the first case, good issues management would have caught the problem before it became a crisis. In the second case, good issues management would have suggested that the company needs a crisis management plan for improbable events. Also, in the second case, issues management would follow up on the crisis to try to close expectational gaps that open as a result of the crisis. Bhopal was a crisis; international chemical plant safety was the issue. In short, a company may have good or bad crisis management, and good or bad issues management; the two are not synonymous.

Finally, some unique organizational problems can arise for issues management, affecting its success (Wartick and Rude, 1986). One is the problem of 20/20 hindsight. Managers love to take credit for success, whether they deserve it or not. Likewise, they can be blamed for failure, even though they could not have prevented the failure from happening. The successes and failures of issues management will be significantly influenced by the organization's culture. In cultures that do not value risk-taking, the "don't screw up" mentality will be prevalent and issues managers will try to make sure that their hindsight is 20/20. In these organizations, the planning value of issues management is lost. In cultures that do value risk-taking, issues managers will be more at the forefront of the issues management process, communicating their findings and logics to decision makers, and hoping for 20/40 foresight instead of 20/20 hindsight.

Resource questions are always important. Companies that are willing to invest resources in serious issues management will have access to a variety of information sources so that issues managers can check out their hunches and validate their conclusions. Companies unwilling to invest such resources will be left relying on few information sources, for example, the state department reports that said, following the opening of the rest of eastern Europe and almost up to the December 24, 1989 execution of the dictatorial Ceaucesceau "first family," that Romania was a benign environment for US business, and nothing much of any concern was going on there. For issues management to provide value to an organization, the resources must be provided to do the job well.

Another form of resource drought occurs when a company says to one of its people, "Hey, this issues management stuff is pretty neat. Why don't you be our issues manager? Here's half a secretary and $5,000 expenses. Now, whenever we have an issue, we'll just turn it over to you, and you can manage it." This issues manager is left out on a *very* thin limb and begins taking the flack for everything that no one else wants to deal with. As we have defined it here, issues management is a specific process of identifying, assessing, and developing responses to controversial, impactful issues based on expectational gaps. It is not a dumping ground for others' problems or for decisions that no one wants to make.

Finally, there is the problem of "response implementation and evaluation" as part of the issues management process, which some like to emphasize and include in issues management and public affairs (Buchholz, 1989; Chase, 1984). Issues managers may develop responses but may not have authority to implement them if they are in staff positions (unless what passes for issues management in the company is really public relations). To avoid this, some companies are specifying issues management as one of the responsibilities of line managers. Consequently, line managers identify and analyze issues, develop responses, *and* implement and evaluate the responses. For MNEs, the bottom line of issues management may be that all managers everywhere are issues managers.

NOTE

1   Much of the discussion in this chapter is based on the literature review and synthesis of Wartick and Mahon (1994).

REFERENCES

Ansoff, Igor. 1975. "Managing strategic surprise by response to weak signals." *California Management Review* 18 (2), 21–33.

Ansoff, Igor. 1980. "Strategic issue management." *Strategic Management Journal* 1, 131–48.

Austrom, Douglas R. and Lawrence J. Lad. 1989. "Issues management alliances: New responses, new values, and new logics." In James E. Post (ed.), *Research in Corporate Social Performance and Policy*. Greenwich, CN: JAI Press, Volume 11, 233–56.

Bergner, Douglas. 1983. "International public affairs: A preliminary report by a PAC task force." *Perspectives* (April), Washington, DC: Public Affairs Council.

Bigelow, Barbara, Liam Fahey, and John F. Mahon. 1993. "A typology of issue evolution." *Business & Society* 32 (1), 18–29.

Blake, David H. 1977. *Managing the External Relations of Multinational Corporations*. New York: Fund for Multinational Management Education.

Buchholz, Rogene A., W. D. Evans, and R. A. Wagley. 1989. *Management Response to Public Issues*, 2nd ed. Englewood Cliffs, NJ: Prentice-Hall.

Business International Corporation, 1991. *Global Strategic Planning: How 17 of the World's Best Companies Are Building Market Share and Achieving Corporate Objectives*. New York: Business International Corporation.

Chase, W. Howard. 1984. *Issues Management: Origins of the Future*. Stamford, CT: Issue Action Publications.

Coates, J. F. 1986. *Issues Management*. Mt. Airy: Lomond Publishing.

De George, Richard T. 1993. *Competing with Integrity in International Business*. New York: Oxford University Press.

Dutton, Jane E. and S. E. Jackson 1987. "Categorizing strategic issues: Links to organizational action." *Academy of Management Review* 12, 76–90.

Dutton, Jane E. and Edward Ottensmeyer. 1987. "Strategic issues management systems: Forms, functions, and contexts." *Academy of Management Review* 12, 355–65.

Eyestone, R. 1978. *From Social Issue to Public Policy*. New York: John Wiley & Sons.

Fahey, Liam, and V. K. Narayanan. 1986. *Macroenvironmental Analysis for Strategic Management*. Minneapolis, MN: West Publishing Co.

Ghoshal, Sumantra. 1988. "Environmental scanning in Korean firms: Organizational isomorphism in action." *Journal of International Business Studies* 19:1 (Spring): 69–86.

Gray, Barbara. 1988. *Collaborating: Finding Common Ground for Multiparty Problems*. San Francisco: Jossey-Bass.

Gray, Barbara, and Donna J. Wood. 1991. "Toward a comprehensive theory of collaboration." *Journal of Applied Behavioral Science* 27:2 (Dec.): 139–62.

Johnson, J. 1983. "Issues management – What are the issues?" *Business Quarterly* 48:3, 22–31.

Lusterman, Seymour. 1985. *Managing International Public Affairs*. New York: Conference Board.

Mahon, John F. and Sandra A. Waddock 1992. "Strategic issues management: An integration of issue life cycle perspectives." *Business & Society* 31, 19–32.

McCann, Joseph E. and Luis Gomez-Mejia. 1986. "Assessing an international 'issues climate': Policy and methodology implications." *Academy of Management Best Papers Proceedings 1986*, Academy of Management, 316–20.

Miles, Robert H. 1987. *Managing the Corporate Social Environment: A Grounded Theory*. Upper Saddle River: Prentice-Hall Inc.

Mitroff, Ian I. 1987. *Business Not as Usual: Rethinking Our Individual, Corporate, and Industrial Strategies for Global Competition*. San Francisco: Jossey-Bass.

Molitor, Graham T. 1978. "Environmental scanning at GE." In G. Steiner (ed.), *Business Environment/Public Policy Papers.* AACSB.

National Association of Manufacturers. 1978. *Public Affairs Manual.* Washington, DC: National Association of Manufacturers.

Nigh, Douglas W. and Phillip L. Cochran. 1987. "Issue management and the multinational enterprise." *Management International Review* 27 (1), 4–12.

Olsen, Michael D., Bvsan Murthy, and Richard Teare. 1994. "CEO perspectives on scanning the global hotel business environment." *International Journal of Contemporary Hospitality Management,* 6:4, pp. 3–9.

Preble, John F., Pradeep A. Rau, and Arie Reichel. 1988. "The environmental scanning practices of US multinationals in the late 1980's." *Management International Review* 28:4, 4–14.

Richardson, Bill. 1995. "The politically aware leader." *Leadership & Organization Development Journal,* 16:2, pp. 27–35.

Rogers, Jerry. 1983. *Global Risk Assessments: Issues, Concepts & Applications.* Book I. Riverside, CA: Global Risk Assessments, Inc.

Solis, Diane. 1993. "To avoid cost of US prescription drugs, more Americans shop south of the border." *Wall Street Journal* (June 29): B-1.

Tombari, Henry A. 1984. *Business and Society.* New York: Dryden Press.

Wartick, Steven L. 1988. "The contribution of issues management to corporate performance." *Business Forum* 13 (Spring), 16–22.

Wartick, Steven L., and John F. Mahon. 1994. "Toward a substantive definition of the corporate issue construct: A review and synthesis of the literature," *Business & Society* 33:3, 293–311.

Wartick, Steven L., and Robert E. Rude. 1986. "Issues management: Corporate fad or corporate function?" *California Management Review* (Fall): 124–40.

Wood, Donna J., and Barbara Gray. 1991. "Collaborative alliances: Moving from practice to theory." *Journal of Applied Behavioral Science* 27:1 (Dec.): 3–22.

9
Managing Global Corporate Social Performance

"How much responsibility does a manufacturer have for the illegitimate use of a product that was designed to do something and when used legitimately really isn't a problem?" asked Tony Anderson, Chairman and CEO of the H. B. Fuller Company. This company's products include Resistol, a toluene-based glue that is unattractive in US and European markets but quite popular in a variety of commercial and industrial settings in Mexico and Central America. Resistol, unfortunately, has become an addictive drug of choice for many Central American street children. These "Resistoleros" inhale the glue for a quick, cheap high, and then often experience violent episodes and serious health problems, including kidney failure and brain damage. Fuller's response has been to stop selling Resistol in small containers that are easily accessible to children, and to try to control the selling practices of their Central American distributors. The firm has also devoted $100,000 a year to educate street kids about the product's hazards when inhaled. In the spring of 1994, Fuller announced that it would develop new polymers for use in a product to replace Resistol (Makower, 1994: 282–4).

Many industries are subject to global controversy and intercultural conflict, including makers of agricultural and manufacturing equipment, transportation and distribution companies, telecommunications, electronics and computers, and even "low-tech" industries such as shoe, apparel, and fabric manufacturing. Will companies in these industries be ready to meet the challenges of international social and political conflict? Will managers be prepared to deal with global stakeholder demands and international social issues? How can a company's managers stay "on track" with their values and objectives in a tumultuous global environment?

Learning to manage global corporate social performance will help managers to meet these challenges. As in other arenas of international business performance, the key to readiness is to think strategically (see Epstein, 1987; Wartick, 1992; Wood and Pasquero, 1992). To this point in the book, the focus has been on examining the philosophical, institutional, and responsive process aspects of corporate social performance. Now it is appropriate to turn our attention to the *outcomes* of business decisions and actions, which are, in fact, the essence of performance. In doing so, the focus shifts to the tools managers can use to assess and report outcomes and to incorporate the new information generated into the company's plans and policies. These tools must be used within a context of managing global corporate social performance from a macro-perspective; that is, a broad-based "satellite view" of the overall characteristics of a global CSP strategy is needed. To this end, a social performance CODE, emphasizing Consistency, Opportunity, Diversity, and Emergency capability in a company's CSP policies and procedures, is provided.

EVALUATING AND REPORTING OUTCOMES

Evaluating and reporting the social outcomes of business activity is best thought of as a continuous process, or cycle, of information-gathering, analysis, discussion, and change. The basic steps of this cycle are illustrated in figure 9.1.

The framework for the evaluation and reporting cycle is, of course, the company's own corporate social performance mission and strategy

Figure 9.1   Evaluating and reporting social performance

```
         Communicate                    Evaluate
         findings to                social objectives,
      relevant stakeholders         actions, and outcomes


         Evaluate                       Communicate
       new actions and                  findings to
       modify as needed              key decision makers

                    Plan and execute
                      new actions
```

Source: Adapted from Donna J. Wood, *Business and Society*. New York: HarperCollins, 1990, p. 585.

as well as the various societal expectations, both legal and extralegal, for acceptable corporate performance. In figure 9.2 the corporate social performance model, first presented in chapter 1 and more fully developed in chapter 4, is reviewed. Across the bottom of the figure are added various management tools that can be used to plan, implement, and assess each component. Of particular importance for managing CSP is an increased understanding and appreciation of the tools used in the third stage of CSP – assessing outcomes.

Impact assessment

Impact assessment describes those activities devoted to identifying and analyzing corporate effects on societies. Assessment may cover a number of bases: for example, the costs (or harms) and benefits of a particular outcome, the progress an outcome represents toward meeting some particular societal or organizational goal, or the company's relative aggregate contributions to a broad distribution of costs and benefits, compared to the performance of other organizations that contribute on the same dimensions. Impacts can probably best be measured if they are linked to specific or generic stakeholders, and several examples of impacts, using a SEPTEmber framework matrixed with a few key stakeholders, appear in table 9.1 (see Wood and Jones, 1995). Below, some of the problems and opportunities of social impact assessment in the global business environment will be considered.

Identifying global social impacts may require new perspectives on business activity. Traditional management perspectives (focusing

Figure 9.2   The corporate social performance model

Table 9.1 Societal impacts of international business activity: a SEPTEmber/stakeholder framework

| Impacts | Stakeholders | | | |
	Employees	Owners	Customers	Community
Social	Occupational identity Training, skills	Status Wealth	Conspicuous consumption Pecuniary emulation	Job base Population bases
Economic	Jobs, income Benefits	Return or loss Stock value	Material wants and needs	Tax revenues Income multipliers
Political	"Safety net" programs Discrimination laws	Corporate governance Owners' rights	Market regulation Information regulation	Plant closing laws
Technological	Productivity gains/losses Job satisfaction	Information	New products Communications	Infrastructure
Ecological	Workplace exposure	Resource depletion lowers profits	Effects of packaging Product disposal issues	Air, water pollution Toxic wastes Solid wastes Resource usage and conservation

narrowly, for example, on stockholder value or customer satisfaction) will not support social impact assessment. New ways of thinking about the company's relationships with its business environment are needed. In particular, managers need to begin thinking about the various environmental segments in which impacts can occur (social, economic, political, technological, ecological); the stakeholders who can be affected; and the similarities and differences among the various nations and cultures in which the company is operating. That is, the lessons so far in this book are all relevant to developing the necessary perspective for social impact assessment. For any product, technology, process, policy, or management function, managers can trace the possible and the likely consequences in terms of resource allocation and depletion; end-user capability and impact; political stability or change; appropriateness of infrastructure in target markets; long-term health considerations; pollution of air, soil, or water; and so on.

Calculating costs and benefits may require creative approaches. Managers are comfortable with cost-benefit analysis of specific project alternatives whose components are readily valued in dollars, yen, pesos, forints, francs, and so on. For international projects, currency exchange rates and a risk factor can be estimated and added into the calculations. However, for many of the impacts that are now being considered, there are no commonly accepted means of valuation, and no ready transfers of value into currency. For example, the 1987 Montreal Protocol on Substances that Deplete the Ozone Layer laid out an internationally negotiated schedule for reduction and eventual elimination of chlorofluorcarbons (CFCs), which deplete the atmospheric ozone layer and allow hazardous solar radiation to reach the earth. However, no one knows precisely what the costs and benefits are of ozone layer depletion, elimination of CFCs, and the treaty itself. Costs and benefits are readily calculable for simple, time-constrained problems. But ambiguous, massive, international-scale problems cannot be played strictly by the numbers.

Furthermore, in cross-cultural situations, the values (both financial and non-financial) placed on a single impact may differ from one culture to the next. CFCs are used primarily in refrigeration and air conditioning units. Highly industrialized societies such as the US and western Europe use huge quantities of CFCs in home and workplace refrigeration, auto air conditioning, refrigerated trucks, and manu-facturing processes – the lifestyle is to some extent CFC-dependent. However, these societies are also the most likely to find a replacement for CFCs and to be able to afford that replacement should it prove more expensive. Developing nations, in contrast, are not so heavily CFC-dependent, nor could they readily develop a substitute chemical or foot the bill for a more expensive replacement. The costs and benefits of CFC elimination are different for these countries.

Creative approaches are needed to overcome the barriers of tradi-tional thinking for companies engaging in social impact assessment (Bruce, 1989). Some economists, for example, have given thought to how the economic costs and benefits of environmental pollution – traditionally thought of (rather, ignored) by economists as an exter-nality or neighborhood effect – can be estimated and valued financially (see Rose, 1970). Regulatory compliance and government relations costs could be allocated over time as costs of production, thereby incorpor-ating into routine management information-gathering the "overhead" costs of events such as misleading advertising, unsafe products or workplaces, or effluent dumping. The contingent valuation method (CVM) is being used to measure pollution's costs and benefits, includ-ing the extent of a polluter's legal liability, changes in health status, and how much should be spent on environmental cleanup efforts.

CVM is based upon survey data concerning some resource, its current condition, and how individuals would pay for improvements in the resource. Recently CVM has been used to provide quantitative measures in US planning of the Clean Air Act of 1991 and wetlands protection bills (Johansson, 1994; Barbier, 1994; Geddis, 1994). This method has been criticized for providing biased estimates and for unreliability (Niewijk, 1994), so the need for further measurement development is far from satisfied.

Estimates of the company's contributions to the overall standard of living in areas where it has physical facilities can be made in conjunction with government statistics. The *maquiladoras*, for example, the foreign-owned manufacturing plants at the Mexican border, have been widely criticized for dumping pollutants and exploiting labor. However, the evidence also shows a higher standard of living for communities with *maquiladoras*, not only because the wage rate is higher than average, but also because jobs are provided for two-earner families.

Implementing social impact assessment requires widespread employee commitment. Normally, putting a new process into effect involves a series of steps that people *do*. An equally important and often-overlooked dimension is the process of developing *feelings of commitment* to the new idea among organizational members. At first, a new idea like social impact assessment is likely to require a top management champion who can guide, nourish, and defend the idea through initial implementation. Eventually, however, the champion must be joined by others who commit to the social impact assessment process, and who then influence others to commit to it as well.

Commitment to social impact assessment is necessary from a practical perspective. When the assessment process is fully institutionalized in a company, it is carried out by managers and workers at all levels of the organization. These hands-on assessors are in the best position to identify new or overlooked impacts, to sense the dynamics of impacts over time, and to suggest improvements in the process itself. Without widespread commitment, impact assessment will be seen as just another paper-shuffling requirement, or at worst, a vehicle for deception, manipulation, or sabotage.

Implementing social impact assessment may require widespread stakeholder involvement. Impact assessment achieves its full value with the participation of stakeholders on whom the impacts are actually occurring. What if a company sincerely tries to assess the effects of its operations on various stakeholders, but cannot or does not get any information from them? Worse still, what if relations with stakeholders are so bad that stakeholders provide wrong information, either deliberately or because their feelings are in the way of accuracy?

Stakeholder management, as discussed in chapter 4, is by no means a manipulative management device for controlling people and organizations in the environment. Instead, it is a long-term process of gaining access to stakeholders and establishing reciprocal relationships of good faith and trust.

Performance evaluation

Corporate social performance (CSP) is an organization-level concept that requires the participation of the individuals in the organization. Performance evaluation represents the best way to communicate social impact assessment results to people in the company, to obtain their ideas about the company's social performance strategy and results, and to provide incentives for them to improve their own contributions to overall CSP.

Wood (1994: 703–5) lists the following as necessary components of a performance appraisal that supports corporate social performance goals:

- Economic and social accomplishments are both considered important.
- Social objectives are set with consideration of the strengths and capabilities of the manager's operating unit.
- Most social accomplishments are measurable; results can be observed, reported, and related to economic accomplishments.
- The manager's rewards – raises, bonuses, promotions – are tied to the achievement of social as well as economic goals.
- Higher executives in the company fully support the manager's attempts to meet social objectives.

In practice, this means that a company must put its money where its mouth is. The CEO's annual speech about social responsibility, the half-page social responsibility section of the annual report, the public affairs department's lectures on stakeholder relationships, or even a company-wide impact assessment process, will all be for nothing if managers discover that the payoffs for them come solely from increasing financial performance. Nor will external stakeholders be fooled for long by pretty words not backed up with actions and appropriate outputs.

Performance evaluation techniques are well-developed in the human resources literature (see, for example, Grider and Toombs, 1993; Rollins and Fruge, 1992; Scutt, 1993; Tinkham and Kleiner, 1993;

Wills, 1993), and need not be repeated here. However, for social objectives to be properly handled in performance evauation, the following points need to be observed:

- Social objectives for each manager must be specific, explicitly stated, measurable, tied to the company's mission and strategy, and attainable (that is, relevant to the manager's work and within his/her ability to accomplish).
- Managers should have adequate resources (budget, staff, authority, and so on) to accomplish social objectives.
- Managers should be held strictly accountable for accomplishment of social objectives.
- Managers and their superiors should work together to assess social performance and to develop a plan for improving in the future.

CORPORATE SOCIAL REPORTING

Corporate social reporting is defined as the voluntary provision of information on the social outcomes of corporate policies, procedures, and activities. Among US companies, social reporting enjoyed a brief flurry of interest in the 1970s, then virtually disappeared as executives began to fear that, as William C. Frederick (1978) put it, this was just another way "to flog business for its social sins." Legally, US companies are required to provide to the government certain information relevant to social impacts, such as occupational health and safety records or environmental pollution indicators, but legal reporting requirements are fairly narrow. At present, only a few US firms issue periodic voluntary social reports, although many large companies include a social responsibility statement in their annual reports. Those US companies engaged in voluntary social reporting tend to emphasize community relations and charitable giving, discussing programs and projects that are often isolated from or tangential to the company's overall mission and objectives. These reports typically do not cover anything close to the entire range of the company's social impacts.

In Europe, some aspects of corporate social reporting have been institutionalized, indeed required by government. As Dierkes and Antal (1986) point out, European corporate social reports tend to emphasize labor–management relations, worker safety and health and other aspects of corporate policy and practice that are particularly relevant to employees. Recently, however, European companies have moved toward including more natural environment information in their social reports. The European Union is moving toward additional, and more uniform, social reporting in these areas, as well as in areas such as product quality, packaging, and labeling standards.

Migros Genossenschaftsbund AG, a giant Swiss retailing cooperative, has been a world leader in voluntary corporate social reporting with its series of biennial *Social Reports,* beginning in 1978. Each report built to some extent on the information provided in the last report, and each added additional sources and types of information. The company's commitment to social reporting allowed it to experiment with different assessment techniques and reporting schemes. Migros's social reports expanded stakeholders' cumulative knowledge about the company, making it more transparent and open to evaluation. In addition, the reports were valuable internal sources of information and analysis for managers seeking to improve corporate performance on various dimensions.

Around the world, it is unusual to find extensive voluntary social reporting among business organizations, although many governments require companies to provide much information that might be considered social in nature. This lack of voluntary social reporting in other countries results from a number of factors, including aggressive profit orientations, philosophical values, lack of stakeholder demand, and so on. A common factor in all cases, however, is the lack of incentive, or managers' failure to perceive an incentive, for companies to engage in such voluntary behavior.

What are the incentives for a company to voluntarily report on its social performance? Dierkes and Antal (1986: 108) note three primary functions of corporate social reporting:

- to support management in integrating a wide range of social considerations into decision making;
- to provide methodologically sound and comprehensive information on the social impacts of business activities; and
- to permit the monitoring, evaluation, and – where necessary – control of corporate social behavior by stakeholders.

Companies can take a variety of approaches to assessing and reporting their social performance. Dierkes (1980) and Dierkes and Antal (1986) list four distinct types of social reporting:

(1) *The inventory reporting approach* makes a selective or comprehensive list of all activities, programs, and outcomes the company considers relevant to its social performance.

(2) *The social indicators approach* compares the company's performance on selected dimensions, for example, pollution control or

minority hiring, with industry averages, social indexes, government standards or targets, or other relevant aggregate statistics.
(3) *The goal accounting and reporting approach*, probably the most commonly used method, describes the company's own objectives
for its social performance, outlines the programs and policies
designed to achieve them, and assesses the company's success
in meeting its social objectives.
(4) *The balance sheet approach*, the least widely used method, attempts
to add up the costs and benefits, successes and failures, of the
company's social performance just as a financial balance sheet of
profit and loss would be prepared.

In figure 9.3, a crosstabulation yields an inventory of the usefulness (noted in the figure as "high" or "low") of the four types of social
reports for each of the three functions.

Not all managers are comfortable with the idea that their decisions
and the company's actions should be more transparent, more open to
external inspection. But social reporting as a way to make business
activities more transparent provides opportunities for international
business firms as well as threats. For example, Migros's social reporting
process allowed the company to identify several ideas for profitable
new business lines, possibilities for cost savings, and issues such as
inequities in pay scales that caused dissension in the workforce and,
perhaps, lower productivity.

Multinational corporations have been remarkably ineffective at
portraying the economic and social benefits their operations provide
to developing host countries. One writer cites Southern Peru Copper
Corporation's almost $1 billion in capital investment and $1.4 billion
in expenditures contributing to the Peruvian economy in the 1970–
79 decade, and Firestone Tire & Rubber Company's $122 million ex-
penditures in Argentina in 1981 (Micou, 1985: 12–13). The movement

Figure 9.3 The usefulness of four types of social reports to management

	Inventory	Social indicators	Goal accounting	Balance sheet
Support management decisions	Low	Low	High	Low
Provide good information	High	High	Low	High
Monitoring and evaluation	Low	High	High	Low

of large auto manufacturers Ford, Suzuki, and General Motors into Hungary will help offset that country's sizeable government deficit (Moore, 1993), and General Electric and other companies moving into the Murcia region of Spain increased the gross regional product of that area by 31 percent over 1990, the highest rate of growth in Spain in recent years ("Murcia," 1993). Coca-Cola's joint venture with a black ownership group in South Africa allows Coke to establish a vital supplier relationship while aiding anti-apartheid efforts (Moskowitz, 1994). And Merck's partnership with a Costa Rican research and conservation institute provides rain forest protection as well as a steady supply of harvested pharmaceutical components, and marks the first time a host developing country will receive royalties from a pharmaceutical multinational company's research (Moskowitz, 1995).

Of course, social reporting is difficult under the best of circumstances and even more so in complex multinational settings. Nevertheless, there are at least four areas in which corporations could assess their positive contributions to host countries:

(1) The multinationals develop human resources through employment, training, and "indigenization" (transferring positions of authority to local managers);
(2) they strengthen the knowledge base through research and development and the transfer of technology;
(3) they raise the standard of living through the creation of wealth, encouraging local industry, and providing consumer goods; and
(4) they enhance the quality of life by assisting programs that raise standards in health, housing, nutrition, and education. (Micou, 1985: 12–13.)

As a tool for managing global corporate social performance, then, social reporting provides numerous benefits. It provides a process and vehicle for the flow of information between the company and its stakeholders. It gives management a rich source of internal data on how well the company is meeting its objectives. It can help all employees recognize that the company takes social performance seriously. It can help managers identify problems, potential savings, and new business opportunities. Finally, social reporting can enhance a company's image in the eyes of its stakeholders.

As with any management information system, corporate social reporting must be credible if it is to fulfill all these possible functions. In exhibit 9.1 the "Four Cs of Credibility" for social reporting (Wood, 1994) are presented.

Exhibit 9.1   Four Cs of credibility for social reporting

Corporate social reporting is credible to the extent that it offers:

Clear presentation
of topics, programs, and results, using readily understandable prose and appropriate graphics and design.

Comprehensive coverage
of topical areas relevant to important stakeholders inside and outside the firm. Stakeholders will notice if a topic or issue important to them is not included in a social report.

Consistent inclusion
of topics from one report to the next. Longitudinal comparisons of a company's social reports are inevitable; thus, it is vital that problems identified in one report be addressed in the next.

Comparable measurement and reporting techniques
from year to year, so that progress can be assessed reliably.

Source: Wood, 1994.

SETTING THE STAGE FOR GLOBAL SOCIAL PERFORMANCE: MANAGERIAL PERSPECTIVES AND CSP

The nature of a company's corporate social performance strategy depends very much on how that company's managers view themselves, and their company, in relation to the rest of the world. Nancy Adler (1991) has observed that managers whose companies are engaged in cross-border business ventures typically have one of three perspectives – domestic, international, or global – in this regard. These perspectives certainly have effects on a company's product strategy, employment practices, organizational structure, and so on. What may be less obvious is that managers' perspective on their firm's relationship to its environment will also affect that company's corporate social performance (Wartick and Cochran, 1985).

Domestic perspective

Managers guided purely by a domestic perspective know their home markets, regulations, and environmental conditions well, but they do not learn much of anything about the foreign environments in which the company does business. The mentality is "us versus them." Such a mentality may be arrogant, as when a high-ranking US steel manager was overheard to complain about having to do business in whatever language those Koreans speak. Or it may be merely ignorant, as when a US babyfood manufacturer shipped its product to Africa with a plump-cheeked white baby on the label, not knowing that Africans use pictures for content labeling. Kenichi Ohmae (1989: 152) describes this perspective as nearsightedness: "when push comes to shove, [managers'] field of vision is dominated by home-country customers and the organizational units that serve them. Everyone – and everything – else is simply part of 'the rest of the world.'"

A US company engaged in international business, whose managers take a predominantly domestic perspective, is likely to focus its public affairs attention on the US federal government and relevant state governments and on domestic image-building. Managers will think of the Japanese or Swedish or Brazilian governments as amorphous entities with which they must deal from time to time, but they will not think of the individuals who represent and act on behalf of these governments, as they do at home. Such a company may actively scan the domestic environment and indeed may understand it deeply, but it will invest minimal attention in scanning and understanding its foreign environments. Its CSP strategy, likewise, will emphasize home-country stakeholders and familiar values and ethical norms. This "domestic near-sightedness" means that managers will overlook many opportunities in their foreign markets and, inevitably, will be threatened and even faced with crisis in those markets.

International perspective

Managers with an international perspective learn to recognize and become sensitive to cultural differences between the domestic market and the foreign markets they serve. They do not think in over-general terms of "domestic versus foreign," but in terms of unique markets: for example, the southern US, western Europe, Japan, China, Israel, central Africa. Companies operating under this perspective consider it important that they be able to conduct business in the language of their markets, but they may not emphasize multilinguality or international experience for all their managers, only for a few specialists.

Taking an international perspective allows a company's managers to see that stakeholder strategies, public affairs, and even definitions of corporate social responsibility and performance are likely to vary in different cultures, sometimes dramatically. Managers are likely to have had training in intercultural sensitivity and so are more able to recognize the cultural and value bases of behavior in their trading partners that would otherwise be unfathomable, or perhaps even offensive. They can recognize the existence of certain types of stakeholders in some markets that do not exist in others, and they know that stakeholders have varying degrees and types of power in different cultures. This is all to the good, and it is possible for some companies to retain this perspective, not moving forward to the global stage, and do very well.

But an international perspective can become confusing and complicated. Strategies and tactics that work for managers doing business in three countries may be unmanageable when 40 or 90 countries are involved. Even worse, an international perspective can lead a company into the murky depths of cultural relativism and the choice of a laissez-faire social performance "strategy" (or more accurately, a non-strategy). That is, managers may throw up their hands in despair at the immense variety of cultural norms, ethics, and expectations they experience, giving themselves permission to follow any ethical or cultural dictum, or none at all. Nevertheless, to the extent that managerial perspectives can be seen in evolutionary terms, then the international perspective may be a necessary step along the way to a true global view.

Global perspective

Finally, a global perspective emerges when headquarters executives see themselves as serving a variety of important – and different – markets that happen to be in different countries (Garland and Farmer, 1986). Ohmae (1989: 153) describes this as the rule of equidistance: "the corporation sees itself as equidistant from all its key customers," and not in terms of domestic versus overseas operations. In product strategy, for example, a global company would not necessarily seek a "universal product," one that could be engineered, produced, and marketed identically throughout the world. Instead, the company would, as Nissan does with automobiles, design products specifically for the "lead countries" in world regional markets, then provide minor adaptations to suit the preferences of other markets or of smaller portions of major markets (Ohmae, 1989). These "global" products are tailored to market segments, but in ways that make sense to the company as well as the market.

Managers in companies with a global perspective are not only multilingual, they are multicultural. The Japanese division will be staffed by Japanese managers, the Argentine division by Argentinians, and so on. Furthermore, headquarters will not be a "domestic" operation, but will reflect the ethnic and cultural diversity of the company's markets. Managers targeted for headquarters, whatever their country of origin, may be moved around the globe to experience various cultures.

In terms of public affairs, issues management, and corporate social performance, companies that take a global perspective may be able to escape the perceptual trap of "home country versus host country" that haunts and sometimes immobilizes both the domestic and the international perspectives. A global company can be "home" wherever its facilities are found, and still maintain a broader, more sophisticated outlook on its worldwide operations. In 1992, for example, the Coca-Cola Company began a television advertising campaign announcing its sponsorship of Olympic teams in *all 148 countries* where Coke products were sold. Similarly, Mars Candy Company ran ads showing people from many cultures sharing M&Ms as they enjoyed the Olympic games. These campaigns are qualitatively different from those of companies that proudly advertise their sponsorship of *United States* Olympic teams.

A decade ago, this idea of being "at home" anywhere in the world seemed a comforting escape hatch to executives who sought to avoid restrictive regulation, ethical challenges, and stakeholder demands in their true home countries. Now, however, the information revolution is virtually complete; global stakeholders have emerged along with global companies; and there is nowhere to hide, no escape from social and political interconnections. In a sense, home is wherever one invests energy and emotion and gathers rewards. Home constraints in industrialized countries are often demands for an improved quality of life. When the world is "home," it becomes possible for corporate managers to transpose quality-of-life expectations to different cultural settings and thus, over time, help to raise the world's standard of living. In this way, managers with a global perspective can avoid the trap of cultural relativism while still respecting cultural uniqueness and differences.

A "SATELLITE VIEW" OF GLOBAL SOCIAL PERFORMANCE: THE CODE FOR CSP MANAGEMENT

If we stand on the figurative mountaintop and look down at an effective corporate social performance strategy, what do we see? Managing global social performance is not easy under the best of circumstances, so it is sensible for managers to have a clear view of the central characteristics of a good CSP strategy. The CODE for CSP management, shown in exhibit 9.2, is a reminder of what is needed.

Exhibit 9.2   CODE for corporate social performance management

Consistency
Internally consistent principles, consistent applications, consistent measuring techniques, consistent reporting practices.

Opportunity
Recognizing opportunities in the environment, providing opportunities for input from all organizational levels, seeing CSP as a set of opportunities to enhance the company's fit with its environments.

Diversity
Accommodate, plan for, manage, and celebrate diversity in environment, cultures, workplaces, employee groups, customers, communities, and other stakeholders.

Emergency capability
Readiness to assume responsibility in a crisis: providing information and technical know-how, rapid deployment of resources, minimizing harms, managing stakeholder relations, solving the problem.

Consistency

When Ralph Waldo Emerson wrote, "a foolish consistency is the hobgoblin of little minds," his emphasis was on *foolish*, not on consistency (Seldes, ed., 1985). A global corporate social performance strategy must have consistency not for the sake of pleasing dusty ritualists who want everything slotted properly, but for the sake of logic, sound ethical reasoning, and clear guidelines for organizational behavior. Here are some key components of CSP consistency.

Internally consistent principles. The driving forces behind the company's strategy and operations must be consistent with each other. It would be difficult, for example, for a company to maintain a consistent CSP strategy if its two motivating principles were the contradictory ones of "profit at *any* cost" and "*always* protect the natural environment." (Internally consistent principles might be "reasonable profit" and "environmental responsibility.")

Another aspect is the need for CSP activities and outcomes to be geared to the company's overall mission and strategy. This does not mean that only activities such as philanthropy should be tied to the company's product/service line; it also means that the company's top executives must think through their entire range of products and services, operations and technologies, policies and practices, to assess their consistency with the company's overall focus.

Consistent application of principles and procedures. In ethical reasoning, it is essential that managers apply a principle, process, or policy similarly whenever the circumstances are similar (Velasquez, 1992). Operating across cultures makes this difficult for managers, because there are important differences in the world's major ethical systems. However, a company is entitled to decide for itself – within limits of the law and major cultural expectations – what its basic principles are, and then to establish procedures to implement those principles in the company's practices, anywhere in the world. For example, a company may decide that its basic principles involve dignity and respect for all humans, truth in advertising, and employees' right to a safe workplace. Such a firm would establish policies and procedures for guaranteeing consistent application of these principles in all its operations.

Consistent measurement techniques. From year to year, and from culture to culture, managers should try to measure social impacts and outcomes with comparable tools. Similarly, information gathered on worldwide stakeholders, and on stakeholders in specific markets, is easier to assimilate and use when it is reasonably consistent across cultures and markets. Measurement consistency will give managers invaluable comparative information on how well they are meeting their objectives in various markets, what impacts they are having, and what stakeholder challenges or opportunities to expect.

Consistent reporting policies and procedures. Finally, a global CSP strategy needs to have procedures for using stakeholder management and social outcomes data both in internal management decision making and in external relations and image management. Reports that vary in content or measurement from year to year, or that raise issues and never address them again, or that do not address issues considered crucial by some important stakeholders, are not very useful and may actually be harmful to the company.

Opportunity

Opportunity is a key component of a global corporate social performance strategy because CSP itself has a positive, forward-looking aspect as well as a backward-looking assessment aspect. The focus here is on recognizing, providing, and acting upon opportunities to enhance a company's social performance and the quality of life for people in its environment.

Recognizing opportunities in the environment. A great deal has been written about the importance of top management's perspective on opportunities and threats in the business environment, and how different perspectives will affect a company's orientation to environmental factors (see, for example, Piercy, 1989; Proctor, 1992a, 1992b). The reality of the global environment magnifies the actual range of opportunity and threat enormously. A coherent CSP strategy should enable managers to look analytically across the spectrum of their company's global activities so they can perceive more opportunities for enhancing corporate performance. For example, providing literacy programs, general educational support, or employee and family health care in developing host countries is a positive-sum game.

Providing opportunities for input. Employees at all levels in the company need to have a means of offering their observations and suggestions on corporate social impacts. Similarly, stakeholders must have opportunities for informing managers about how the company's operations affect them. For example, the presence of labor and often government representatives on European boards of directors provides a formal avenue for expression of these stakeholders' concerns and interests in the firm's operations.

Using opportunities to fit the firm to its environment. In today's complex and interlocked business environment, corporate social performance is a key component of an overall strategy to mold the organization to its environment, and vice versa. For example, Japanese companies are known more for "sticking to the knitting" than for corporate philanthropy, but Japanese firms operating in Europe and North America have had to alter their view of charity to better fit in with these cultures. Some examples: Nomura Securities Co. paid $2.8 million for a new wing of London's Tate Gallery; Toyota Motor Co. established a scholarship fund for young black Americans; Nippon Television Network Corp. paid for the restoration of Michaelangelo's masterpiece paintings on the ceiling of the Vatican's Sistine Chapel ("Altruism," 1988: 13).

Diversity

The need for a global CSP strategy to accommodate and reflect diversity appears to be in direct competition with the need for consistency. However, every global CSP strategy must be able to accommodate, plan for, manage, and celebrate diversity in the environments where the company does business.

Planning for diversity means accepting that the world is not suddenly going to become homogeneous and that a global company will, for the foreseeable future, need to adapt itself to various cultures, workforces, product/service demands, legal and regulatory environments, and so on.

Accommodating and managing diversity can be as simple as making sure that all employees engaged in international operations are sensitized to cultural differences and similarities and are taught ways of handling awkward moments. Or it can be as complex as the company considers necessary, given its specific environment and its internal organization. In a global company, managers need to have routine access to language training, dictionaries and linguistic references, translators and interpretors. Conferences may need to be run with simultaneous translation in several languages.

Culture is perhaps an even more difficult issue than is language. Superficial cultural differences – styles of dress, table habits, living arrangements, courtesies, and so on – are easy to accommodate once managers have learned to be sensitive toward and respectful of these differences. Some cultural differences, on the other hand, are more deeply rooted and more difficult to handle, such as the different treatment of women in various cultures, or ideas about racial or class superiority. On deep issues such as these, the company's top management team, in conjunction with the board of directors, will need to decide where it stands and what it can live with, and then implement those values throughout the firm in operational processes, policies, and incentive systems.

Celebrating diversity is the usually-overlooked facet of global environmental diversity. Managers are accustomed to thinking and acting in terms of control, order, certainty, and smooth trends. It can be difficult to simply relax and acknowledge that human and cultural diversity is fascinating and enriching. A global CSP strategy will not aim for creating or assuming sameness among cultures; it will build stakeholder relationships based on what is strong and beautiful in each culture, and act to preserve and celebrate different cultures.

Emergency capability

This fourth factor in the CODE for global social performance is absolutely essential for any large multinational corporation today. Crises happen even in the best-managed companies – tanks leak, planes crash, valves fail, employees make mistakes, products are sabotaged. Sometimes in international business it seems more surprising when things go right than when they go wrong. A global CSP strategy will emphasize the need to be ready to assume immediate responsibility in a crisis.

Several good works exist on crisis management (see, for example, Mitroff, 1993; Pauchant, 1992). In general, it is important to make sure that the company's CSP strategy allows a crisis team to be assembled quickly, information to flow freely and accurately, technical know-how to be applied immediately to contain the problem and minimize harms, stakeholders to be brought into the crisis management process, and the problems to be corrected as soon as possible.

Companies that are responsive to their stakeholders in a crisis situation are likely to be forgiven quickly. Companies that stonewall, deny responsibility, bluff, or take narrow legalistic approaches to crisis may never be forgiven (see Pagan, 1986). Thus, building solid, trustful stakeholder relations over time is an effective aspect of a global CSP strategy with respect to crisis management.

CONCLUSION: IMPACTS OF GLOBAL CSP STRATEGY

In R. Edward Freeman's (1984) stakeholder perspective of the firm, there is a role for what he calls "enterprise strategy." Rather than asking the business-level strategy question: "What business are we in? What business should we be in?" managers should ask themselves, "What do we stand for?" The answer to this enterprise-level question tells a great deal about the company's core values, where it will put its energies, and how it will invest its human and financial resources.

Is it possible for a company to decide that it stands for outstanding global social performance? Can a company's enterprise strategy have to do with enhancing its social, political, economic, technological, and ecological relationships with the markets, cultures, and peoples of the world? We posit that such a strategy is possible, and that numerous companies are already moving toward it.

The Swiss cooperative Toni Yogurt, briefly described in chapter 4, is a case in point. Toni's CEO in the 1970s, Walter Regez, wanted the company to stand for environmentally *and* economically sound business practices. This enterprise-level mission meant that the company had to take a serious look at its packaging, and the decision was made to go with recyclable glass. The resulting marketing strategy pushed the entire dairy industry of Switzerland into an ecological competition, with major payoffs in reduced energy consumption and natural resource use, heightened consumer awareness, and technological innovations. About Toni's efforts, scholar Thomas Dyllick (1989: 661) writes,

Trying to evaluate the ecological success of Toni's strategy . . . , it will not be sufficient to judge Toni's comparative success on its own. Its real success has to be seen in the *collective ecological improvements* by the whole industry, brought about by Toni's bold move to integrate the ecology into its marketing strategy. By pushing ecologically ahead, it succeeded in shifting the main competitive focus of the industry from price to ecology. Toni, being only a minor competitor with some 2% market share in the mid-seventies, was able to change the strategic rules of the game to its own advantage, thereby causing all competitors to improve on the ecology of their packaging as well. This has to be considered the true ecological success of Toni's strategy.

Some important points need to be made about the Toni example. First, in no way does the company's commitment to reducing environmental wastes interfere with its financial performance objectives. Indeed, *Toni's financial performance was greatly enhanced* by its recycling strategy. Second, Toni's leadership in container recycling *changed the rules of the game for all competitors*, making it advantageous for every company in the industry to use recyclable packaging, and creating a frantic scramble among companies trying to match Toni's lead. Third, Toni's success is likely to be a significant *incentive for further creativity and innovation in the company* as its executives seek to combine social and financial performance objectives for the good of the company, the stakeholders, and the earth. Who loses with a strategy like this?

An enterprise strategy that focuses on outstanding global social performance can allow a company to be a powerful change agent in the cultures where it operates and, eventually, in the entire global community. Such a strategy and opportunity carry enormous responsibilities – for companies to act in good faith, with thoughtful foresight and careful evaluation, to improve the quality of life for citizens of those cultures and for the people of the world. The possibilities that companies *can* do so have never looked better.

REFERENCES

Adler, Nancy J. 1991. *International Dimensions of Organizational Behavior.* 2nd ed. Boston, MA: PWS-Kent Publishing Co.
"Altruism motivated by a big dose of self-interest." *International Management* (Dec. 1988): 13.
Barbier, Edward B. 1994. "Valuing environmental functions." *Land Economics* 70:2, 153–73.
Bruce, Leigh. 1989. "How green is your company?" *International Management* (Jan.): 24–7.

Dierkes, Meinolf. 1980. "Corporate social reporting and performance in Germany." In Lee E. Preston (ed.), *Research in Corporate Social Performance and Policy*, Vol. 2. Greenwich, CT: JAI Press, 251–90.

Dierkes, Meinolf, and Ariane Berthoin Antal. 1986. 'Whither corporate social reporting – is it time to legislate?" *California Management Review* 28:3 (Spring): 106–21.

Dyllick, Thomas. 1989. "Ecological marketing strategy for Toni Yogurts in Switzerland." *Journal of Business Ethics* 8: 657–62.

Epstein, Edwin M. 1987. "The corporate social policy process: Beyond business ethics, corporate social responsibility, and corporate social responsiveness." *California Management Review* 29:3 (Spring): 99–114.

Frederick, William .C. 1978. "Auditing corporate social performance: The anatomy of a research project." In Lee E. Preston (ed.), *Research in Corporate Social Performance and Policy*, Vol. 1. Greenwich, CT: JAI Press, 123–38.

Freeman, R. Edward. 1984. *Strategic Management: A Stakeholder Perspective*. Marshfield, MA: Pitman (now New York: Ballinger/HarperCollins).

Garland, John, and Richard N. Farmer. 1986. *International Dimensions of Business Policy and Strategy*. Boston: PWS-Kent/Wadsworth.

Geddis, Robert. 1994. "When does the cost of monitoring outweigh the benefit?" *Iron Age New Steel* 10:7, 47.

Grider, Doug, and Leslie Toombs. 1993. "Current practices of performance appraisal as a linking mechanism for human resource decisions in state government." *International Journal of Public Administration* 16:1 (Jan.): 35–56.

Johansson, Per-Olov. 1994. "Altruism and the value of statistical life." *Journal of Health Economics* 13:1, 111–18.

Makower, Joel. 1994. *Beyond the Bottom Line: Putting Social Responsibility to Work for Your Business and the World*. New York: Simon & Schuster.

Micou, Ann McKinstry. 1985. "The invisible hand at work in developing countries." *Across the Board* 22:3 (March): 8–15.

Mitroff, Ian I. 1993. *Crisis Management: A Diagnostic Guide for Improving Your Organization's Crisis-Preparedness*. San Francisco: Jossey-Bass.

Moore, P. 1993. "Hungary." *Euromoney*. (March): 133–36.

Moskowitz, Milton. 1994. "Company Performance Roundup." *Business & Society Review* 91, 54–63.

Moskowitz, Milton. 1995. "Company Performance Roundup." *Business & Society Review* 93, 70–80.

"Murcia makes good." 1993. *Corporate Location* (August): 556.

Niewijk, Robert K. 1994. "Misleading quantification." *Regulation* 17:1, 60–71.

Ohmae, Kenichi. 1989. "Managing in a borderless world." *Harvard Business Review* 67:4 (May–June), 152–61.

Pagan, Rafael D., Jr. 1986. "The Nestlé boycott: Implications for strategic business planning." *Journal of Business Strategy* 6:4 (Spring): 12–18.

Pauchant, Thierry C. 1992. *Transforming the Crisis-Prone Organization: Preventing Individual, Organizational, and Environmental Tragedies*. San Francisco: Jossey-Bass.

Piercy, Nigel. 1989. "Making SWOT analysis work." *Marketing Intelligence & Planning* 7:5, 6, 5–7.

Proctor, R. A. 1992a. "Structured and creative approaches to strategy formulation." *Management Research News* 15:1, 13–18.

Proctor, R. A. 1992b. "Selecting an appropriate strategy." *Marketing Intelligence & Planning* 10:11, 21–4.

Rollins, Thomas, and Mike Fruge. 1992. "Performance dimensions." *Training* 29:1 (Jan.): 47–51.

Rose, Sanford. 1970. "The economics of environmental quality." *Fortune* (Dec. 23).

Scutt, Linda. 1993. "Evaluating appraisal." *Training Tomorrow* (July): 22–3.

Seldes, George (ed.). 1985. Ralph Waldo Emerson, "Self-Reliance", as quoted in *The Great Thoughts*. NY: Ballantine Books.

Tinkham, Robert, and Brian H. Kleiner. 1993. "New approaches to managing performance appraisals." *Work Study* 42:7 (Nov./Dec.): 5–7.

Velasquez, Manuel G. 1992. *Business Ethics: Concepts and Cases.* 3rd edition. Englewood Cliffs, NJ: Prentice-Hall.

Wartick, Steven L. 1988. "The contribution of issues management to corporate performance." *Business Forum* 13 (Spring), 16–22.

Wartick, Steven L. 1992. Comment on the papers by Freeman, Hogner, and Wood and Pasquero." Conference on Perspectives on International Business. Columbia, SC: University of South Carolina, Center for International Business Education and Research (May 21–4).

Wartick, Steven L. and Philip L. Cochran. 1985. "The evolution of the corporate social performance model." *Academy of Management Review* 4, 758–69.

Wills, Gordon. 1993. "Your enterprise school of management." *Journal of Management Development* 12:2, 25–35.

Wood, Donna J. 1994. *Business and Society.* 2nd edition. New York: HarperCollins.

Wood, Donna J., and Jean Pasquero. 1992. "International business and society." Conference on Perspectives on International Business. Columbia, SC: U. of South Carolina, Center for International Business Education and Research (May 21–4).

Wood, Donna J., and Raymond E. Jones. 1995. "Stakeholder mismatching: A theoretical problem in corporate social performance research." *International Journal of Organizational Analysis* 3:3 (July): 229–67.

10

Business and Societies: the Future

How fast can the world change? In January 1990, US chief executive officers were expressing cautious optimism about the events in Eastern Europe the previous year, although some worried that a possible reunification of East and West Germany could create "another unfriendly nation." On the other hand, hardly anyone thought that changes would happen as fast as they did. Sunkist Growers' CEO remarked to a *Fortune* reporter: "It's a long way between the first hole in the Berlin Wall and the reunification of the Germanies" (Alpert, 1990: 126). Yet reunification occurred only a few months later, on October 24, 1990. Five years later, reunification was in full swing. Thanks to a DM200 billion investment from West German and foreign enterprises, manufacturing productivity in the former East Germany increased dramatically. Nevertheless, unemployment was also at record levels, indicating still more changes in store for the united Germanies (Jones, 1995; Hall and Ludwig, 1994).

The future of international business and society relationships cannot be seen clearly, but certain dim outlines appear when we examine several shaping factors. One path of influence lies in global sociopolitical, technological, and economic forces that are under no one's control but will affect everyone. Also, the decisions and actions of sovereign nation-states and international organizations will have important impacts on business and society relations. And, the future will be shaped by the perceptions, choices, and actions of individual managers and their business organizations. International managers must be ready to face this uncertain future, equipped with a grasp of the interactive power of global trends, national actions, organizational and individual choices.

This final chapter will recap the major messages of the book, pose some unresolved problems in the field of international business and society, and speculate on future business–society relationships in an ever-smaller world.

RECAPPING THE INTERNATIONAL DIMENSIONS OF BUSINESS AND SOCIETY

Business and society is the study of relationships between business organizations and the social, political, technological, economic, and natural environments in which they exist and operate. In this section, the conceptual tools available for international business and society analysis are reviewed.

SEPTEmber analysis. The following scheme can be used to break down the global business environment into more manageable dimensions:

- *Social environment:* culture, values, population, forms of social organization.
- *Economic environment:* conditions of production and distribution.
- *Political environment:* influence, law, public policy, and governance.
- *Technological environment:* tools and methods of production, resource manipulation, communication, and knowledge production and use.
- *Ecology or natural environment:* natural resources, the emotional and spiritual benefits of natural beauty, and sustenance for life itself. (Wood, 1994.)

Categorizing events, trends, opportunities, threats, and so on, into social, economic, political, technological, and ecological domains is a good way to begin to get a grip on the complexity of the global business environment. Furthermore, once events are categorized in this way, managers can begin to sort out the interactions among the dimensions, observing, say, how a new environmental law in Europe will change the way a chemical company must relate to the other environmental sectors.

Institutional–ideological model. This refinement of the SEPTEmber model (Wilson, 1977) emphasizes the importance of the interrelationships of ideologies (or belief systems) and institutional behaviors; it is built on the core of possibilities established by technology and the natural environment. In the international domain, the IIM is especially powerful because it does not link specific organizations with specific institutions or ideologies, but with the processes and functions those organizations are undertaking in the social system. This makes it easier for multinational managers to understand, in various countries, how a religious group could be running a government, how an educational system could be completely sponsored by voluntary organizations, how health care is handled by ad hoc social activists, or how a government could own all the significant means of production.

Business–government relations. Government serves the functions of establishing rules of social control and redistributing society's resources. Several factors influence alternative business–government relations frameworks in terms of both what is and what could be. The dynamics of change in worldwide business–government relations are being driven by worldwide forces of disintegration and consolidation, increasing leadership of international organizations. MNE managers need to know that this dynamism can present opportunities as well as threats. Tools such as corporate political action and strategic uses of regulation and public policy can be helpful to MNE managers as they work to redefine their firms' relationships with national governments and international quasi-governmental bodies.

Corporate social performance. CSP is defined as "the exercise of the principles of social responsibility, the processes of social responsiveness, and the social impacts of business activity" (Wood, 1991). This integrative framework of social structures, management processes, and outcomes gives multinational managers a perspective on how to link the various components of corporate performance together, as well as how the performance of their companies will be evaluated.

In terms of international CSP, some multinational enterprises are choosing to take a leadership role, exceeding public standards or expectations, not just matching them. This strategy can result in important self-interest advantages. For example:

> IBM has gained a reputation for finding the highest standard in the world in any particular [technological] area and then adopting a more stringent norm as company policy. According to European IBM environmental coordinator Ian Holm, the policy has allowed the US giant to transfer its production processes "anywhere on the world market without extra cost or delay." (Bruce, 1989: 25.)

At the same time, IBM has taken the lead in meshing concern for the environment with overall business strategy, developing a progressive cradle-to-grave policy for managing the ecological impacts of its products and manufacturing processes (Kenward, 1992).

Stakeholder analysis and management. A stakeholder is defined as "any group or organization that can affect or is affected by the achievement of the corporation's objectives" (Freeman, 1984). The stakeholder theory of the firm, in contrast to the neoclassical and behavioral theories, envisions business organizations as engaged in a network of relationships with other people, social groups, and organizations. These relationships may involve employees, owners, customers, communities, suppliers, governments, international agencies, terrorists, religious groups, and more. It is stakeholders who provide the inputs and consume the outputs of business activity. Stakeholders set expectations for business activity; stakeholders experience the effects of business behavior; stakeholders evaluate the company's performance and judge it acceptable or not (Wood and Jones, 1994).

Stakeholder relations are more complex and difficult, but also richer and potentially more rewarding, in international contexts. A company's key stakeholders may differ considerably across cultures; a single worldwide stakeholder may have different interests and power relations in different parts of the world; and global stakeholder relations will shift over time. These complexities of international stakeholder relationships make it more important for the MNE manager to conceive of the firm not as a series of material inputs and outputs, but as a network of stakeholder relationships.

Ethical analysis. At the core, the individual is the locus of all ethical decision making. Ethical conflicts emerge for individuals not from conflicts between right and wrong, but through dissonances between things that are thought to be right *or* things that are thought to be wrong. Working through ethical conflicts can be handled through a process of moral reasoning in which ethical principles of utility, rights, and justice are applied to a set of facts and observations, and a decision is made based on how the various factors are weighted. In the international domain, managers will find differences in ethical standards and customs, and must be wary of the dangers of ethnocentrism in handling conflicts that arise because of these differences. However, the existence of cultural differences does not excuse managers from engaging in moral reasoning, nor does it relieve them of responsibility for the consequences of their actions.

Organizational ethical climate. Three approaches to handling business ethics in the international domain are ethical imperialism, "when in Rome," and the transnational approach, with the latter having clear advantages over the first two. Organizations can impose structures such as codes of ethics, ethics training programs, and rewards systems to facilitate ethical decision making. In the informal culture of the firm, shared values, and incentives for moral, immoral, or amoral behavior were discussed as major factors affecting ethical decision making.

Issues management. Issues management ties together the tools and concepts of international business and society analysis. Issues management is defined as "the process by which the corporation can identify, evaluate, and respond to those social and political issues which may impact significantly upon it." (Johnson, 1983: 22) For any business organization, an issue is a problem that (1) rests on an expectational gap (occurring when there are inconsistencies in views of what is, and/or what ought to be), (2) is controversial, and (3) has a present or future impact on the company.

Issues develop over an identifiable life cycle based on changes in public attention over time. Life cycles are made up of three stages separated by discrete events. In the early, or nascent, stage, expectational gaps are opening and closing, becoming controversial, and implying impact, but public attention doesn't rise until some dramatic event or "trigger" moves the issue into its middle, or developing, stage. In this middle stage, the issue is undergoing redefinition and controversy builds until a trigger event – a resolution of some sort – pushes it into the mature stage. Then, depending on who is monitoring the effectiveness of the resolution, the issue may or may not resurface. Based on this understanding of what an issue is, issues management uses three types of techniques: (1) issues identification and environmental scanning to find expectational gaps, (2) issues analysis to assess controversies and impacts, and (3) response development to help close expectational gaps.

The principal caveat concerning international issues management is that *all* managers must be issues managers. Otherwise, IM can become a marginal staff function that does not serve the purpose of informing, planning, and guiding the company through turbulent waters or, even worse, issues management may not exist in the firm at all, leaving managers with no guidance on how to respond to the many complex factors that will affect their decisions (Wartick and Mahon, 1994).

Social reporting and evaluation. Finally, attention was given to explicitly assessing and disclosing the outcomes of business decisions and actions. A number of tools are available for evaluating and reporting outcomes and for incorporating the new information generated into the company's plans and policies. An important process within corporate social reporting is a social performance CODE, which emphasizes consistency, opportunity, diversity, and emergency capability in a company's policies and procedures.

THINKING ABOUT INTERNATIONAL TRENDS

There are many, many trends which could and should be examined with respect to the future of international business and society. For example, there appears to be a worldwide conflict brewing between fundamentalist political and religious views of social organization, and liberal or social democratic views. Also of enormous importance are the implications of technology that changes so fast that humans can no longer understand and control it. (In mid-1994, for example, nations learned of the new "threat to domestic labor" from foreign workers who telecommute via computer modem and fax.) The long-term business implications of population trends, or the movement of manufacturing to developing nations, or the reciprocities between illegal international drug trafficking and legitimate international business operations are also worthy of attention. Certainly, exploring the political and technological implications of the Cold War's end and the desire of weapons manufacturers on both sides to stay solvent by arming all other nations to the teeth is a provocative trend.

Two trends exemplify the enormous implications of worldwide changes for business and society relationships. These are: (1) an institutional trend toward international regulation and supranational government, and (2) an ideological trend toward consolidation of the world's major ethical traditions into a single set of fundamental principles. Both consolidating trends are being driven by changes in the technological and ecological core; specifically, the rapidity and low cost of information technology and the degradation of cross-border and commons areas of the global natural environment.

Supranational government?

National sovereignty still rules, although one can observe certain cracks in the foundation. The unprecedented deployment of United Nations troops to countries in chaos, such as Somalia, Rwanda, and Bosnia, is one sign that the future may not favor national sovereignty as much as supranational government, at least in some critical domains such as peacekeeping and humanitarian aid.

Issues such as the creation of additional common-market or free-trade zones, the increasing inability of nations to control transborder information flows, and the rise of modern-day labor migrations via telecommuting, literally bring the nations of the world closer together. Imagine the impact on your business if your employees could be working from anywhere in the world. How would you handle routine personnel issues such as compensation, training and development, and evaluation? What laws would govern your treatment of employees?

Concern for the natural environment, finally, appears to be one of the most critical driving factors toward less sovereignty and more supranational government. A number of important environmental protection treaties have been signed in recent years (see Getz, 1994), and the 1992 Rio Summit on environmental protection laid the groundwork for many other such agreements. When nations agree to give up some portion, no matter how small, of their sovereign rights to control their territory, in exchange for better protection of commons areas that affect all nations, then a step has been taken toward collaborative problem-solving and away from coercive posturing.

The forces for national sovereignty are very strong and deep-rooted. The 1995 terrorist bombing of the federal building in Oklahoma City occurred apparently as a response to an imagined "world government" movement. The French, German, and English resistance to a common currency in the European Union is a strong issue of national sovereignty. The splintering of Russia and Eastern Europe into small, self-contained governing units also speaks to the depth of national sovereignty as a core value in many of the world's peoples. And yet, global forces such as the needs of international capital and labor movement, the difficulties of global environmental protection, and increasing attention to human rights issues may push all nations toward yielding some portion of their sovereignty to the common good.

Universal ethical standards?

Over the years, the United Nations has gradually expanded its pronouncements on human rights until a great many aspects of human and social behavior, and of national policy, are now included. In exhibit 10.1, the UN's Human Freedom Index appears, along with the most recent available ranking of countries along these dimensions. The foundation for this index is the idea that human freedom is an ultimate good, a condition to be sought and worked for, and the basis of human rights and just distribution.

Exhibit 10.1 The human freedom index

Key indicators of freedom

The right to
- travel in own country
- peacefully associate and assemble
- monitor human rights violations
- travel abroad
- teach ideas, receive information
- ethnic language

The freedom from
- forced or child labor
- extrajudicial killings or "disappearances"
- capital punishment
- unlawful detention
- censorship of mail or telephone tapping
- compulsory party or organization membership
- compulsory religion or state ideology in schools
- compulsory work permits
- torture or coercion
- corporal punishment
- arts control
- political censorship of press

The freedom for
- peaceful political opposition
- multiparty elections by secret and universal ballot
- social and economic equality for ethnic minorities
- independent newspapers, book publishing, radio and television networks
- political and legal equality for women
- social and economic equality for women
- independent courts and trade unions

The legal right to
- being considered innocent until proved guilty
- free legal aid when necessary, and counsel of own choice
- freedom from police searches of home without a warrant
- freedom from arbitrary seizure of personal property
- a nationality
- open and prompt trial

The personal right to
- interracial, interreligious, or civil marriage
- equality of sexes during marriage and for divorce proceedings
- homosexuality between consenting adults
- practice any religion
- determine the number of one's children

Country rankings

High Freedom Ranking (31–40)
38 – Sweden and Denmark
37 – Netherlands
36 – Finland, New Zealand, Austria

35 – Norway, France, West Germany, Belgium
34 – Canada, Switzerland
33 – USA, Australia
32 – Japan, United Kingdom
31 – Greece, Costa Rica

Medium Freedom Ranking (11–30)
30 – Portugal, Papua New Guinea
29 – Italy, Venezuela
27 – Ireland
26 – Spain, Hong Kong, Botswana
25 – Trinidad/Tobago, Argentina, Jamaica
24 – Ecuador
23 – Senegal
21 – Panama, Dominican Republic
19 – Israel
18 – Brazil, Bolivia
16 – Peru
15 – Mexico
14 – South Korea, Colombia, Thailand, India, Sierra Leone
13 – Nigeria, Benin
11 – Singapore, Sri Lanka, Tunisia, Egypt, Ghana

Low Freedom Ranking (0–10)
10 – Poland, Paraguay, Phillipines, Tanzania
 9 – Malaysia, Zambia, Haiti
 8 – Yugoslavia, Chile, Kuwait, Algeria, Zimbabwe, Kenya, Cameroon
 7 – Hungary, Turkey, Morocco, Liberia, Bangladesh
 6 – East Germany, Czechoslovakia, Saudi Arabia, Mozambique
 5 – Cuba, Syria, North Korea, Indonesia, Vietnam, Pakistan, Zaire
 4 – Bulgaria, USSR
 3 – South Africa
 2 – China, Ethiopia
 1 – Romania, Libya
 0 – Iraq

Source: UNDP, Human Freedom Index, 1991. Ranks 88 countries by
48 indicators of democracy available in 1985. Since then, many countries
have moved upward by holding multiparty elections, such as the Eastern
European nations.

Ethics scholars, scanning the array of human rights treaties and
statements, are attempting to extract a core list of "universal human
rights" that could guide business decisions and behaviors in the international domain. Exhibit 10.2 is one such list.

Exhibit 10.2   Donaldson's list of universal human rights

---

(1)   The right to freedom of physical movement.
Examples of violations: house arrest or imprisonment without fair trial; prevention of citizens from traveling abroad.

(2)   The right to ownership of property.
Examples of violations: Denial of property rights because of race, religion, gender.

(3)   The right to freedom from torture.
Examples of violations: political or war-related rapes, mutilations, beatings, forced starvation or dehydration, non-consensual medical experimentation.

(4)   The right to a fair trial.
Examples of violations: violence from assassination squads, political "disappearances," illegal arrest, detention without trial, rigged trial.

(5)   The right to non-discriminatory treatment.
Examples of violations: employment or educational discrimination on the basis of characteristics such as race, sex, religion, creed, etc.

(6)   The right to physical security.
Examples of violations: bombing of civilian areas, terrorist activity, creation of political, religious, or cultural refugees.

(7)   The right to freedom of speech and association.
Examples of violations: state-controlled print and telecommunications media; imprisonment for "incorrect" views or organizing; banning voluntary organizations.

(8)   The right to minimal education.
Examples of violations: intensive use of child labor in third-world craft industries such as textiles, carpets; failure of schools to ensure literacy for every graduate.

(9)   The right to political participation.
Examples of violations: Disenfranchisement of adults (e.g., blacks in South Africa), restrictions on political organizing or voice, limited access to decision makers.

(10)   The right to subsistence.
       Examples of violations: blockades, failure to provide international
       relief for regions hit by drought, lack of "safety net" for the very
       poor in many countries.

Sources: List of rights from Donaldson, 1989, 1991, 1992. Examples from
Wood, 1994

There can certainly be debate and controversy about whether each
of these items is indeed a "universal human right." Members of some
cultures, for example, are very reluctant to grant universal status to
the right to freedom of speech and association because, they argue,
such a right guarantees that terrorists and enemies of the state will be
able to thrive. Furthermore, not all cultures abide by democratic principles, and so the right to political participation might be questionable
to members of such cultures. As a final example, the right to non-
discriminatory treatment might be agreed to in some cultures for
men, but not for women.

Which position is right? The ethicists' intent (as ours) is not to
pronounce what is and is not a human right, but to open discussion
and debate so that international managers can be aware of human
rights concerns in international business and can move toward more
inclusion of ethical matters in their decision processes. German theologian Hans Küng (1991), for example, suggests that the foundation
of ethics in religious teachings should be more thoroughly studied
across cultures. It is his belief, after a lifetime of such study, that
fundamental ethical principles (such as rules prohibiting murder,
cheating, and incest) are indeed universal across the world's major
religions.

In the discussion over universal rights and cultural relativity, we
must remember that ethical standards and principles do evolve and
change over time. The early Hebrews owned slaves, aggressively
attacked neighboring peoples, and were instructed by Mosaic law to
take their rebellious sons outside the city gate and stone them to
death. The early Americans as well owned slaves, and men had the
right to beat their wives and children in the name of "discipline."
Other religious and cultural traditions contain stories equally horrify-
ing to today's human race. The Hindu practice of *sati*, burning a
widow to death on her husband's funeral pyre, was once very common but is now illegal in India (Rajan, 1990). Nigerian culture has
long supported female "circumcision," an extremely painful practice
with "devastating health consequences," but world opinion has turned
against this coercive, dangerous practice as a violation of women's

human rights ("What's culture," 1993). All of these principles and practices have moderated over time, and there is reason to suppose that ethical principles will continue to evolve toward some universal understanding of human rights and justice.

Effects on business–society relationships: the role of multinational enterprises in global trends

In 1986, sociologist Peter Berger wrote an empassioned defense of capitalism. In it he argued that the ideological framework of the Cold War, then beginning to wind down, was essentially bankrupt:

> We cannot point in the present world, and perhaps never could have, to any society which is either a case of pure market mechanisms, or pure political allocation. Every society which we call capitalist in the world today has massive processes of political allocation, and even the oldest societies which have called themselves socialist have massive underground market economies which, in some of these countries, play an enormous role. (Berger, 1986: 18.)

Berger's position is that those who attack the economic form of capitalism, and its attendant political form, democracy, are political and intellectual elites (p. 25) whose interests are threatened by poor people becoming less poor, or perhaps even wealthy, through entrepreneurship. The anti-capitalist arguments focus on the ideas that capitalism generates inequality within and between societies, that it is politically oppressive and ecologically unsound, and finally that it is dehumanizing (p. 19). On the contrary, Berger argues, capitalism, more than any other system of distribution:

- has tremendous "power for dealing with human misery" (p. 26) not only through the production of goods and services but also through its emphasis on research and innovation;
- has a high "correlation . . . with political liberty and human rights" (p. 27);
- permits and even fosters "a plurality of values" (p. 27) rather than a single, unified approach to social and political life.

Ann McKinstry Micou (1985), vice president of the United States Council for International Business, supports Berger's theme and offers practical counsel to MNE managers. She has observed in *Across the Board*, a popular management magazine, that multinational corporations are not very skilled in self-defense when criticized for social irresponsibility in developing nations. In evidence, she quotes modern theologian Richard John Neuhaus (1983):

the business response to critics is often one of accepting the basic arguments of the opponents of business and then, in a very apologetic and
defensive manner, attempting to demonstrate that business is not quite
the ogre that it is portrayed. For example, much of what is called
"external relations" or "corporate responsibility" gives the argument
away before it begins by saying, "Yes, we do make a profit, but we also
help out this poverty group in Bedford Stuyvesant, we also give money
to the Metropolitan Opera."

Aside from macroeconomic factors such as higher employment, enhanced gross national product, and improved balance of payments for
host countries, Micou (1985: 9–10) offers many examples of how
developing countries benefit from MNC operations:

- With 12 other American-based firms, Pfizer has established a system
  in Gambia for distributing pharmaceuticals and improving health
  care. Working with the Gambian medical and health department,
  the firms have helped the government develop efficient procure-
  ment policies, stock-management systems, and distribution networks.
- Beyond the usual employee benefits, Champion International Corporation subsidizes 13,000 meals a day for its Brazilian workers
  and offers a cooperative supermarket with goods sold at 17 percent less than local prices. Kaiser Aluminum & Chemical Company
  and the Reynolds Metals Company have made it possible for Ghana
  to construct a hydroelectric power project that has eased the country's dependence upon foreign oil. Tenneco has formed a joint
  venture with a Khartoum engineering company to establish a model
  farm in the Sudan. Fluor, the large engineering and construction
  firm, has trained more than 100,000 people in host countries –
  20,000 in South Africa alone – in everything from construction
  supervision to civil/structural engineering.
- Union Carbide has built and equipped a technical college in Zimbabwe. Chase Manhattan Bank has conducted a pioneering agricultural credit program in Panama. Monsanto has developed an
  energy-saving farming system in Kenya, introducing a conservation tillage method and an environmentally safe, easy-to-use weed-
  killer. Ford Motor Co. S.A., in a program that is 18 years old, has
  built 128 schools in Mexico, serving 170,000 children annually.
- Reebok participates in a collaborative venture called "Witness,"
  which provides hand-held video cameras and fax machines to
  human rights activists for documentation of human rights abuses
  around the globe (Makower, 1994).
- In 1992, Levi Strauss discovered that its Bangladeshi contractor was
  using child labor, in violation of Levi Strauss's mission statement

and contractor policy. Rather than fire the children and deprive their families of badly needed income, the company developed a program to pay the children to attend school, and the contractor agreed not to hire any more child labor (Makower, 1994).

Bob Dunn, formerly of Levi Strauss & Company, emphasizes that "as a business we have a responsibility to act in a way that's consistent with our values, that includes making some positive contributions in the countries where we do business" (Makower, 1994: 262). As an example of how multinational enterprises can give back something to communities and countries, Reebok International, the tennis shoe company, has developed a policy statement on business partners and the protection of human rights. Highlights of their code appear in exhibit 10.3.

Exhibit 10.3　Reebok's human rights production standards

Nondiscrimination. Reebok will seek business partners that do not discriminate in hiring and employment practices on grounds of race, color, national origin, gender, religion, or political or other opinion.

Working hours/overtime. Reebok will seek business partners who do not require more than 60-hour work weeks on a regularly scheduled basis, except for appropriately compensated overtime in compliance with local laws, and we will favor business partners who use 48-hour work weeks as their maximum normal requirement.

Forced or compulsory labor. Reebok will not work with business partners that use forced or other compulsory labor, including labor that is required as a means for political coercion or as punishment for holding or for peacefully expressing political views, in the manufacture of its products. Reebok will not purchase materials that were produced by forced prison or other compulsory labor and will terminate business relationships with any sources found to utilize such labor.

Fair wages. Reebok will seek business partners who share our commitment to the betterment of wage and benefit levels that address the basic needs of workers and their families so far as possible and appropriate in light of national practices and conditions. Reebok will not select business partners that pay less than the minimum wage required by local law or that pay less than prevailing local industry practices (whichever is higher).

Child labor. Reebok will not work with business partners that use child labor. The term "child" generally refers to a person who is less than 14 years of age, or younger than the age for completing compulsory education if that age is higher than 14. In countries where the law defines "child" to include individuals who are older than 14, Reebok will apply that definition.

Freedom of association. Reebok will seek business partners that share its commitment to the right of employees to establish and join organizations of their own choosing. Reebok will seek to assure that no employee is penalized because of his or her non-violent exercise of this right. Reebok recognizes and respects the right of all employees to organize and bargain collectively.

Safe and healthy work environment. Reebok will seek business partners that strive to assure employees a safe and healthy workplace and that do not expose workers to hazardous conditions.

Source: Reebok International Limited, 100 Technology Center Drive, Stoughton, MA 02072.

The benefits and costs of MNE activity in various nations and cultures of the world will continue to be a subject of great concern among the world's citizens and their governments. MNE managers need to be able to assess the impacts their companies have on local cultures and economies. The tools discussed in this book can help managers do just that.

FINALLY, WHAT IF . . .

If nothing else, the future is certainly full of possibilities. In the first chapter of this book a few "what if" questions, all of them possible and all with serious consequences for business, were examined. It was difficult then to sort through all the possible implications, to come up with ideas about what the business effects might be and how businesses might respond. In this last chapter, some additional "what if" possibilities are raised, and you can certainly add your own. Having learned something about the international dimensions of the business environment, the relationship between ideology and societal institutions, stakeholder relations, public affairs and issues management, and the nature of corporate social performance, exploring the future of business and societies should be substantially easier.

Exhibit 10.4 presents a list of WHAT IF statements, with varying degrees of probability and business impact. What happens when the

---

Exhibit 10.4   WHAT IF... some possible events

- Many citizens in Eastern Europe are talking about their countries being "colonized," becoming "the newest block of Third World nations." They don't think this is a good thing! But, WHAT IF they were to take this idea seriously, and enter into political coalitions with existing groups of developing nations? WHAT IF they were to discover new powers and opportunities by defining themselves as "third world countries"?
- WHAT IF NAFTA were extended to Central and South America?
- WHAT IF a major global defense company, say, Siemens of Germany or Rockwell of the US, decided to hire and train an army?
- WHAT IF the reunified Germans start World War III?
- WHAT IF the ozone layer really does get depleted? What if the entire Amazon rainforest is really cut down?
- WHAT IF interactive cable TV is installed in all third world homes?
- WHAT IF C-Span makes a deal with Apple, to install interactive computer-television technology in every US home, then begins recording citizen votes on public policy issues? What if they take the idea global?
- WHAT IF the United Auto Workers union successfully organizes Japanese, Korean, and East European auto workers?
- WHAT IF all the US states west of the Mississippi declare their independence from the federal republic, on the grounds of irreparable cultural and political differences, and the declaration of independence is written in Spanish?
- WHAT IF Canada and Mexico simultaneously waged wars of aggression against the US? Who else in the world would send troops to help? Whom would they help?
- WHAT IF the world's religious fundamentalists form a coalition and simultaneously seize political power in their respective nations? What if these groups seize control of some of the world's largest, or richest, nations?
- WHAT IF the European Union legalizes cocaine?
- WHAT IF corporations with more than 2,000 employees were prohibited worldwide? What if they were only prohibited in Europe, Japan, and North America?
- WHAT IF all university-based business programs in the world were made obsolete by interactive telecommunications technology? WHAT IF five years of post-secondary arts, humanities, and sciences education became mandatory throughout the world?

- WHAT IF the US adopted the Japanese K-12 system of education? What if the Japanese adopted the US K-12 system of education? WHAT IF education throughout the world was privatized?
- WHAT IF, following the Cold War meltdown, the world's military intelligence specialists all go to work in industrial espionage?
- WHAT IF the US successfully markets its military as the world's police force? What if they invite the former Soviets to join in a joint venture?
- WHAT IF *in vitro* reproductive technology is perfected to the point of no longer needing "human carriers" for fetal development?
- WHAT IF all cancers could be cured with a shot? WHAT IF a cure for AIDS is never found?
- WHAT IF the US decides to annex the Philippines?
- WHAT IF agribusiness takes over world food production and distribution and actually figures out how to feed the world? What if, instead, they hold the world hostage for more. . . . (whatever – you fill it in).
- WHAT IF the US becomes Spanish, Canada becomes French, Germany becomes Turkish, Argentina becomes German, England becomes Indian, Romania becomes Hungarian, and Japan becomes American?

SEPTEmber framework is applied to each one? The variety of effects each event would have, and the interconnectedness of these events as they affect global business, become clearer. Likewise, when a corporate social performance framework is applied to the WHAT IF events of exhibit 10.4, the future shapes of CSP values, objectives, processes, and outcomes become clearer. Similarly, looking at these events from the perspective of business–government relations, or ethical analysis, or public affairs and issues management, gives new ideas about how companies might respond to the demands of the future.

What if, in your next few years as an international manager, you had to deal with a half-dozen or maybe twenty of these "WHAT IFS"? Would you be able to ride the rapids, or would you be up the creek without a paddle?

REFERENCES

Alpert, Mark. 1990. "Wary hope on Eastern Europe." *Fortune* 121:2 (Jan. 29): 125–6.

Amine, Lyn S. 1986. "Multinational corporations in Eastern Europe: Welcome trade partners or unwelcome change agents?" *Journal of Business Research* 14 (April): 133–45.

Berger, Peter. 1986. "The moral crisis of capitalism." Pp. 17–29 in R. B. Dickie and L. S. Rouner (eds.), *Corporations and the Common Good.* Notre Dame, IN: Univ. of Notre Dame Press.

Bruce, Leigh. 1989. "How green is your company?" *International Management* (Jan.): 24–7.

Donaldson, Thomas. 1989. *The Ethics of International Business.* New York: Oxford University Press.

Donaldson, Thomas J. 1991. "Rights in the global market." Pp. 139–62 in Freeman, R. Edward (ed.), *Business Ethics: The State of the Art.* New York: Oxford University Press.

Donaldson, Thomas. 1992. "Can multinationals stage a universal morality play?" *Business & Society Review* (Spring): 51–5.

Freeman, R. Edward. 1984. *Strategic Management: A Stakeholder Approach.* Boston: Pitman.

Getz, Kathleen A. 1993. "Selecting corporate political tactics." Pp. 242–73 in Barry M. Mitnick (ed.), *Corporate Political Agency.* Newbury Park, CA: Sage Publications.

Getz, Kathleen A. 1994. "Implementing multilateral regulation: A preliminary theory and illustrations." *Business and Society* 34: 280–316.

Hall, John, and Udo Ludwig. 1994. "East Germany's transitional economy." *Challenge* 37:5, 26–32.

Johnson, J. 1983. "Issues management – What are the issues?" *Business Quarterly* 48(3), 22–31.

Jones, Colin. 1995. "On your own." *Banker* 145:829, 27–9.

Kenward, Michael. 1992. "The big blue giant turns green." *Director* 46:4, 35.

Küng, Hans. 1991. *Global Responsibility: In Search of a New World Ethic.* New York: Crossroad.

Makower, Joel. 1994. *Beyond the Bottom Line: Putting Social Responsibility to Work for Your Business and the World.* New York: Simon & Schuster.

Micou, Ann McKinstry. 1985. "The invisible hand at work in developing countries." *Across the Board* 22:3 (March): 8–15.

Neuhaus, Richard John. 1983. "Religion's animus toward business." US Council for International Business.

Rajan, Rajeswari Sunder. 1990. "The subject of sati: Pain and death in the contemporary discourse on sati." *Yale Journal of Criticism* 3:2 (Spring): 1–27.

Reebok International Limited, 100 Technology Center Drive, Stoughton, MA 02072.

United Nations Development Programme, 1991. *Human Development Report.* New York: UNDP.

Wartick, Steven L., and John F. Mahon. 1994. "Toward a substantive definition of the corporate issue construct: A review and synthesis of the literature." *Business & Society* 33:3 (Nov.).

Weber, Max. 1958. *The Protestant Ethic and the Spirit of Capitalism.* New York: Scribner.

"What's culture got to do with it? Excising the harmful tradition of female circumcision." 1993. *Harvard Law Review* 106:8 (June): 1944–61.

Wilson, Ian H. 1977. "Socio-political forecasting: A new dimension to strategic planning." Pp. 159–69 in Archie B. Carroll (ed.), *Managing Corporate Social Responsibility*. Boston: Little, Brown.

Wood, Donna J. 1991. "Corporate social performance revisited." *Academy of Management Review* 16:4: 691–718.

Wood, Donna J. 1994. *Business and Society*, 2nd edition. New York: HarperCollins.

Wood, Donna J., and Raymond E. Jones. 1994. "Research in Corporate Social Performance: What Have We Learned?" *Proceedings* of the Conference on Corporate Philanthropy, organized by the Center for Corporate Philanthropy, University of Indiana Bloomington, and Case Western Reserve University, May 1994.

Index